The Rise and Fall of War Crimes Trials

This book is the first comprehensive analysis of the politics of war crimes trials. It provides a systematic and theoretically rigorous examination of whether these trials are used as tools for political consolidation or whether justice is their primary purpose. The consideration of cases begins with the trial of Charles I of England and goes through the presidency of George W. Bush, including the trials of Saddam Hussein and those arising from the War on Terror. The book concludes that political consolidation is the primary concern of these trials – a point that runs contrary to the popular perception of the trials and their stated justification. Through the consideration of war crimes trials, this book makes a contribution to our understanding of power and conflict resolution and illuminates the developmental path of war crimes tribunals.

Dr. Charles Anthony Smith is a professor in the political science department at the University of California, Irvine. His research encompasses work in public law in both comparative and international frameworks as well as on the judiciary in the United States using a variety of methodologies. He has published articles in *Law & Society Review*, *Human Rights Review*, *Journal of Human Rights*, *Journal of International Relations and Development*, the *Election Law Journal*, and the *International Political Science Review*, among others. Smith's law practice focused on complex litigation in federal court and intellectual property.

The Rise and Fall of War Crimes Trials

From Charles I to Bush II

CHARLES ANTHONY SMITH

University of California, Irvine

CAMBRIDGE
UNIVERSITY PRESS

CAMBRIDGE UNIVERSITY PRESS
Cambridge, New York, Melbourne, Madrid, Cape Town,
Singapore, São Paulo, Delhi, Mexico City

Cambridge University Press
32 Avenue of the Americas, New York NY 10013-2473, USA

Published in the United States of America by Cambridge University Press, New York

www.cambridge.org
Information on this title: www.cambridge.org/9781107680715

First published 2012
First paperback edition 2013

A catalogue record for this publication is available from the British Library

Library of Congress Cataloguing in Publication Data
Smith, Charles Anthony, 1961–
   The rise and fall of war crimes trials : from Charles I
   to Bush II / Charles Anthony Smith.
      p.   cm.
   Includes bibliographical references and index.
   ISBN 978-1-107-02354-3 (hardback)
   1. War crime trials – History.   2. International criminal
   courts.   3. Charles I, King of England, 1600–1649.   4. Bush,
   George W. (George Walker), 1946–   I. Title.
   KZ1168.5.S65   2012
   341.6ʹ9–dc23   2011052727

ISBN 978-1-107-02354-3 Hardback
ISBN 978-1-107-68071-5 Paperback

Contents

Contents

Acknowledgments

As a practicing lawyer prior to my academic career, I sat
in one of my conference rooms with my law partners and
watched the return of the verdict in the O. J. Simpson murder trial. The press had taken to referring to the trial as "The
Trial of the Century." This case displaced the many previous
claimants to the title "Trial of the Century" from the murder trial of Fatty Arbuckle to the Lindbergh kidnapping and
the Manson Family murder prosecutions. While the other
lawyers in the room discussed the nuance of the evidence
that had failed to convict (we all had predicted an acquittal),
I could not help but think that this hyperbolic categorization
of this sensational murder trial put the Nuremberg Trials
in a peculiar perspective. This led me to read, for the first
time, the transcripts from Nuremberg because I realized I
knew very little about what was surely the true Trial of the

Acknowledgments

Century. To this day I suggest any student that aspires to practice law read Robert Jackson's opening statement from Nuremberg as an example of litigation at its very finest. This book is an attempt to present the story of the systematic evolution of war crimes trials. Although this volume originated as a concept in a room mostly reserved for depositions, it has come to press through the assistance, guidance, and insight of those in the halls of the academy, and I owe those many people a tremendous debt.

The generosity of friends and scholars who have taken the time to comment on this manuscript and lend their guidance to me as I moved the project forward is remarkable. Specifically, the faculty at Utah State University and the University of California, San Diego, were incredible, insightful, and supportive. In particular, this volume would not have happened without the early guidance and insight and perpetual mentoring of David Goetze. I also owe a great deal to Amy Bridges, Harry Hirsch, Gary Jacobson, and Martin Shapiro for their collective and individual insights and wisdom. I am very grateful for the thorough research assistance from Zak Gershman, Josh Russ, Adam Shniderman, Josh Vrotsos, and Curt Brown. I am deeply grateful for the professionalism and helpfulness of the employees at the archives located in the National Prisoner of War Museum at Andersonville Prison in Georgia and at the International Criminal Court at The Hague. As I presented portions of the manuscript at conferences, including the annual conferences held by Law & Society, the Midwest Political Science Association, RC 09 of the International Political Science Association, and the American Political Science Association, I had the great fortune to receive terrific feedback from various chairs, discussants, co-panelists, and audience members. I owe a particularly important debt to Leslie Goldstein, Mary Volcansek, Michael Tolley, the late Neil Tate, Jim Gibson, Jim Kelly, Roy Flemming, and Rich Hiskes, who each contributed to my understanding of how best to approach the project. In the later stages of the project, Alison Brysk, Rachel Cichowski, Russ Dalton, Bernie Grofman, Tony McGann, Mark Petracca, Marek Kaminski, Dan Pinello, and Wayne Sandholtz were generous with their insights and thoughts and proved invaluable in the final stretch of navigation. I am also grateful for the financial support of the Center for the Study of Democracy at UCI. I owe a special thanks to Latha Varadarajan for her detailed comments on the manuscript which, without question, improved the project. I would be remiss if I did not single out Heather Smith-Cannoy and Ben Bishin for recognition for their contributions. They each embody everything that could be hoped for in a colleague or friend and demonstrated limitless generosity with their time, insights, and assistance. I am also extremely grateful to the anonymous external reviewers as well as the editorial team at Cambridge. The insights from the reviewers improved the manuscript in both obvious and nuanced ways. John Berger

Acknowledgments

and the entire editorial team made this a remarkable experience through their professionalism, thoroughness, and commitment to the project. Finally, like everything else in my life since my very first conversation with him, Julio Rodriguez made this better through sharing his wisdom, insight, and clarity of vision.

1

Introduction

Overview

The law has contemplated punishment for violent acts toward other humans as long as there has been law. Individual accountability for aggression and other acts of rights deprivation is the bedrock of municipal criminal law and forms the foundation of a large portion of the civil codes of virtually every legal system. In contrast, states and those who act on behalf of states, until relatively recently, have mainly operated with impunity toward individuals and have operated in a vacuum of accountability for transgressions toward individuals. Although the rise of the liberal state brought with it an improvement in the protection of human rights as states evolved to become more cognizant of the claims of the individual (Ratner and Abrams 2001, pp. 3–4), a legal mediation of the treatment of individuals by states developed in the shadow of privilege of near absolute internal sovereignty. Accordingly, the initial development of accountability for improper actions by the state arose in the dual-tract context of the laws and customs of war and in the context of interactions with noncitizens (McCormack 1997; Smith 2008). Individual criminal accountability for those who commit egregious acts on behalf of states flourished in the context of a post-belligerence or transitional justice frame.

Often, contestation over appropriate prosecutions of state actors has been couched in terms of whether the proposed prosecutions were practical (e.g., Aukerman 2002, p. 39). Others have insisted that there is a general imperative seated in international law that requires prosecution for gross human rights violations by state actors (e.g., Orentlicher 1991). Generally, analysis has converged on the notion that prosecutions are one of the best mechanisms, even perhaps the best mechanism, for the provision of post-transition justice (Penrose 1999). Other avenues for the delivery of postconflict justice, such as truth commissions, are thought of as morally inferior and sub-optimal with outcomes that sacrifice justice for political expediency (Dwyer 1999; Minow 1999; Neier 1998). For much of the scholarly community, accountability and punishment for criminal actions undertaken on behalf of the state are the driving imperatives that demand prosecutions (Crocker 1999). Others enter the debate as champions for situating the specific mechanism for transitional justice in terms of the goal-specific structures, for instance democratic consolidation, and in terms of culturally specific processes, shaped by the locale of the conflict (Aukerman 2002). Much of the literature considers the overall evolution of discrete aspects of the jurisprudence of war crimes trials, from questions about universal jurisdiction (Morris 2001, p. 43; Smith and Smith 2009, pp. 32–5) to considerations of the relative value of international versus domestic venues (Kritz 1996) and the appropriate scope of sentencing (Nino 1991). Missing from the literature is a thorough explication of the political origins of these types of trials and the manner in which the construction of each tribunal has shaped the path of development of future tribunals. The purpose of this volume is to demonstrate the evolutionary path and jurisprudential trajectory of the development of war crimes tribunals.

The first efforts to prosecute political leadership for actions taken on behalf of the state during times of conflict were revolutionary attempts to hold those who enforced the law accountable to it. As the trials developed over time with each successive conflict and each postconflict consideration of what to do about the criminals of war, the search for justice and accountability was constrained by political expediency and the tangible needs of the victors who sought to mete out justice. Although the approbation of the actions classified as war crimes amounts to a public airing of the norms and expectations of the larger community, these public displays of the mechanics of justice are undertaken without fear of prosecution for those involved in the creation or perpetuation of the postconflict tribunals. Perhaps even more important, these trials are constructed for the purposes of political consolidation rather than the dispensation of justice. Although the evolution of war crimes trials has taken a path that approached justice as the goal of the proceedings only to ultimately revert to political consolidation and expediency as the purpose of the prosecutions, there remains a value to the proceedings even if not all war criminals are held accountable for their crimes and the powerful states are completely insulated from prosecution. The prosecution of individuals for criminal conduct and acts of state during times of war or conflict has evolved over time into a mediated resolution of the tension between the demands of justice and the necessity of consolidation of power. Despite the best efforts of some of the architects of postconflict prosecutions, ultimately the search for justice through war crimes trials has been co-opted by political concerns and the trials have reverted to show trials that rival the initial forays into political prosecutions.

The initial foray into the prosecution of civilian and military leaders in a nominal court of law began inauspiciously with Charles I of England, who was executed after a show trial orchestrated by Oliver Cromwell. After the Civil War in the United States, Captain Henry Wirz, a commandant of a Confederate prison, was executed after a public show trial. However, when the Nuremberg Trials were conducted after World War II, the process of a demonstrably fair prosecution through a legitimate legal forum triumphed over the early models of mere summary prosecution by the victors. In the decades since the trials at Nuremberg, the prosecution of the perpetrators of human rights violations on an ad hoc basis has come to be expected by the international community after the resolution of any conflict that gives rise to the types of bad acts that have been variously called war crimes, crimes against humanity, or gross violations of human rights. These ad hoc tribunals have established a jurisprudence of prosecution that has evolved with each successive set of trials or tribunals. In contrast to the more recent permanent court, the International Criminal Court (ICC), the ad hoc prosecutions took the form of trials or tribunals, with varying procedural rules and jurisdiction over various crimes. The nominal purpose of the tribunals invariably is the establishment or re-implementation of justice.

The ad hoc trials have been designed, at least nominally, to redress human rights violations as an integral part of the restoration of justice after the cessation of conflict. The prosecutions have been conducted either domestically or through an international structure. Conventionally, these tribunals prosecute individuals who, on behalf of a governmental entity during conflict, have acted contrary to the emerging norms of appropriate conduct during conflict. Typically, some wrongful use of force against civilians by the agents of government is a necessary element to the crimes that are the focus of prosecution. Moreover, the wrongful acts by these agents of government are categorically of a type that is claimed to be universally abhorrent. The categories of acts that fall into this range of universally unacceptable have been variously catalogued from the indictment of Charles I through each successive war crimes trials subset including those crimes identified in the ICC statute and the indictment of Saddam Hussein. The ICC was created in part to bring efficiency and predictability to these types of prosecutions. Specifically, the institutionalized court might have reduced the selective justice and idiosyncratic operation of the ad hoc tribunals. The ICC also presented the possibility that universal jurisdiction would continue to evolve as an accepted international norm. That is, with the ICC came the hope that certain especially heinous acts would be considered so terrible that a global jurisdiction would provide the foundation to proceed against the perpetrators regardless of the geographic limits of the crimes.

The question addressed here through an examination of the development of war crimes trials is whether human rights tribunals, either ad hoc or standing, are products of the high call to justice or instead are tools utilized in the normal dimensions of political processes and political consolidation. Whether human rights tribunals in general are juridical rather than political has yet to be established. It is not surprising that there has been an absence of a systematic analysis of the concept of war crimes trials. These trials are constructed after some outrageous level of violence has occurred and only after at least some of the perpetrators of that violence have been defeated. Perhaps obviously, those who stand before any specific tribunal as the accused typically complain that the prosecution is politically motivated and fundamentally unfair. Perhaps because the motives of any of the defendants in the role of systemic critic of the prosecution and the court are tainted by self-interest, little attention has been given to the question of whether the nature of these tribunals is fundamentally juridical or political.

Whether the purpose of the trials is justice or the appeasement of various political factions and political consolidation can be examined through an analysis of the degree to which justice was served through the conduct of the trials. In order to examine the relative degree of commitment to justice among the various trials, some definition of justice must be operationalized. Although *justice* has come to be thought of as a more admirable concept than *politics*, the foundations of a jurisprudence that precedes the functional construction and implementation of the law are soundly rooted in political discourse. For the purposes of assessing the development and conduct of war crimes trials, a straightforward notion of justice as a product of substantive due process and procedural due process, which aspires to achieve the dual goals of deterrence and retribution, is parsimonious and clear. If the substantive due process elements of the trial fall short, then the defendant cannot be treated fairly regarding the content of the charges. If the procedural due process elements of the trial are insufficient, then the evidence against the defendant is never adequately tested and a robust defense is not possible. Deterrence as a goal is critical because both the specific defendants and others similarly situated in the future must be discouraged from engaging in comparable acts in the future. Retribution as a goal is the notion that the specific victims and society collectively are entitled to be put back in *status quo ante*, or the condition they were in before the criminal act occurred.

Whether the trials are driven by the demands and constraints of political consolidation can only be determined after some operationalization of political consolidation. That is, *political consolidation* here means the effort at maintaining and solidifying the newly secured or defended control over the institutions of government. The shifts in political power that precede the initiation of human rights tribunals vary in their degree of societal upheaval and in the degree to which the victorious party is able to assert political control. That is, after the conflict subsides, the victorious – those who come to be in charge – have control over the institutions of the governments at issue to varying degrees.

Some shifts in power are complete and those in power have little to be concerned with regarding their treatment of the perpetrators of the violations, as the accused no longer have any meaningful political power. This situation arises in the event of a total military victory. The defeated have no recourse if their treatment by the victorious rises to little more than summary justice. Other shifts are complete but the control over the institutions of government remains unstable. The maintenance of power is at least partially dependent on the continued suppression of those elites no longer in power, but where unfair treatment of the former leaders could be risky for the new rulers. This occurs when the vanquished elites maintain some ability to resurrect a popular political base and possibly challenge the newly installed regime. Some shifts in power are incomplete and those with new power depend on those with old power for some critical aspect of system maintenance and control. This situation is typical when those who have lost power still maintain or can exert some control over a necessary element of governance, such as the financial infrastructure or portions of the military. Some power shifts result in an indeterminate resolution. For those instances in which no clear winner of the conflict emerges, something akin to an uneasy balance of power among competing factions continues after the conflict seems to have concluded. Here, balance arises when the end of the conflict is brokered rather than achieved by one party through political or military means.

Given the variety of ways in which conflicts can end and the variety of ways power can be obtained and maintained, the degree of justice achieved in human rights tribunals may be a function of the political expediency of those who come to power instead of the implementation of an abstraction of a universally recognized concept.

The evolution of war crimes trials has developed in both a transnational environment and a domestic environment. Of course, conflict has taken place in both transnational and domestic venues, so naturally the resolution of conflict and postconflict political developments should be expected in both. The trials have evolved in the context of a search for transnational justice and domestic justice, and each type of trial or series of prosecutions has affected the subsequent efforts regardless of whether those efforts were transnational or domestic. Each given instance of postconflict prosecution might be considered so specifically tied to the discrete facts of the conflict as to render it a singular occurrence that could not be credibly compared to other similar processes. However, the historical path of development of these postconflict processes reveals that these cases share a great deal in common and each has guided the development of the subsequent trials. Moreover, the transnational prosecutions have so informed the development of the more recent municipal prosecutions that to consider one without the other would overlook a critical dimension of the pedigree of the municipal trials. Additionally, because many prosecutions that appear in a transnational context involve only municipal crimes, there is little indication that the international community makes any meaningful distinction between the two types of trials. There likewise is little indication that such a distinction would give additional traction to any systematic analysis of war crimes trials.

For each case examined here, the political context of the end of the conflict is analyzed before considerations of the issue of justice are addressed. The variables that act as indicators of the extent to which each case was concerned with justice include the degree to which substantive due process and procedural due process were present in the trial. Further, the degree to which retribution and deterrence were the goals of the process gives insight into the intent behind and purpose of the proceedings. Finally, for each case, a comparison of the distribution of political power and the degree of justice achieved illuminates the function of the trials. This comparison establishes whether the degree of justice achieved is a function of the demands of political consolidation. The analysis also addresses whether human rights tribunals serve a legitimate political purpose beyond the confines of justice.

The Evolution of Justice and the Concept of Law

The philosophy of law and the evolved concepts of modern Western jurisprudence are grounded in Plato's dialogues (Hall 1973, p. 6). A critical, and perhaps first, imperative of the philosophy of law is the notion of justice. *Justice* is seen as a determination of the morality, or the rightness, of the treatment of the citizenry by its government through the enactments and decisions of the government. Accordingly, the question of what acts deserve to be categorized as just has persistently arisen in the discourse of politics (Ibid.).

In *The Politics*, Aristotle conceptualized law and justice with the argument that "in seeking justice they are seeking impartiality; for law is impartiality" and "justice is held by all to be a certain equality" (Aristotle 1994, pp. 114 and 103). Justice, then, begins at the outset with the idea of equal or impartial treatment. For St. Augustine, justice was a prerequisite to any claim to legitimate governance or any claim of a right to rule by law. He dismissed states run without justice as the foundation of their claim to legitimacy by arguing that states without justice were "but robber-bands enlarged" (Hart 1961, p. 152). St. Thomas Aquinas expanded these early concepts of justice and its definitional parameters by introducing the notion of continuity or predictability over time. His definition of justice as "a habit whereby a man renders to each one his due by a constant and perpetual will" suggests that, under the ambit of justice, right and wrong remain the same over time and circumstance and societal responses to right and wrong are likewise stable (1913–25, part II, q. 58).

John Locke built upon these conceptualizations by identifying a nonarbitrary aspect of justice that dictates that all be accorded the same treatment in a *predictable* fashion: "[T]he legislative ... authority cannot assume to itself a power to rule by temporary arbitrary decrees, but is bound to dispense justice ... by promulgated standing laws, and known authorized judges" (Locke, Wootton ed. 1993, pp. 330–2). H. L. A. Hart incorporated these ideas about continuity and predictability into the modern notion of justice by noting that to be just, the law demanded "a uniform or constant feature, summarized in the precept 'Treat like cases alike' and a shifting or varying criterion used in determining when ... cases are alike..." (Hart 1961, p. 156). As an aside, the type of justice provided for by human rights tribunals is what

Locke would designate as commutative justice (Bodenheimer 1962, p. 26). That is, *commutative justice* is corrective justice or justice that concerns "the dealings of individuals with one another and the adjustments to be made in case of the performance of illegal or improper acts" (Ibid.). This is distinct from *distributive justice*, which addresses the allocation of goods and things among individuals.

The nonarbitrary nature of corrective justice manifests itself in two related but distinct forms: substantive due process and procedural due process. *Substantive due process* entails resolving what acts will be categorized as criminal. Substantive due process ensures that the content of the law is fair. That is, the premise of substantive due process is to ensure that the law is not arbitrary or unreasonable. *Procedural due process* entails resolving how the prosecution of the crime at issue will occur. Jeremy Bentham distinguishes between substantive due process and procedural due process as follows: Substantive law is "principal" while procedural law is "adjective" (Postema 1977). Gerald Postema explains this distinction by suggesting that procedural law is "adjective" in two specific dimensions. First, procedural due process is adjective law because it is dependent on substantive due process for its context and intelligibility just as the adjective is dependent on the noun. Second, the adjective procedural law modifies the principal substantive law. That is, "the law of procedure exists only for the sake of giving efficacy ('execution and effect') to substantive law" (Postema 1977, pp. 1396–7). The end and only purpose of the procedural law is to secure the proper execution of the substantive law (Ibid.). Put more colloquially, the substantive law answers questions of *what* is a crime while the procedural law answers questions of *how* society might respond to the crime. The purpose of both substantive due process and procedural due process is to facilitate "the direct end of justice: rectitude of decision"; that is, the end of justice is to achieve the right result (Ibid., pp. 1399–1400).

Locke's conceptualization of corrective justice, construed as criminal law, is something very closely related and akin to Hart's concept of a simple model of a coercive law or demand (Hart 1961, p. 41). For Hart, an "order backed by threats is essentially the expression of a wish that others should do or abstain from doing certain things" (Ibid.). The function of these coercive orders can be split into two distinct goals: deterrence and retribution. The purpose of the threat of a sanction is first to deter those who would disregard the order and second to punish those who do, in fact, disregard the order (Bodenheimer 1962, pp. 161–231).

The extent to which any particular human rights trial or tribunal is driven by and achieves something approaching justice can be determined by a study of these two predicate aspects and these two goals of justice. That is, the predicate aspects of justice are substantive due process and procedural due process executed with the goals of deterrence and retribution. The question of substantive due process involves the range of crimes and the identities of the accused. The question of procedural due process involves the manner in which the trials are conducted, including whether there is a predetermined outcome, a right to a full and fair defense, and a right of appeal. The question of deterrence involves placing the charged defendants on notice of the future consequences of similar criminal conduct and placing other prospective wrongdoers on sufficient notice of the potential consequence of their actions to dissuade them from replicating the crimes at issue. The question of retribution involves the degree to which the perpetrators are punished and the victims individually and society as the collective are made whole.

Each case considered here began with some initiation of the process by some official with some claim and declaration of the search for justice. For each case, the parameters of both substantive due process and procedural due process were set forth in the initiating declaration. Though stated in a variety of different ways, each case established or at least nominally identified deterrence and retribution as the explicit goals of each tribunal. Although each case is defined by the specific facts of the conflict and the resolution of the conflict that precede the trial, the tribunals share many common elements and characteristics. For each case, the processes by which the tribunals are derived and accomplished exhibit the clear characteristics of politics and the consolidation of power. It may not be the case that justice and the consolidation of political power are irreconcilable rivals. However, as the cases demonstrate, justice as operationalized here may be a luxury that can be pursued fully only after political control is no longer in question.

Politics and Power

Of course, before assessing whether the tribunals are actually a vehicle for political consolidation first and a vehicle of justice second, some clear understanding of what is meant by the consolidation of political power has to be constructed. Max Weber famously noted that politics is a realm of power and violence (1946, pp. 77–8). The state, according to Weber, enjoys a monopoly over the legitimate use of force or power within its boundaries or jurisdiction (Ibid., p. 78). Blais has suggested that the "study of power *is* the study of politics" (1974, p. 45). Laswell and Kaplan argue that the study of the political is the "study of the shaping and sharing of power" (1950, p. xiv). To define what is political with the concept of power presents the dilemma of defining power. James has commented, cynically, that the popularity of power as a concept is due to its sloppy nature (1964, p. 47). Lending support to James, Kaufman and Jones wrote of power: "[W]e 'know' what it is, yet we encounter endless difficulties in trying to define it" (1953, p. 205). Partridge is even more discouraging when he argues that power "is a concept ... too amorphous, sprawling or chameleon-like ever to be amenable to exact identification..." (1962, p. 107).

Rather than abandon the notion of power as too vague or broad to provide a useful explanation of any phenomena, an understanding of power as politics in the context of the human rights tribunals can be constructed for the limited purpose of this analysis. In *The Metaphysics*, Aristotle defined power in a relational fashion as the beginning of a change or movement (Clegg 1979, p. 41). Hobbes also construed power in a relational fashion. Hobbes's fictional ruler served to end the disorder of the state of nature and impose the order of Leviathan. The legitimate dominion of one supreme ruler over individuals represents the ideal of Hobbes's concept of power: The ruler is power (Ibid., pp. 26–36; Parenti 1978, pp. 3–4). The Hobbesian notion of power as dominion or control has been expanded to encompass causal relationships. As Simon put it, "for the assertion 'A has power over B' we can substitute the assertion 'A's behavior causes B's behavior'" (1957, p. 5). Dahl (1963, p. 41), March (1955, p. 437), and James (1964, p. 50) all concur in this causal analysis whereas McFarland has boldly stated there is "considerable agreement among political theorists that the power relation is a type of causality relation" (1969, p. 34). Riker goes even further by arguing that "power is potential cause" (1964, p. 347). Partridge views power as the present ability to produce effects in the future (1962, p. 116). Lukes ponders "is it not the supreme exercise of power to get another ... to have the desires you want them to have...?" (Lukes 1974, p. 23).

Robert Dahl presented a straightforward conceptualization of power defined as "A has power over B to the extent that he can get B to do something B would not otherwise do" (Dahl 1956, pp. 201–15). Peter Bachrach and Morton Baratz introduced a negative dimension of power or inhibitory power (Bachrach and Baratz 1962). Using Dahl's example, Bachrach and Baratz structure negative power as the idea that when B fails to do something she wants to do because A is opposed, then A has power over B. Bachrach and Baratz go further than Dahl and also argue that power is exercised indirectly when A reinforces social or political values in a manner that limits public contestation to issues A views as innocuous or acceptable for public discourse (Ibid.). These definitions of power both represent inherently conflictual relationships among various actors in any given society. Steven Lukes brings a third dimension of consideration to the debate that contemplates that the preferences of B are manipulated by A (Lukes 1974). That is, the first two facets of power consider the direct actions or the inactions of individuals or presumably institutions while this third facet approaches considerations of the formations of desire that might develop contrary to self-interest. The fourth facet of power as developed and presented by Michel Foucault does not accept that the actors identified as the As and the Bs in the other three conceptions of power are extant or given (Foucault 1980). The subjects of power are social constructs with a historically describable formation rather than an organically bounded one. The first face of power is concerned with who exercises power. The second face is concerned with which issues have spurred the use of power. The third face (closely intertwined with the second) addresses who is harmed by the exercise of power. For the fourth face of power, the issue becomes one of the construction of A and the construction of B as outputs of power (Digeser 1992). These broad theoretical discussions of power have been embraced by the discipline in disparate contexts from international relations to urban politics.

Laswell and Kaplan begin their consideration of power with the assertion that the function of government is power (Laswell and Kaplan 1950, p. 6). By *power*, they mean the "making of important decisions and the importance of the decisions is measured by their effect on the distribution of values" (Ibid., p. 7). *Values* are those things desired by individuals such as income and safety (Ibid.). Laswell and Kaplan measure the power of individuals and groups by their "degree of participation in the making of important decisions" (Ibid.). Thus, to Laswell and Kaplan, the study of politics and power is the study of influence and the influential (Ibid.). Dahl has acknowledged this notion of influence and concluded "the making of governmental decisions is not a majestic march of great majorities united upon certain matters ... it is the steady appeasement of relatively small groups" (Dahl 1956, p. 146). International interactions also must be considered through the lens of power (Barnett and Duvall 2005).

The degree to which the trials examined are political can be measured by considering the extent to which they serve to consolidate power. In this context, the trials serve to consolidate power to the extent the trials expand the political influence or control of the mechanisms of government of those conducting the trials or appease some constituent group upon which those conducting the trials rely. If the trials are shown to be mechanisms for the consolidation of power, then whether the purpose of the trials also includes some dimension of justice should be assessed. Importantly, the separate goals of justice and consolidation of power may not be mutually exclusive or even especially rivalrous. Although the two goals may compete for primacy of purpose of the trials, it is certainly possible the prosecutions could serve both ends. Perhaps more interest in justice means less interest in the use of the trials to consolidate power while more interest in power consolidation means less concern can be given to justice. In other words, justice may be a concern only after power has been secured and there is no substantial need for additional consolidation.

The Cases

The cases are presented in chronological order because each subsequent trial was conducted with the knowledge gleaned from the historical record of those that came before it. Often the trials make explicit reference to the predecessor tribunals. The prosecutorial effort and the defense approach to challenging those prosecutions are shaped by the historical trajectory of the jurisprudence and practical implementation of the previous trials. The cases are also clustered by institutional variation. That is, whether the tribunal is international or domestic and whether the parties to the tribunal were engaged in the conflict that led to the tribunals is also considered. For each case considered here, the degree to which justice was served through the tribunals as well as the degree to which political ends were served is assessed. The underlying purpose of this analysis is not to provide a justification for the actions of those perpetrators of human rights violations that invariably stand as the accused or to serve as a frame through which those perpetrators can be presented as victims. Rather, the purpose is to determine if political considerations have diminished the juridical considerations and if more complete justice could be achieved through a less political process.

The analysis of cases begins in Chapter 2 with the trial of Charles I of England in January of 1649 and the post-Civil War trial and execution of Captain Henry Wirz in 1865. The trial and execution of the monarch underscored Cromwell's victory and the clear conclusion to the English civil war. The de jure solution of a trial won out over a simple execution or regicide because, as one supporter of Cromwell said, "tho we defeat him a hundred times, he is still the King" (Williamson 1957, p. 22). This prosecution came about after the conclusion of a conflict for the nominal purpose of punishing the defeated leader for crimes such as the murder of civilians, torture of captives, and forced conscription. The trial of Charles I is the antecedent to modern war crimes tribunals. The trial of Captain Henry Wirz in the fall of 1865 followed, and at least in part, was in retaliation for President Abraham Lincoln's assassination and was seen as a requisite step toward the prosecution of Confederate president Jefferson Davis. The nominal crimes that led to the hanging of Wirz were war crimes committed by him in his role as commandant of a Confederate prison located in Andersonville, Georgia. In particular, he was charged with the murder and abuse of prisoners as well as engaging in a conspiracy with the military and civilian leadership of the Confederacy to cause the deaths of Union prisoners. Between February 1864 and May 1865, more than thirteen thousand Union soldiers died while imprisoned at Camp Sumpter, more colloquially referred to as Andersonville Prison. These initial forays into holding individuals responsible under the law for acts of the state during war laid the foundation for the institutionalization of war crimes tribunals after World War II.

Before Nuremberg, several prosecutions were contemplated then abandoned. Although considered, prosecutions of Napoleon and the Bonapartists in 1815 and later against Wilhelm II and other alleged war criminals after World War I never occurred. The planned trials that arose out of the Armenian genocide in 1915 collapsed in abject failure with no major international power interested in pursuit of those who engaged in the slaughter. As considered in Chapter 3, once the Nazis were defeated and World War II came to a close, however, the Allies institutionalized the concept of war crimes tribunals through the Nuremberg Trials. Nuremberg became the standard by which future war crimes trials would be judged. Although a paragon of virtue and success from both a procedural due process and substantive due process standpoint, the Nuremberg Trials failed to provide the victim class with either restitution or a substantial role in the proceedings. An effort to replicate in Tokyo the jurisprudential successes of Nuremberg failed. The defects of the Tokyo trials were expansive and substantial. From rules of evidence that overwhelmingly favored the prosecution to the ability to prosecute representatives of classes of criminals, the Tokyo trials failed to establish any modicum of justice. Indeed, the emperor, the head of state during the belligerence, was never mentioned at any of the trials and was not charged or prosecuted in any way.

Although the Tokyo trials fell far short of an exercise in justice and the Nuremberg Trials failed to address restitution, combined they formed the foundation of an international expectation of postconflict prosecutions. That is, these two efforts institutionalized the expectation that war crimes tribunals would follow war when the rules of engagement were disregarded. The international community's embrace of prosecutions for war crimes and crimes against humanity led to a comparable expectation at the domestic level. In Chapter 4, I turn to domestic war crimes tribunals. Domestic war crimes tribunals followed the demise of authoritarian and undemocratic regimes around the world. This chapter considers the trials that arose after the Dirty War in Argentina, the Truth and Reconciliation Tribunals after the demise of apartheid in South Africa, and the lustration process in the Eastern European states after the fall of the Soviet Union as exemplars of domestic war crimes tribunals. In each case, the architects of the trials were bounded by the political landscape.

In Argentina, President Alfonsin was elected based on a promise to prosecute those responsible for the massive human rights violations. However, he was constrained by the reality that the military continued as an institution after the election. He could not prosecute too much or too many members of the military or he would have faced a coup from a renewed military establishment. In the end, Alfonsin provided as much justice as he believed he could without jeopardizing the peace. In South Africa, after years of domination, the white minority owned most of the economic resources in the country. If Nuremberg-style tribunals were implemented, the white flight and ensuing economic drain might have undercut any possibility that the African National Congress could govern. Since white South Africa had capitulated – holding elections was an admission of wrongdoing – the victorious ANC could afford to be magnanimous. Moreover, they simply could not afford to be vengeful without the risk of total economic collapse. In the former Soviet states of Eastern Europe, the abuse of the citizenry was so ubiquitous by those who worked in the governmental institutions that widespread prosecutions for the bad acts that occurred during the Soviet era would have decimated the capacity to govern or provide for even a nominal administration of state.

This leads to a consideration of the third-party war crimes tribunals in Chapter 5. Third-party war crimes tribunals are those in which the administrators of the trials do not belong to the victim class and were not directly involved in the conflict that preceded the trials. In these cases, ad hoc human rights trials that arise from domestic conflict are conducted by the international community. That is, countries uninvolved in the conflict that gave rise to the allegations of atrocities are in charge of the prosecution and resolution of the claims. The International Criminal Tribunal for the former Yugoslavia (ICTY) and the International Criminal Tribunal for Rwanda (ICTR) are considered here. Both the ICTY and the ICTR suffered from severe limitations of efficacy and accomplishment. The ICTY faced hurdles such as the difficult notion of plea bargains with perpetrators of atrocities and a lack of cooperation among the home population of the defendant class. The ICTR was so inefficient that the people of Rwanda in essence circumvented both it and the formal domestic proceedings through the *gacaca* process. These trials administered by a third party prepared the way for the globalization of war crimes trials through the International Criminal Court. That is, the ICTY and the ICTR served as precursors and prototypes for the International Criminal Court. The globalization and formal institutionalization of war crimes tribunals through the ICC is considered in Chapter 6. The purpose of the ICC is to serve as an independent and permanent tribunal with jurisdiction over the crime of genocide, crimes against humanity, war crimes, and the crime of aggression. This chapter addresses the scope and the limitations of the ICC, including severe jurisdictional limitations such as complementarity. While the ICC is perhaps the logical outcome of the evolution of these tribunals, its jurisdictional limitations mean it is unlikely to prosecute any but the politically weakest global actors. Chapter 6 concludes with a brief consideration of the prosecutions, investigations, and adjudications to date as well as the pending cases before the ICC. Each of the active cases arises out of conflict in sub-Saharan Africa. Considering the establishment of the ICC and the long history of ad hoc tribunals, the global community might reasonably expect some prosecution for war crimes and other crimes against humanity no matter where those bad acts occur. The very idea of the ICC seems predicated on that expectation. In fact, however, the jurisdictional constraints severely limit the countries and actors who could be subject to any process before the ICC.

Despite the global expectation of trials and the now established institutional structure in which to hold them, there are conflicts that have ample incidents of the categorical crimes but no possibility of war crimes prosecutions. While terrorism, included in Chapter 7 with the wars in Iraq and Afghanistan, may arise out of similar concerns about self-determination and sovereignty, the externalities of terrorism know no bounds. Shortly after the attacks of September 11, 2001, the United States invaded Afghanistan. This advent of the Western War on Terror and terrorism as the preeminent security concern among industrialized nations suggests that the use of war crimes tribunals to prosecute nonstate or nonquasi-state actors has become normalized beyond the unique circumstances of Sierra Leone.

Quasi-state actors are those who claim a governmental right to act even when the international community may not recognize that right or that state. War crimes prosecutions of individuals *as* individuals and not in their roles as instruments of state action are unprecedented. Moreover, in the United States, the concept of a military tribunal has been merged into the concept of a war crimes trial for the purposes of prosecuting members of the Taliban in Afghanistan and other captives of the War on Terror. Modern terrorism has altered the role of war crimes tribunals as dramatically as it has altered the realities of war. Modern war is closely related to terrorism although the prosecutions that have arisen in the context of actual war have been different than those that arose in the context of terrorism.

Chapter 7 also considers the trials that arose after the United States invaded Iraq. From the outset of the first movements of belligerence toward Iraq, war crimes trials were contemplated for members of the Saddam Hussein regime. This chapter assesses the effect that this modern war has had on the institution of war crimes tribunals. It also assesses the consequences of planning for war crimes tribunals at the outset of the offensive action. The prospect of war crimes tribunals is now used before the cessation of conflict as public relations weapons alongside the normal propaganda of war.

Chapter 8 draws conclusions from the cases presented. The history and evolution of war crimes tribunals suggest that politics is of primary concern. Inevitably, concerns about justice give way to political considerations. In essence, retribution and deterrence are luxuries for those who are victorious on the battlefield. Justice from the perspective of victims is a scarce commodity even when procedural due process and substantive due process have become institutionalized by the international community. In the final analysis, politics prevails in even the best of circumstances and justice is relegated to the status of a symbolic excuse for prosecution.

2

Antecedents and Origins of War Crimes Tribunals

The Trial of Charles I and the Trial of Captain Henry Wirz

Charles I of England was the first head of state nominally tried for war crimes. His trial was the first foray into the realm of postconflict justice for heads of state although it was driven by nothing more than the political ambitions of his enemies. Still, the idea of holding the sovereign responsible for criminal conduct during times of conflict was a remarkable development that created the foundation upon which future claims of criminal liability would be constructed. The controversial prosecution and execution of Charles I did not introduce an immediately accepted new legal regime into the extant international jurisprudence, but rather initiated the possibility of postconflict prosecutions as a legitimate avenue for the delivery of justice. By the time the Civil War in the United States ended, many in leadership positions in the victorious Union were determined to prosecute

Confederate president Jefferson Davis for war crimes. The prosecution of Captain Henry Wirz, the commander at Andersonville Prison, was seen as the necessary first step toward the desired prosecution of Jefferson Davis because the suffering that occurred at the prison was one of the few opportunities to claim sufficient atrocities by the Rebel forces to justify prosecutions. Like the trial of Charles I, the prosecution of Wirz was motivated by a desire to punish the defeated and consolidate political power after a military victory. In the case of Wirz, the public was so disenchanted by the overtly political nature of the prosecution that it made a judicial pursuit of Jefferson Davis politically untenable. In this chapter, I begin with a description of the trial of Charles I followed by that of Captain Wirz. I then develop the argument that these cases laid the foundation for future prosecutions.

The Trial of Charles I

Charles I of England was tried and executed in January of 1649. While the case of Charles I may not instantly bring to mind notions of prosecutions in response to human rights violations, a review of the enabling legislation passed by Parliament and the transcripts of the trial reveals that it was conceptually the first step down the developmental path to modern war crimes trials. Charles I became king of England in 1625 and governed while engaged in a perpetually difficult relationship with Parliament. Over a thirteen-year period, the king requested funds from Parliament for wars against Scotland and Ireland three separate times. Parliament provided a portion of the requested funds the first two times only in exchange for his agreement to transfer some of his authority to Parliament. After the third request, Parliament refused to provide funds under any circumstances. In response to Parliament's refusal to fund his war and its rebuke of his authority, the king entered the House of Commons with armed soldiers, intent on arresting several members of Parliament. Not only was the king unable to actually take any member of Parliament into custody, his actions were deemed so outrageous by the public and Parliament that he was forced to flee London.

The king of course did not simply abandon his rule or claim to the right to govern. Rather, he fled London in order to form an army so he could reclaim his position as functional, as well as titular, head of state. England was suddenly engaged in civil war. The king's loyalists were known as the Cavaliers. They were pitted against the supporters of Parliament called the Roundheads. Eventually, as the Roundheads gained an advantage in the conflict, a fissure developed between Parliament and the army it formed to battle the king. The split was ideologically driven. Thomas, Lord Fairfax, the leader of the Parliamentarians, was in favor of a constitutional monarchy with shared power between the Parliament and the king. Oliver Cromwell, the leader of the army, now nominally independent from Parliament, favored a very weak king with no power arising from a constitutional base (Williamson 1957, pp. 15–17; Wingfield-Stratford 1950, pp. 3–11).

After Cromwell's army gained a stable advantage and was essentially in control of the mechanisms of state for England, the constitutional issue that dominated the political discourse concerned the basis of government. One vision of government was rule by a single house of Parliament, elected biennially with no regard to property ownership as a requisite to suffrage (Williamson 1957, p. 18). The plan for Parliament divorced from property ownership contemplated a "constitutional levelling" that, with no regard for wealth or standing, would disperse power among the citizens. Colonel Thomas Rainsborough was the leader of the Levellers. Because Cromwell was opposed to the plan of the Levellers, he aligned with Fairfax against Rainsborough to seek some form of constitutional monarchy. Thus, Cromwell's coalition with Fairfax supported a continuation of Parliament as it was, without a powerful king. That is, they wanted to establish a modified version of the traditional way to rule.

The personal and professional rivalry of Cromwell and Rainsborough was as intense as their two visions of government were irreconcilable. In the fall of 1647, Rainsborough is reported to have hissed at Cromwell as an aside: "One of us must not live" (Ibid.). Once Cromwell had Rainsborough killed in October 1648, the execution of Charles I became a foregone conclusion. In essence, as long as Rainsborough was alive and leading the left, Cromwell worked for the restoration of the king even if to a weakened and powerless throne. While Cromwell was no fan of the monarchy conceptually and in particular held Charles I in contempt, his faction was too small to form a long-term, stable power coalition without alignment with one of the other groups. Once Rainsborough was dead, Fairfax perceived Cromwell as the only threat to his consolidation of power and their alliance began to dissolve. Once Cromwell realized the threat Fairfax represented, Cromwell adopted the policy and position of the Levellers, the destruction of the monarchy, so he could create an alliance with the leaderless Levellers (Ibid., pp. 18–21).

Two events made Cromwell's decision to abandon a resurrected monarchy an easy one. Charles I set his own execution in motion through his efforts to deceive Cromwell (Wedgewood 1964, p. 4; Williamson 1957, p. 19; Wingfield-Stratford 1950, p. vii). Even as Charles I negotiated with Cromwell for a return to his throne during the so-called Hampton Court negotiations, he sent a letter to the queen of France to give her his assurance that he had no intention of abiding by any agreement reached with Cromwell. He went so far as to assure her he intended to hang Cromwell at the earliest possible opportunity. After Cromwell's spies intercepted the letter and delivered it to him, Cromwell no longer made any effort to construct or even consider restoring the monarchy as a resolution to the ongoing dispute.

For some of the other members of Parliament, a more serious and outrageous act than the professed intent to kill Cromwell was the procurement by Charles I of Scottish mercenaries to invade the shores of England. The procurement contract gave the Scottish mercenaries the authority to use "all possible measures for suppressing the opinions and practices of Independents and all such doctrines and practices as are contrary to the light of nature or to the known principles of Christianity" (Williamson 1957, p. 20). In exchange, the Scottish were to be given admission to the English Privy Counsel as well as one-third of all available patronage positions once Charles I was restored to the monarchy (Ibid.). This effort by Charles I to "establish Presbyterianism at the point of Scottish swords as the State religion of England" was considered an unforgivable act of malfeasance and a near complete abdication of his duties to England by the leaders of the British army as well as by Cromwell and the members of his coalition. To Cromwell and the members of the British army, the Scots were invading foreigners hired by a disgraced, desperate, and crownless king. The act of engaging the Scottish army to invade England was, Cromwell wrote, "a more prodigious Treason than any that had been perpetrated before" because it was meant to "vassalize us to a *foreign* nation" (Ibid., p. 21, emphasis in original). By the end of November 1648, Cromwell had decided he had to kill the king as a "cruel necessity" (Ibid., p. 22). In Cromwell's mind, the king had made clear beyond any doubt that he was not going to allow Cromwell to be the functional ruler of England. Accordingly, the death of the king was a prerequisite to Cromwell's consolidation of power.

Charles I could not be allowed to live if Cromwell was to implement his vision of an England without a king. As one supporter of Cromwell stated, "though we defeat him one hundred times, he is still the King" (Ibid.). While Cromwell had effectively seized power from a military victory frame of view, his hold on the authority of office was tenuous. Charles I could become a resurrected monarch with even a minor shift in public support. In an effort to consolidate and legitimize his overthrow of the king and assumption of power, Cromwell opted to ignore the long history of tyrannicide in Europe in favor of a new concept. He would not merely kill the defeated king; he would place the sitting monarch on trial and defeat him again in a court of law (Mayfield 1988, pp. 34–8). The appeal to the rule of law as a justification for their actions was a mechanism used by Cromwell and his faction simply to facilitate the implementation of the style of government that they desired. The premise of how this approach would help consolidate power was straightforward. Specifically, if even the monarch was subject to the dictates of the law, then the law would be supreme over everyone. Those who constructed the law would also be bound by it. Merely killing the king would leave the premise or idea of the monarchy intact, even if the actual monarch was executed. A prosecution would strip the office as well as the officeholder of the divine and untouchable aura reserved for royalty. From a practical standpoint, the trial would repeal the law that assumed infallibility on the part of the king.

The trial of Charles I was justified under the same rationale as, and closely resembled, modern human rights trials. The trial arose after the conclusion of a conflict for the nominal purpose of redressing the wrongs committed by the captured agents of government against civilians and those who prevailed in the conflict. The king's alleged crimes included murdering civilians, torture, and involuntary conscription. These crimes are all well within the range of crimes considered and prosecuted by modern war crimes tribunals. If the trial of Charles I resembles some rough equivalent to a modern human rights trial, then the question becomes one of whether justice was served or whether this prosecution was merely an effort by Cromwell and the other victors to consolidate power. The presence or absence of justice in the proceeding can be assessed by an examination of the procedural due process and substantive due process of the trial as well as a review of the degree to which deterrence and retribution were the goals of the trial. The documentary history of the trial edited by Lagomarsino and Wood (1989) provides an accessible and reliable record.

On January 1, 1649, the remaining members of the House of Commons approved an ordinance calling for the trial of Charles I because:

Charles Stuart hath acted contrary to his trust in departing from the Parliament, setting up his standard, making a war against them, and thereby [hath] been the occasion of much bloodshed and misery to the people.... [H]e gave commissions to [foreign] rebels ... [and] what he has done contrary to the liberties of the subject and tending to the destruction of the fundamental laws and liberties of this kingdom (Lagomarsino and Wood 1989, pp. 1–3, 15–16).

The House of Commons approved the ordinance that provided for the king's trial. The difficulty that arose from the vote is that Charles I was to be tried for crimes that amounted to treason. However, the previous definition of treason also affirmatively contemplated a specific intent to harm the well-being of the king. Obviously, the king could not be deemed to have committed treason under the prior law short of a showing of self-harm, attempted suicide, or reckless self-endangerment (Wedgewood 1964, p. 6). So in order to have a law that Charles I could have violated, the House of Commons then declared: "[I]t is treason for the King of England for the time being to levy war against the Parliament and Kingdom of England" (Ibid., p. 17).

When the House of Lords refused to affirm or even vote on the prosecution ordinance, the House of Commons elected to proceed without the House of Lords. The House of Commons passed another ordinance that declared anything it passed "hath the force of law, and all people of this nation are included thereby, although the consent and concurrence of King or House of Peers (Lords) be not had thereunto" (Ibid., pp. 2, 22–3). The House of Commons indicted the king, then voted to rewrite the law of treason so that a crime existed that could justify the prosecution, and then declared itself the supreme power in England. Finally, the House of Commons passed another ordinance calling for a "High Court of Justice for the Trying and Judging of Charles Stuart, King of England" (Lagomarsino and Wood 1989, pp. 24–6). The ordinance contained in part the following accusations:

> Whereas it is notorious that Charles Stuart, the now King of England ... hath had a wicked design totally to subvert the ancient and fundamental laws and liberties of this nation, and in their place to introduce an arbitrary and tyrannical government, and that besides all the other evil ways and means to bring this design to pass he hath prosecuted it with fire and sword, levied and maintained a cruel war ... against Parliament and kingdom whereby the country has been miserably wasted ... Thousands of people murdered, and infinite other mischiefs committed ... (Ibid.).

The ordinance established the existence and membership of the High Court and granted it jurisdiction for the purposes of "hearing, trying, and adjudging of the said Charles Stuart" (Ibid.).

The trial of Charles I is flawed beyond redemption from a substantive due process standpoint. While the charges seem plausible as human rights violations and comport in general with the successive war crimes trials, the postindictment redefinition of treason suggests bold manipulation of the process and overt expediency in construction of the prosecutorial framework. That the tribunal was created and constructed specifically to try only one criminal from the entire conflict and that the substance of the charges had to be tailored to construct a charge that could stand against Charles I indicates that the tribunal was more concerned with the specific criminal target than the crimes as presented by the prosecution.

Procedurally, the trial fares even worse. The procedure for the trial was established in the authorizing statute. The charges against Charles I would be read, the court would take his answer, followed by an examination of witnesses under oath or "otherwise," and taking any other evidence. After the evidence, the court would proceed to a final sentence and execution of the sentence (Ibid.). Since the crime of treason was first enacted by statute in England in 1352, the law had never provided the accused with counsel or allowed the accused to obtain their own counsel (Lagomarsino and Wood 1989, p. 6). The process established for the trial of Charles I had no avenue or possibility of appeal, pardon, or reconsideration. Charles I could not challenge any evidentiary ruling, any ruling on any motion, and, most critically, any final judgment. The commissioners and judges of the court were the only participants able to call witnesses or present evidence. Accordingly, Charles I faced his accusers without counsel, with no capacity to present a defense or challenge the prosecutorial evidence, with no right of cross examination of any kind, and without the ability to appeal the decision in any way.

The king was brought into the House of Commons and stood before the High Court. For the first time, as the formal charges were read to him, Charles I learned why he faced trial (Ibid., pp. 61–4). The crimes charged included specific actions by the king that caused:

> many thousands of the free people of this nation to be slain ... invasions from foreign parts ... procured by him ... By which cruel and unnatural wars by him ... levied ... much innocent blood of the free people ... Hath been spilt ... By all which it appeareth that he ... is the occasioner, author and continuer of the said unnatural, cruel and bloody wars, and therein guilty of all the treasons, murders, rapines, burnings, spoils, desolations, damage and mischief to this nation. (Ibid., pp. 62–3).

The court sought to portray itself as an instrument of justice by repeating the mantra of generalized injustices perpetrated by the king. The indictment is not a roster of specific acts on specific dates that harmed specific people. Rather, it represents a general language of complaint that does little more than indicate that Charles I engaged in a war in England.

When the court instructed Charles I to respond to the charges with a plea, he instead immediately raised objections to the proceedings. He responded to the charge not with an answer of guilty or not guilty, but rather with a demand that the court identify the authority by which it intended to pass judgment over him (Ibid., p. 64). The king said, "[L]et me know by what lawful authority I am seated here and I shall not be unwilling to answer" (Ibid.). A lengthy exchange followed between Charles I and the court that never progressed past the king's argument there was no basis in law upon which the court could proceed and the court's retort that the trial would go forward. After this circular argument had gone on for some time, the court returned the king to confinement and took a recess to consider how to more formally respond to the king's objections. Even if the argument of a complete absence of jurisdiction somehow could be overlooked, Charles I had no legal counsel and was completely unrepresented. He was prohibited from introducing any evidence against the charges or challenging any evidence that might be introduced by his accusers. The entirety of the participation by the king in the trial for his life was limited to his answer to the complaint – in short, nothing more than a plea without evidence.

The court met in private chambers during the recess so the members of the court could consider how to craft a response to the king's objection to the proceeding. They arrived at a parsimonious solution to the problem raised by the king. They resolved that Charles I would not be allowed to make the argument again (Ibid., p. 71). The king's challenge to the court's ability to make its members judges and the complete absence of any avenue or mechanism through which an appeal could be pursued were of particular concern for the court (Ibid.). Upon reconvening, the court announced that it had considered the king's complaints and the king should be satisfied the court did in fact have the authority to judge and sentence him (Ibid.). Further, there would be no additional consideration of the argument and the court would no longer hear or acknowledge any additional challenges to its authority or the procedure of the trial (Ibid.).

The first defense against the charges was the complete absence of procedural due process. This was also the most difficult argument for the court because it threatened the claim of legitimacy of the process. The court could not provide procedural due process for Charles I and continue to exercise its clearly unfounded jurisdiction. To acknowledge the king's due process argument and remedy the defects was to acknowledge the absence of a legal right to proceed.

Charles I was brought back before the court and again the king challenged its authority (Ibid., p. 74). John Bradshaw, Lord President of the Court, angrily responded to the king with a demand of capitulation of the argument and submission to the jurisdiction of the court: "[Y]ou appear as a prisoner ... if you ... dispute the authority of the court, we may not [engage in that argument] ... you are to submit unto it" (Ibid., pp. 75–7). As Charles I continued to protest, the lord president attempted to end the debate with the king and force him to end his argument: "[T]hey have considered ... their jurisdiction. They do affirm their own jurisdiction" (Ibid., p. 76). The king again objected, pointing out that the House of Commons never before in the history of England acted as or conducted any proceeding as a court of justice.

He demanded, "I would know how they came to be so" (Ibid., p. 77). The king refused to abandon his argument and would not answer the charges as demanded by the court. The court ordered that a plea of no answer be registered in the record and once again returned the king to his cell for confinement. The court then recessed (Ibid., p. 79).

The king prepared a speech to present in his defense. Although the court refused to allow Charles I the opportunity to make his argument, he argued in the written speech that "the King can do no wrong" (Ibid., p. 80). Charles I made a concise statement of his challenge to the legality of the proceeding: "[T]he law upon which you ground your proceedings must be either old or new. If old, show it; if new, tell what authority … hath made it, and when" (Ibid.). The court of course understood that the king was correct in his complaint. Accordingly, in order to proceed, the court had no choice but to ignore his argument.

Charles I also argued that the substance of the trial was as indefensible and specious as the assertion of jurisdiction by the court. Charles I defended the acts that formed the basis of the charges as the proper acts of a patriot and the expected actions of the king. This line of argument is an early precursor and foreshadow of the "good soldier" defenses of the modern trials; the king argued "[B]y this time it will be too sensibly evident that the arms I took up were only to defend the fundamental laws of this kingdom" (Ibid., p. 81). Thus, the king argued that the court had no authority to conduct the proceedings and that the charges levied against him only arose out of his legitimate, proper, and dutiful defense of England.

When Charles I was brought before the court for a third time, he was not allowed to address the court (Ibid., p. 83). The prosecutor or solicitor asked for and received leave of the court to proceed with the presentation of evidence and, since the charges against Charles I were true, to then proceed to judgment (Ibid., p. 84). The solicitor ended his address to the court with the following: "I do humbly pray – and yet, I must confess, it is not so much I as the innocent blood that hath been shed, the cry whereof is very great for justice and judgment – and therefore I do humbly pray that speedy judgment be performed against the prisoner" (Ibid.).

Charles I once again sought to explain his objection to the proceeding. This time he wanted to assert the defense and satisfy the people of England that he only acted to defend the ancient laws entrusted to him (Ibid., pp. 86–8). The court refused to allow him to present his argument and responded to his rhetoric with overt contempt: "[M]en's intentions ought to be known by their actions. You have written your meaning in bloody characters throughout the whole kingdom" (Ibid., p. 87). The court then ordered a default – an admission through nonresponse – be entered against him and replace the no answer plea entered on his behalf earlier (Ibid.).

Even though the king had already been convicted, the court determined it was time to introduce evidence into the trial. The court took testimony for two days that confirmed the charges (Ibid., pp. 88–100). The witnesses presented to the court testified they saw Charles I give direct orders to kill civilians, seize property, and hire foreigners to invade England (Ibid.). Testimony was admitted that the king forced unwilling civilians into conscription and that he persecuted citizens of England who would not accept the episcopacy in their churches through torture and the seizure of property (Ibid.). Among other atrocities, the testimony established that to defy the Christian sensibilities of Charles I was to risk the amputation of ears and the mutilation of noses (Ibid.). These charges of torture, forced conscription, and other human rights violations against Charles I, without exception, easily fit within the parameters of more modern human rights trials.

Upon the completion of the presentation of evidence, the court resolved:

> that the condemnation of the King shall be for a tyrant, traitor, and murderer; that the condemnation of the King shall be likewise for being a public enemy to the Common wealth of England; that this condemnation shall extend to death (Ibid., p. 100).

The court met the next day to write the actual sentence and on the subsequent day Charles I was brought back to the House of Commons to receive the sentence in person (Ibid., pp. 102–11).

After additional unsuccessful attempts by Charles I to point out the court's lack of jurisdiction, Lord President

Bradshaw presented his closing argument prior to sentencing by the court (Ibid., pp. 118–28). Although Bradshaw did not give the argument until after the conviction of Charles I and the subsequent evidentiary phase of the proceedings was over, his speech was a justification of the trial and an attempt to finally respond to the king's allegation of a lack of jurisdiction. Bradshaw argued that any king first ruled by the will of the people and that will was revocable. Bradshaw asserted that "the end of having kings or any other governors is for the enjoying of justice, that's the end" (Ibid., p. 120). Bradshaw then introduced a deterrence dimension to the trial when he put future kings and governors on notice:

> Now sir, if so be the King will go contrary to that end, or any other governor will go contrary to the end … he must understand that he is but an officer in trust and he ought to discharge that trust and … the people … are to take order for the animadversion [criticism] and punishment of such an offending governor (Ibid.).

Having established that the trial should serve as a deterrent for future kings and having put forth a warning to others in power that they would answer to the people if they abused their power, Bradshaw then argued that the purpose of Parliament was retribution for the people. "Sir, Parliaments were ordained for that purpose, to redress the grievances of the people. That was their main end" (Ibid., p. 121). He further asserted, "[I]f wrong be done by the King … justice hath power to reform the wrong" (Ibid.). Bradshaw concluded his overall justification of the prosecution and trial generally by a proclamation that warned other government officials: "[L]et all men know that great offices are seizable and forfeitable" (Ibid., p. 125). Bradshaw's speech unequivocally set forth the dual formal goals of the proceeding as retribution and deterrence.

The sentence of Charles I recounted the charges and proceedings of the trial and concluded:

> For all which treasons and crimes, this court doth adjudge that he, the said Charles Stuart, as a tyrant, traitor, murderer, and public enemy to the good people of this nation, shall be put to death by the severing of his head from his body (Ibid., p. 109).

On January 30, 1649, the sentence was carried out and Charles I was beheaded.

Despite Lord President Bradshaw's claims that the rationale of the trial was driven by concerns about deterrence of future misbehavior by future governors and kings and retribution for England, the House of Commons abolished both the monarchy and the House of Lords within one week of the king's execution (Ibid., p. 144–5). The lawless consolidation of power after the king's execution cannot be reconciled with the claimed desire to hold the agents of government in check through establishing the rule of law as the ultimate authority. Bradshaw and the others in the House of Commons claimed to act against the king so as to deter those in authority from future bad acts and yet, judging by their conduct, no others beyond those in the House of Commons needed to be deterred. Any concern for retribution ended at the drop of the king's head into the basket at the foot of the executioner. That is, the House of Commons undertook no effort to establish any compensation for the victims of the king's alleged crimes. Both retribution and deterrence were wholly absent from consideration after the trial had ended and the execution had been accomplished.

Though there is historical dispute as to the legitimacy of the authorship of *The King's Book*, the diary purportedly was written by Charles I as he was detained for the trial and execution. There, Charles I wrote a response to the question of whether the trial was a political or juridical event (Almack 1901, pp. ix–xxiii):

> My Enemies ... will, it may be, seeke to adde (as those did who crucified Christ) the mockery of Justice, to the cruelty of Malice: That I may be destroyed, as with greater pomp and artifice, so with lesse pity, it will be but a necessary policy to make My death appeare as an act of justice, done by subjects upon their soveraigne ... who being sworn and bound by all that is sacred before God and Man, to endeavor My preservation, must pretend to cover their perjury (Ibid., p. 268).

Charles I parsimoniously summed the defects in the procedural due process when he woefully pointed out, "It is, indeed, a sad fate for any man to have his Enemies to be Accusers, Parties and Judges" (Ibid.). The king challenged the validity of the substantive due process when he wrote "those who have had the chiefest hand, and are most guilty of contriving the publique troubles, must by shedding My bloud seem to wash their own hands of that innocent bloud, whereof they are now most evidently guilty" (Ibid.).

The trial of Charles I had little to do with justice and a great deal to do with the consolidation of power. That justice was served at all cannot be argued persuasively. The trial itself was premised upon a political strategy developed and implemented by Cromwell to enable him to rule without fear of a rival emerging with a viable claim to legitimacy. The trial was little more than an ad hoc process designed and manipulated in progress to result in conviction. The substantive dimensions of the prosecution were comprised primarily of the foregone conclusion of guilt on the part of Charles I. Justice was little more than a verbal camouflage used to conceal the unambiguous political intent of those in power. Retribution and deterrence were given pro forma attention by the prosecutor and used as justifications for the proceeding in order to accomplish the true goal of the trial – the execution of the king in particular and the diminution of the monarchy generally. As Lagomarsino and Wood declare, "Baldly stated, the plain fact was that Charles I had lost a civil war and was therefore made to pay the price for his loss" (1989, p. 2).

Cromwell claimed to seek "justice" through beheading Charles I. More plausibly, he perceived he could only quash the lingering symbolic power of the crown through the death of the monarch. The execution of Charles I did not, however, end the monarchy as Cromwell had hoped. The political consolidation at the root of Cromwell's judicial approach to the elimination of Charles I was short-lived. Indeed, in 1661, shortly after the monarchy was resurrected, Cromwell, who succumbed to illness in 1658, was exhumed and symbolically executed by decapitation on the twelfth anniversary of the execution of Charles I. Cromwell's sacrifice of justice on the altar of political consolidation did him no good because in the end, he was unable to dissuade the population from their preference for a monarchy. Had Charles I defeated Cromwell, no doubt Cromwell's head would have been the first to fall. The winner defined justice and constructed the framework of a trial for his political purposes. Although Cromwell ultimately failed, his efforts to claim that leaders in war were subject to the constraints of law succeeded in some measure. While some pointed to the example of Charles I and sought to prosecute Napoleon and the Bonapartists in 1815, exile was the final judgment. The next major war crimes trial did not occur until after the Civil War in the United States. The road from Charles I to Captain Henry Wirz was long in years, but short in concept.

The Trial of Captain Henry Wirz

From the outset of the American Civil War, both sides captured large numbers of soldiers. As the prisoner of war population increased, the drain on resources, combined with public sentiment, led the Union and the Confederate governments to reach an accord for a prisoner exchange system (Laska and Smith 1975, p. 79). An agreement was executed on July 22, 1862 that structured the exchange of prisoners and allowed both sides to dramatically limit their prisoner populations. The agreement began to strain under the pressures of war in the summer of 1863. The South objected to the release of former slaves captured fighting for the Union. Both sides argued over whether the agreement covered captured civilians. In July 1863, the South returned thirty-five thousand freed Confederate prisoners to combat in violation of the terms of the prisoner exchange agreement. Ulysses S. Grant, then the general in chief of the Union Army, suspended the prisoner exchanges. Grant recognized there were more Confederate soldiers in prison than Unions soldiers and that the Southern forces were more desperate for men than the Union forces (Catton 1959, pp. 5–6). Moreover, he believed that a cessation of the prisoner exchange would help end the war. In a telegram dated August 14, 1864, Grant wrote to General Benjamin Butler, the officer charged with oversight of the exchange program, "It is hard on our men not to exchange them, but it is humane to those left in the ranks of our battles" (Laska and Smith 1975, p. 80).

By the fall of 1863, the Confederate prisons were overflowing and the Confederate secretary of war, James Seddon, ordered Captain Sidney Winder to find a proper location and build a new prison (Wirz Trial, U.S. War Dept., War of Rebellion Official Records 1880–1901; vol. 6, p. 965–6 and vol. 8, p. 732). Andersonville, Georgia was chosen as the site for the new prison and construction began in January 1864. The site was chosen in part because it had a stream running through it that could provide clean water. Additionally, it was far away from any current battle zones so a minimal guard force would be necessary since a Union assault on the compound would be unlikely. A large number of prisoners could be detained at a minimal cost of greatly needed Confederate soldiers. Also, because Andersonville had a population of about twenty people and was little more than a railroad stop and a post office, there would be little local objection to construction of the prison (Futch 1968, pp. 3–4). Although the compound was formally named Camp Sumpter, it was colloquially referred to as Andersonville Prison from the outset. The location, now operated by the National Parks Service, is known today as the Andersonville National Historic Site and also hosts the National Prisoner of War Museum.

The design of the prison was straightforward. Like many Confederate prisons, it could be described as a stockade around a field. Trimmed and sharpened pine logs twenty feet long and eight to twelve inches thick were buried five feet in the ground to form the primary containment wall. Sentry boxes stood at regular intervals along the walls and an outer perimeter that was about twelve feet high was constructed. Outside the exterior walls, armed guards were located in dirt bunkers as the final barrier to escape. The original prison covered about seventeen acres of land and was later enlarged to about twenty-six acres. It was designed to hold ten thousand prisoners (Laska and Smith 1975, p. 81).

The first 500 prisoners arrived on February 20, 1864, prior to completion of construction (Futch 1968, p. 8). By April, 7,160 men were imprisoned. By July, more than twenty-five thousand men were held there. The prison population was increasing at a rate of several hundred a day and by August 1864 over thirty-three thousand men were crammed into the confines of a camp designed for only ten thousand. Although the original plans contemplated barracks for the prisoners, the high cost of materials meant no shelter was constructed (Wirz Trial, U.S. Dept. War, War of Rebellion, Official Records 1880–1901, vol. 6, pp. 956–66; vol. 8, p. 732). Prisoners were left to their own devices to construct crude tents, shrub huts, or any shelter at all to keep them out of the rain and sun. The Confederacy had been unable to clothe its own soldiers for some time. Prisoners could not expect any type of personal supplies to be provided. Those confined in Andersonville only had the clothing they brought through the gates. Additionally, there was not a sufficient supply of food for the prisoners. Even when they managed to find a meal, since the cooking facilities were inadequate for the size of the prison population, they ate raw grain or corn. The initial draw for the location – the water source running the length of the compound – turned into one of its largest problems. Because the camp was seriously overcrowded, had no sanitation system, and the meager hospital/morgue was located within the camp, the creek became a conduit of disease throughout the compound (Futch 1968, pp. 3–62). One Confederate guard described the conditions at Andersonville as follows: "They [the Union soldiers] have ... caused us such suffering, I feel no pity for them.... It is a singular sight to look down into this inclosure [*sic*] [Andersonville]. The suffering within both mind and body is fearful and one can only compare it to Hades on Earth" (Kennedy, Diary, June 18, 1864, p. 85). The population peaked in the early fall of 1864 and as the Confederacy retreated, it took fewer prisoners. Moreover, after August 1864, the death rate exceeded the rate of new arrivals. Some months had merely high rates of mortality – in August of 1864, over three thousand men out of thirty-three thousand died in the hospital or stockade. Other months were staggering in the magnitude of deaths – October 1864 saw almost 4,690 deaths out of a population of less than ninety-five hundred (Ransom 1881, 1974 ed., p. 367).

On April 8, 1865, Confederate general Robert E. Lee surrendered a massive number of troops to Union general Ulysses S. Grant. Although Lee's surrender marked the beginning of the formal end of the Confederacy, some among the rebellion hoped to rally the remaining troops to fight on. Part of this effort included a plan to kidnap President Abraham Lincoln to force the return to a prisoner exchange policy – the only avenue available to re-man the Confederate forces. The kidnapping plot turned into an assassination and seven days after the large-scale Confederate surrender, Lincoln died from his wounds on April 15. By the end of

April 1865, the Union army had marched through Atlanta and Macon and had control of the territory surrounding the prison (McElroy 1879, p. 639). By then, over thirteen thousand men had died there (Belknap 2002, p. 467).

As early as the winter of 1864, the Joint Committee of the U.S. Congress on the Conduct of the War asserted there was a Southern conspiracy to cause the deaths of Union soldiers in the prisons (H.R. Report No. 67, 38th Cong. 1st Sess., 1864). A special commission came to the conclusion that "a predetermined plan ... for destroying and disabling soldiers" held as prisoners of war had originated with "rebel counsels" (Laska and Smith 1975, p. 83). The miserable conditions at Andersonville had become widely known and notorious. Lincoln's assassination altered the public sentiment in the North from one of reconciliation to one of punitive vengeance (Ibid.).

When General J. H. Wilson of the Union cavalry, headquartered in nearby Macon, Georgia, learned that the commandant of Andersonville Prison was still at the compound, he dispatched a squad of men to arrest him (McElroy 1879, p. 639). Captain Henry Wirz, the officer in charge of Andersonville Prison, was arrested on May 7, 1865.

Wirz was born in Switzerland in 1822 and moved to the United States to open a medical practice in 1854 (Rutherford 1921, p. 3). He called himself a physician, but seems to have received no formal medical training (Laska and Smith 1975, p. 85). At the start of the war, he was living in Louisiana. He enlisted in the Confederate army and was placed in Company A of the Fourth Battalion of Louisiana Volunteers (Rutherford 1921, p. 4). During the Battle of Seven Pines, which took place from May 31 to June 1, 1862 near Richmond Virginia, he was gravely wounded. His right arm just above the wrist was shattered, and while it was not amputated, it never fully healed nor did he regain any meaningful use of it (Laska and Smith 1975, p. 86; McElroy 1879, p. 640). Although after the injury, Wirz received a field promotion to captain, he was no longer physically fit for actual combat. He was reassigned under the command of Brigadier General John Winder, who was in charge of the Federal prisoners of war (Futch 1968, p. 6). Wirz was first put in charge of a prison in Alabama, but eventually was assigned to Andersonville. General Winder was closely involved with Andersonville from its inception. He arranged for his son, Captain W. Sidney Winder, to select the site and his nephew, Captain Richard Winder, to oversee construction for the prison (Laska and Smith 1975, p. 80).

From the moment he was arrested, Wirz was aware of his dire circumstances. On the day of his arrest, he wrote a letter to General Wilson insisting he planned to leave the country for Europe if only he was given safe conduct (McElroy 1879, p. 640). Wirz also made a preemptive claim that he should not be blamed for the horrors of the prison. He wrote: "The duties I had to perform were arduous and unpleasant, and I am satisfied that no man can or will justly blame me for things that happened here, and which were beyond my power to control. I do not think I ought to be held responsible for the shortness of rations, for the overcrowded state of the prison (which was itself a prolific source of fearful mortality), for the inadequate supply of clothing, want of shelter, etc. etc." (Wirz letter to Wilson, May 7, 1865 cited in McElroy 1879, p. 640). Wirz unknowingly foreshadowed his defense at trial when he wrote, "Still I now bear the odium, and men who were prisoners have seemed disposed to wreak their vengeance upon me for what they have suffered – I, who was only the medium, or, I may better say, the tool in the hands of my superiors" (Ibid.).

Although he recognized there was a great deal of hostility toward him, Wirz and his supporters later claimed he had surrendered under the belief that he was protected by an umbrella grant of a general amnesty. In short, the foundation of the claim of amnesty was that when Confederate general Joseph E. Johnston surrendered to Union general William T. Sherman on April 18, 1865, they agreed to a broad grant of a "general pardon" for the soldiers under Johnston's command (Ruhlman 2006, p. 167). Wirz's supporters claimed his trial and execution were illegal because he was taken into custody despite this pardon (Page and Haley 1908, p. 236; Ruhlman 2006, p. 167). Of course, if Wirz actually believed he was covered by a pardon, there would have been little reason to prepare the letter to Wilson that pled for leniency and safe passage.

On May 20, 1865, General Wilson ordered the arresting officer, Captain Henry Noyes, to take Wirz and, importantly, the hospital records of Andersonville Prison to Washington,

DC (Futch 1968, p. 117). Although Abraham Lincoln's death was well beyond any sphere of influence that could credibly be attributed to Wirz, unquestionably his fate became bound to the investigation of the assassination.

Lincoln had appointed former secretary of war Joseph Holt the judge advocate general (JAG) in September 1862 (Ruhlman 2006, p. 173). The JAG operated under the auspices of the War Department as its chief prosecutor. On June 20, 1864, Congress established the Bureau of Military Justice as a specific division of the War Department and expanded the duties of the JAG. The expanded responsibilities included oversight of military tribunals, interpretive duties regarding military law, and control over the enforcement of military justice (Wirz Trial U.S. Dept. War, War of Rebellion, Official Records 1880–1901, vol. 4, p. 774). The JAG was charged with calling and swearing in witnesses and the introduction of evidence through testimony and otherwise. Distinct from a civilian prosecutor, the JAG also had the specific obligation to advise the presiding court about facts or any other matter to avoid error in the proceedings. The JAG was also directed to provide legal guidance and advisory opinions to the court (Ruhlman 2006, p. 175).

The creation of the Bureau of Military Justice led to an expansion of the use of military tribunals as a primary vehicle for prosecution of those engaged in the rebellion. Although *Ex Parte Milligan* (71 U.S. 2 [1866]) seemed to limit the scope of military tribunals by rejecting the argument that the Bill of Rights provided no protections during war, thousands of military tribunals were empanelled and used for the dispensation of justice until the Southern states were readmitted to the Union in 1877. After the assassination of Lincoln, Secretary of War Edwin Stanton used the Bureau of Military Justice and the office of the JAG to prosecute the Lincoln conspirators. Secretary Stanton, Judge Advocate General Holt, the editors of the *New York Times*, and popular sentiment in the North all held Confederate president Jefferson Davis, General Robert E. Lee, and other Confederate military and civilian leadership liable for the assassination of Lincoln as well as the deaths of Union soldiers in captivity (Belknap 2001–2002, p. 467; Ruhlman 2006, p. 176). However, the prosecutions of the Lincoln conspirators proved controversial and unpopular (Belknap 2001–2002, pp. 462–7). The civilians implicated in the plot were tried and convicted by a military commission based on perjured testimony, with no opportunity to appeal. Indeed, shortly after the trials, one of the witnesses, Sanford Conver, was prosecuted for perjury and sentenced to ten years in prison (Belknap 2001–2002, p. 465). The office of the JAG also convened a federal grand jury in Norfolk, Virginia to present bills of indictment against Davis and Lee, charging them with treason. The lack of public support for the Lincoln conspiracy prosecutions paled in comparison to the reaction to these efforts to prosecute the Confederate leadership. The country was tired of war and committed to reconciliation. Although Ulysses S. Grant lobbied President Johnson to issue a pardon, neither Johnson nor Stanton was persuaded by the appeal for clemency. Stanton viewed the prosecution of Wirz as the vehicle through which he could silence the growing Northern clamor to free Jefferson Davis (Ruhlman 2006, p. 179). Stanton hoped to prove through the Wirz trial that the Confederates had conspired to kill imprisoned Union soldiers (Ibid.). The prosecution and conviction of Wirz was a necessary first step toward establishing a foundation of culpability upon which a prosecution of Jefferson Davis could be constructed.

Despite reservations about the propriety of the Lincoln conspiracy trials, the War Department lawyers viewed them as a foundational precedent upon which they could proceed against Wirz (Laska and Smith 1975, p. 95). Wirz was charged with two counts. First, Wirz was charged with "combining, confederating, and conspiring ... to injure the health and destroy the lives of soldiers in the military service of the United States, there held and being prisoner of war within the lines of the so-called Confederate States, and in the military prisons thereof, to the end that the armies of the United States might be weakened and impaired in violation of the laws and customs of war" (McElroy 1879, p. 641).

The second count of the indictment against Wirz contained thirteen specific charges of the murder and maltreatment of prisoners under his control (Page and Haley 1908, pp. 191–204). Although each of the thirteen specifications contained precise details as to the date of the alleged acts, the manner in which the deaths and poor treatment occurred, including details such as whether a musket or a pistol was used to kill the victims, none of the alleged victims were named. Some specifications directly accused Wirz of killing a prisoner while others accused him of ordering the execution of a prisoner or malicious treatment of a prisoner that led to a death. Indeed, each specification contained the phrase "whose name is unknown" and none of them identified any victim by name (Ibid.).

Originally, the list of unindicted co-conspirators included Confederate president Jefferson Davis, General Robert E. Lee, Georgia Confederate commander Major General Howell Cobb, two surgeons from the Andersonville prison hospital – R. R. Stevenson and Isaiah White – as well as John Winder, Richard Winder, and Sidney Winder (Belknap 2001–2002, p. 468; Ruhlman 2006, p. 182). Secretary Stanton saw the Wirz trial as an opportunity for redemption after the unpopular Lincoln conspiracy trials and a chance to definitively implicate Jefferson Davis and the other Confederate leaders in the assassination (Ruhlman 2006, p. 178). However, President Johnson and Stanton, as well as others in the cabinet, did not want to relocate Jefferson Davis to Washington where he would get even more attention and perhaps generate sympathy among the public (Laska and Smith 1975, pp. 100–3). The original charges were publicly read on August 21, 1865, but the proceeding ended as soon as Stanton realized Holt included charges against the Confederate leadership in the indictment (Ibid., p. 101). Stanton adjourned the proceedings until further notice and on August 22, Major General Lew Wallace, the president of the commission, announced President Johnson had dissolved the commission and closed the proceedings (Ruhlman 2006, p. 183). New charges were prepared that were identical to the first set except the co-conspirators were limited to lower ranked officers and those directly affiliated with the operation of the prison and a broad indictment of "others unknown" was tacked onto the roster of defendants (Laska and Smith 1975, p. 102).

When Wirz was again arraigned on August 23, 1865, his lawyers presented several affirmative defenses in the form of objections that they claimed defeated the indictment (McElroy 1879, p. 641). In response to the new indictment, the defense sought a delay in the proceedings in order to prepare. Wirz also argued that double jeopardy barred the second prosecution since he had pled to the charges two days earlier and those were dismissed when the commission was dissolved (Laska and Smith 1975, p. 108). The defense contended that Wirz was either entitled to defend against the original charges or should be set free. The commission rejected the argument, ordered Wirz to plead to the new charges, and proceeded with the trial (Ibid.). The defense then argued that Wirz had been offered protection by General Wilson and was therefore exempt from prosecution. Alternatively, Wirz claimed immunity under the surrender terms reached between Generals Sherman and Johnston. The defense also asserted that the military tribunal lacked jurisdiction because the war had ended. Moreover, even if the tribunal could exist outside the scope of conflict, it lacked jurisdiction in this case. The final avenue of defense was that the charges were overly vague regarding the time, location, and manner of the claimed offenses (Page and Haley 1908, p. 204). The tribunal overruled all of the objections and Wirz's legal team entered not guilty pleas to all charges (McElroy 1879, p. 641).

In light of the refusal to grant the requested one-week delay and the cursory rulings on the affirmative defenses, the two lawyers representing Wirz withdrew from the case. General Wallace allowed the withdrawals and announced from the bench that the judge advocate general – the man who had spent the prior three months preparing the case for prosecution – would assume the defense of Wirz (Laska and Smith 1975, p. 108). For a brief period, it appeared Colonel Norton Chipman – the lead prosecutor for the office of the judge advocate general – would prosecute and vigorously work toward a conviction of Wirz, give "impartial advice" to the commission regarding evidence as well as instruct the commission on the proper application of law to the facts, and defend Wirz. The first two roles for Chipman were unavoidable given the statutory construction of the commission, but had he also served as Wirz's defense counsel, the proceedings would have been beyond any possibility of judicial redemption. Wirz was spared the indignity of his prosecutor also controlling his defense when an associate of Stephen Douglas, Louis Schade, and Otis Baker announced they would take over his defense (Ruhlman 2006, pp. 186–7).

Schade and Baker first moved to end the proceedings or reduce the charges against Wirz. They argued the commission lacked the appropriate jurisdiction to prosecute a foreign soldier for acts committed in war. Following the arguments made by the first defense team, Schade and Baker also argued Wirz was protected from prosecution either by the Johnston and Sherman parole agreement or by the promise of safe passage by Noyes (Wirz Trial U.S. Dept. War, War of Rebellion, Official Records 1880–1901, pp. 10–19). The terms of the Johnston and Sherman parole agreement also were the foundation for the defense argument that the charges should, at a minimum, be reduced as it would have extinguished any conspiracy engaged in prior to the broad parole (Ibid., p. 10). Chipman countered that Wirz was not in fact a soldier of a foreign nation, but rather was nothing more than a disloyal citizen (Ruhlman 2006, p. 188). The prosecution claimed the right to place citizens on trial through a military process during times of rebellion and pointed to the Whiskey Rebellion and the trial of Aaron Burr as support for the position (Wirz Trial U.S. Dept. War, War of Rebellion, Official Records 1880–1901, pp. 10–19). Chipman also argued that if Noyes had actually promised any safe passage, it was only for safe passage from Andersonville to Macon, Georgia (Laska and Smith 1975, p. 110). The commission ruled that only the president had the authority to forgive or pardon crimes committed during war and that the defense motions were irrelevant (Wirz Trial U.S. Dept. War, War of Rebellion, Official Records

1880–1901, pp. 13–17). At that point, with the summary and complete defeat of the pretrial motions, Schade and Baker believed that Wirz's fate was sealed and they decided to resign just as the first legal team had (Ruhlman 2006, p. 189). Although Wirz persuaded them to continue his defense, there was little they could do besides enter not guilty pleas on all counts (Ibid.).

The prosecution presented evidence through October 18, 1865. Over 160 Union soldiers who claimed to have been imprisoned in Andersonville testified (Page and Haley 1908, p. 207). Surgeons from the camp hospital and the prior commander of the camp testified to the miserable conditions after Wirz assumed command and to the unremarkable nature of the prison before he was stationed there (Ruhlman 2006. p. 189). Of course, the dramatic growth of the prisoner population happened during the period when Wirz was in command. His defense was simple: Wirz had provided the best accommodation possible for the prisoners brought to the compound given the resources he had available (Ibid.). He was not responsible for either the number of prisoners held or the lack of provisions available to distribute.

Once the evidence established Wirz was in charge of the internal operations of the prison, that the conditions in the prison were quite bad, and that the southern Georgia region had abundant food and resources that could have been used to improve those conditions, the prosecution turned to perhaps the primary purpose of the trial, the effort to implicate Jefferson Davis in the deaths of the prisoners

(Wirz Trial U.S. Dept. War, War of Rebellion, Official Records 1880–1901, pp. 100–2, 239–43, 276, 371–84). After the defense objections to the prosecutorial efforts to implicate Davis were overruled, Chipman turned to demonstrating that Wirz was a brutal commandant with no regard for the well-being or safety of his prisoners. Recall that the specifications that charged Wirz with killing particular prisoners identified the victims as unknown. That is, despite the parade of witnesses used to convict Wirz, not one person testified to the identity of any actual person killed or harmed by him as claimed in the indictment. The extensive prison records, which were known to exist and were available for use at the trial, make this omission in evidence especially problematic. The list of the dead from Andersonville identifies almost thirteen thousand people by name, state of origin, date of death, and headstone marker number, as well as a categorical breakdown of the cause of death for each prisoner (Ransom 1881, 1974 ed., pp. 269–368).

Robert Kellogg, a former prisoner, was called to testify early in the trial. He testified that although he had not witnessed maltreatment of any prisoner by Wirz, much less the murder or killing of any prisoner by Wirz, he believed Wirz must have treated prisoners badly and even killed some prisoners because so many other prisoners claimed it as fact (Wirz Trial U.S. Dept. War, War of Rebellion, Official Records 1880–1901, pp. 61–6). Other former prisoners testified that Wirz had stolen money and possessions from prisoners and had killed several men – none of whom were the victims identified in the indictment (Ibid., pp. 136, 142, 155–6, 163–9, 193–5, 323–5, 398). At least some of the testimony that purported to establish misconduct by Wirz was demonstrably false as Wirz was absent from the camp during some of the alleged actions that gave rise to the prosecution (Ruhlman 2006, p. 192).

Of the many witnesses who lacked credibility, perhaps the most notorious was the witness identified by the prosecution (and himself) as Felix de Labaume. Labaume claimed to be the grandnephew of Marquis de Lafayette – the French nobleman who joined forces with George Washington during the American Revolution (Belknap 2001–2002, p. 468). Labaume testified that he was fighting with the 39th New York Infantry when he was captured and taken to Andersonville. While imprisoned there, he witnessed a host of terrible acts by Wirz and others at the prison (Ruhlman 2006, pp. 192–3). Labaume testified that Wirz forced men to live off rat meat, deprived the prisoners of water as punishment, and gagged and bound them in chains (Laska and Smith 1975, pp. 118–19). Before he completed his testimony, Stanton arranged for Labaume to be appointed to a post in the Department of the Interior (Page and Haley 1908, p. 206). Although his testimony was compelling and implicated Wirz in a host of atrocities, Labaume had never been detained in Andersonville prison. In fact, Felix de Labaume was actually Felix Oeser and, prior to the Wirz trial, had been in the custody of federal marshals for deserting from the 7th New York Volunteers (Belknap 2001–2002, p. 468).

Several of his former comrades in arms from the 7th New York recognized him as Oeser and, once the press reported his true identity, he was summarily dismissed from the Department of the Interior but never charged with perjury (Page and Haley 1908, p. 206).

Only one person was identified by name as a prisoner personally killed by Wirz. George Gray testified that while he and a prisoner named William Stewart carried the corpse of another prisoner to the morgue at Andersonville, Wirz shot, killed, then robbed Stewart (Laska and Smith 1975, p. 119). Although Gray testified that these acts by Wirz occurred in mid-September, no charges as filed alleged any murder or bad act at all by Wirz in September (Page and Haley 1908, pp. 191–204). The court remedied this defect during its deliberations by changing the date alleged in specification three – the June 13 fatal shooting of an unknown prisoner – to September 13 (Laska and Smith 1975, p. 120).

A prisoner named Thomas Herburt, nicknamed "Chicakmagua" after the location of the battle in which he lost one of his legs, presumably died because Wirz ordered him shot (Wirz Trial U.S. Dept. War, War of Rebellion, Official Records 1880–1901, pp. 181–3, 711–12). Herburt suffered from some sort of psychological infirmity and was shot on May 15, 1864 on Wirz's order while in the space next to the prison wall beyond a barrier called the deadline. In essence, the deadline marked the beginning of a zone next to the prison walls in which the prisoners were not allowed. The premise of the deadline, a common design feature in both civilian and military prisons all over the country, was that it provided a safeguard against prisoners storming the walls (Ruhlman 2006, p. 197). If a prisoner crossed into the zone between the deadline and the prison wall, the guards would warn the prisoner to retreat. Noncompliance with orders to retreat could be met with shots from the guards, which could of course include lethal shots (Laska and Smith 1975, pp. 80–1). When Herburt ignored repeated orders to return to the area behind the deadline, witnesses said Wirz ordered the guard to shoot (Ruhlman 2006, p. 196). Wirz testified he had left the area and was headed to his quarters when he heard the shots that killed Herburt (Wirz Trial U.S. Dept. War, War of Rebellion, Official Records 1880–1901, pp. 711–12). Because the rules regarding the deadline were well-known and posted, at least some scholars have suggested Herburt in essence committed suicide to escape an intolerable existence (Ruhlman 2006, p. 195). Like William Stewart, although Herburt was well-known by name among many prisoners, he was not listed in the charging documents as a victim (Page and Haley 1908, pp. 191–204). While specification eight charges that an unknown soldier was shot at the direction of Wirz on May 15, 1864, over 700 prisoners died that month (Ransom 1881, 1974 ed., p. 366). No evidence was introduced that connected Herburt to the vague charge as the victim.

Although the defense attorneys, Baker and Schade, were able to cross examine the prosecution witnesses, they were less successful at presenting witnesses for the defense.

While the prosecution responded to favorable testimony with a range of rewards from government jobs to pardons, as a man on trial for his life and likely to be executed, Wirz had nothing of value to offer those who might testify. Moreover, the government had several months in which to build its case against Wirz, while the defense attorneys did not join the case until after it was under way. One of the greatest limitations of the defense was their obligation to rely on Chipman, the prosecutor, to subpoena their witnesses. Though Chipman, Baker, and Schade subpoenaed over 100 witnesses, only thirty-two witnesses actually testified for the defense (Wirz Trial U.S. Dept. War, War of Rebellion, Official Records 1880–1901, pp. 292–3, 327, 415, 529–30, 605, 695–9). As difficult as it was to rely on the prosecutor to serve the subpoenas, it was even more problematic for the defense that the witnesses were subject to prosecutorial approval not only of their identity but also their testimony (Ruhlman 2006, p. 198). When the defense attempted to demonstrate that some of the prosecution witnesses committed perjury through their testimony, Chipman objected that the defense was impugning and slandering loyal American soldiers and the court agreed (Wirz Trial U.S. Dept. War, War of Rebellion, Official Records 1880–1901, pp. 292–3, 327, 415, 529–30, 533, 593, 605, 695–6).

In spite of the severe limitations on a vigorous defense, in the end, Wirz's legal team presented a credible exoneration of him. Three Catholic priests who frequently tended to the dead and dying at the camp testified that they never saw him engage in the types of acts contained in the indictment (Ibid., p. 436). Four Confederate surgeons testified that the horrible conditions were the result of overcrowding and scarcity of resources and that Wirz could not have prevented the suffering (Ruhlman 2006, p. 199). Moreover, the prosecution simply did not present any evidence that the particular crimes alleged to have been committed by Wirz were in fact committed by him. That is, despite days of testimony about the Confederate leadership and its management of the war, no evidence was presented which indicated any effort to intentionally cause the deaths of Union prisoners detained at Andersonville. No evidence was introduced that indicated Wirz engaged in any act that could rise to a conspiracy to kill Union prisoners. Finally, no evidence was introduced that actually connected Wirz to the vaguely described murders specified in the indictment. In short, the prosecution presented no evidence of a conspiracy, no evidence Wirz was involved in any conspiracy, and no evidence that Wirz engaged in the specific murders alleged.

In what can only be described as an abuse of discretion, the prosecutor took it upon himself to assign a court recorder rather than Baker or Schade to give a closing statement on behalf of Wirz (Wirz Trial U.S. Dept. War, War of Rebellion, Official Records 1880–1901, pp. 701–3). The summation pointed out the absence of evidence in support of any of the charges and also pointed out the obvious fabrication of some of the witnesses (Ibid., pp. 710–11). The court recessed and on October 20, 1865, Chipman began the summation for the prosecution (Ibid., pp. 704–41). Chipman spent a great deal of time accusing the Confederate leadership of willful neglect of Union prisoners and spent a great deal less time actually pointing to evidence that suggested Wirz was guilty as charged of conspiracy or murder (Ibid.). When Chipman addressed the individual murder charges contained in the indictment, he essentially just read the charges and then claimed testimony supported those charges. Although October 24, 1865 was the date the court had determined would be the end of the trial, Chipman agreed to allow additional witnesses and the trial continued until November 4, 1865 (Page and Haley 1908, p. 212).

As the trial concluded, Wirz wrote a letter wherein he acknowledged the certain outcome of the trial and his likely execution (Wirz Trial U.S. Dept. War, War of Rebellion, Official Records 1880–1901, pp. 751–61). He expected to be and was found guilty on all counts, except for three of the specifications in Count II (Laska and Smith 1975, p. 127). He was found not guilty of specifications four and ten in Count II which alleged he shot and killed unnamed prisoners and specification thirteen of Count II which asserted he had beaten a prisoner to death (Page and Haley 1908, p. 214; Ruhlman 2006, pp. 205, 235–9). The not guilty verdict, at least as to specification ten of Count II, is not entirely surprising as two doctors testified at the close of the trial that the physical infirmities Wirz suffered as a result of his perpetually wounded arm meant he did not have the strength to "use the right arm very aggressively without injury to the bones, which are partially destroyed" (Wirz Trial U.S. Dept. War, War of Rebellion, Official Records 1880–1901, pp. 805–8).

Wirz was sentenced to be hanged until dead at a time and place to be set by the president of the United States. On November 6, President Andrew Johnson set November 10, 1865 as the date Wirz would be executed for his crimes (Haley and Page 1908. p. 215). The only avenue of appeal available to Wirz was a direct plea to President Johnson for a commutation of the sentence. Although he wrote a letter imploring Johnson to execute him or set him free, while reasserting his innocence, no one from the Johnson administration responded. In an ironic turn of fate, Wirz was hanged on a scaffold erected on the future site of the Supreme Court. In 1908, James Madison Page, who served as a second lieutenant in the 6th Michigan Cavalry, published his defense of Wirz and a recounting of the story of Andersonville (Page and Haley 1908). Page wrote that once the sentence was carried out the military commission dissolved:

> Thus ended the greatest judicial farce enacted since Oliver Cromwell, *et al.*, instituted the Commission to "try and condemn" Charles I. The condemnation of Henry Wirz was the more pronounced of the two, for the remains of Charles I were accorded something like a decent burial, whereas the body of Major Henry Wirz was consigned without ceremony to the prison-yard at Washington (Haley and Page 1908, p. 216).

There can be little doubt that justice was not served, or even considered, as a primary dimension of the prosecution of Wirz. He was convicted of involvement in a conspiracy to cause the deaths of Union prisoners and of ten specific murders. No evidence at all was introduced to support the claims against Wirz contained in the conspiracy charge. Moreover, although the conspiracy charges contemplated a concerted effort on the part of Wirz and others to cause the deaths of the prisoners, in the end, he was prosecuted for shortages of goods, including food and medical supplies, wholly outside of his control. The records are unambiguous that the deaths at Andersonville were primarily caused by sanitation and nutrition issues. The individual charges of murder were also substantively deficient. While the prosecution was able to cobble together a host of details regarding the time, place, and manner of the alleged murders and the prosecution was able to produce scores of witnesses who claimed to have heard about these murders, only two people were ever identified as having actually been one of the ten victims. Of the two alleged victims, no record exists of one of them ever being in the prison. The absence of identifiable victims or firsthand witnesses casts a shadow of impropriety across every aspect of Count II.

Procedurally, the trial cannot withstand even a cursory analysis. At the outset, the multiple roles of the prosecutor are so problematic that even if the rest of the process had somehow been legitimately constructed, the trial would still be suspect. The prosecutor's ability to interpret the law for the commission as well as make functional evidentiary rulings meant that the prospects of admission of any exculpatory evidence were grim at best. Additionally, that the prosecutor could manipulate the subpoena power of the defense team and limit the cross examination of the prosecution's witnesses meant that an effective defense was almost impossible to construct. The expansive use of hearsay evidence by the prosecution stands in stark contrast to the refusal of the court to allow similar exculpatory hearsay. Of course, even beyond the ubiquitous power of the prosecutor, the procedural manipulation to the disadvantage of the defendant was unconscionable. From amending the indictment during the deliberation of his guilt so that the counts would conform to the dates entered into evidence to the permissive introduction of hearsay evidence as the primary inculpating testimony in the trial, Wirz was never given an opportunity to test the evidence presented against him or challenge the claims presented.

Deterrence and retribution were not part of the equation in the prosecution of Wirz. The indictment did not contemplate a victim class. Wirz was convicted of a conspiracy and the deaths of ten unidentified prisoners. As an impoverished former Confederate bound to be hanged, there was no avenue through which any claimant on behalf of any victim of his actions, even if the alleged victims could somehow be identified, could have sought redress. Moreover, none of his alleged co-conspirators or superiors were ever convicted or indicted for any action affiliated with Andersonville.

No other prison warden was charged with any crime. There is simply no indication that deterrence was given any consideration. Retribution is only present as a consideration in the crudest sense. That is, retribution as a dimension of the trial of Henry Wirz exists only to the extent vengeance for the assassination of President Lincoln can somehow be thought to encompass some element of retribution. Wirz was prosecuted and hanged merely in an effort to underscore the defeat of the Confederacy and – hopefully – implicate the former Confederate leaders, especially Jefferson Davis, in the assassination of President Lincoln.

In the final analysis, the Wirz trial is hardly better than the trial of Charles I. While Wirz technically had legal representation, the complete absence of procedural due process undermined any ability of his lawyers to actually defend him. Substantively, the Wirz trial was not driven by quite as blatant of a set of expedient charges as Charles I suffered, but Wirz cannot be considered to have been prosecuted for acts he actually committed. Because neither trial was primarily directed toward achieving the goals of justice, deterrence and retribution were given little more than mild acknowledgments that were self-serving for those that sought to consolidate power. Still, as unrelated to the dispensation of justice as the trials of Charles I and Wirz were, they formed a foundation upon which future trials could be constructed that could indeed hold the heads of state and the leaders in war responsible for horrific acts. The prosecution of Wilhelm II and other alleged war criminals after World War I was contemplated but never occurred. The planned trials that arose out of the Armenian genocide in 1915 also collapsed because there was no international interest in pursuing the prosecutions. The political desire to pursue these prosecutions was simply not strong enough to ensure the difficulties in trying heads of state or their agents would be borne by war-weary victors for the sake of justice. However, the atrocities and ferociousness of World War II permanently altered the assessment of the value of postconflict prosecutions.

3

The Institutionalization of War Crimes Tribunals

The Nuremberg Trials and the Tokyo Trials

The technological advancements of warfare between the First and Second World Wars and the venality and viciousness of the Nazi campaign combined to make World War II a remarkable conflict in its scope and impact. The victorious Allies were committed in a variety of dimensions to the idea that the war had been so horrible that civilization could not withstand another similar conflict. While the occupation and rebuilding of both Germany and Japan were integral aspects of the postconflict strategy, the concept of legal responsibility for some of the criminal acts committed during the conflict took hold as a necessary step toward a consolidated and lasting peace. These two sets of trials took widely divergent paths. While those at Nuremberg embraced concerns about substantive due process and procedural due process as inherent to a just proceeding, the trials in Tokyo reverted to a show trial model with an almost complete disregard for concepts of justice. Nuremberg became the standard by which future trials would be judged while the proceedings in Tokyo were all but forgotten. These trials demonstrate not only the movement forward of the jurisprudence of post-conflict justice, but also the perils of implementation of transitional justice when concerns about political consolidation are paramount. Despite the shortfalls of both sets of trials and the substantial shortfalls of the Tokyo trials, the concept of war crimes trials became institutionalized because of these efforts.

The Nuremberg Trials

After a decade in power, Adolf Hitler and his "thousand year Reich" began to irrevocably falter. In the fall of 1942, the broad coalition of allies that had united in opposition to Hitler defeated Field Marshall Erwin Rommel in Egypt. Four months later, in February 1943, the German Sixth Army, under Field Marshall Freidrich von Paulus, surrendered at Stalingrad. By the close of summer 1943, Hitler had planned and lost the Battle of Kursk in Russia, the Allies were on the ground in northern Africa and Italy, and Japan had been defeated at the Battle of Midway. Although Germany was in retreat on every front, Hitler fought on and continued to occupy many parts of Europe and parts of the Pacific. The technology generally available and the strategies specifically utilized by Hitler and the Nazi regime during World War II raised the costs and consequences of war to new and terrible levels. Although Russia, England, and the United States had very different views as to the proper resolution of postwar political considerations regarding Germany, each was committed to ensuring Germany did not again attempt continental or global conquest (Smyser 1999, pp. 5–11).

As the Third Reich approached utter collapse, on April 30, 1945, Hitler appointed a successor as chancellor and then committed suicide. His successor, Admiral Karl Donitz, executed an instrument of surrender of the German armed forces on May 7. Although the German military had capitulated, the civilian government continued to operate from Flensburg as the Allies rounded up and arrested them. Finally, on June 5, 1945, the Allies formally took sovereignty over Germany through the Berlin Declaration.

After the complete defeat of the Axis powers at the end of World War II, the victorious Allied nations faced a host of postconflict problems. The Allies hoped to avoid a repeat of the missteps after World War I, so they agreed on a commitment to resurrecting the German economy. However, there was broad disagreement over many other issues including the borders of Poland, the nature of the influence the Allied powers would separately have in the states formerly occupied by Germany, and the nature of the relationships among the Allies now that the unifying dimension of their relationships – the war – had ended.

Despite some opposition from Russia, the Allied powers ultimately resolved one of the points of contention through an agreement to create special tribunals for the purpose of prosecuting some of the significant German military personnel. They faced prosecution for crimes committed during the war. The desire to construct the trials to prosecute Japanese personnel originated with the United States only after the prosecution of the Germans. Although a variety of trials for illegal or wrongful actions during the war were held in various occupied territories, including trials of low-level German officers and Russian or French collaborators as well as civil trials seeking compensation for a host of property crimes, the criminal proceedings in Nuremberg against twenty-four high-ranking Nazis are the trials most often associated with Nuremberg. The twenty-four defendants were selected because each was the highest ranking surviving principal within their respective spheres of influence. That is, each defendant was the surviving officer with the greatest authority over the acts that were the basis of the prosecutions. Before the proceedings began, two of the original twenty-four defendants avoided the possibility of prosecution when one defendant committed suicide and the other was subsequently determined by the prosecutors to be too ill to stand trial (Rosembaum 1993, p. 19–20). This section addresses only the trials – the Nuremberg Trials – of the twenty-two Nazis, which occurred from October 18, 1945 to October 1, 1946.

The additional, later trials included those of various German civilians and lower-level military personnel and the trials in Tokyo, as well as the trials outside Germany prosecuting civilians and military personnel in the juris-diction of the various alleged wrongdoings. The so-called Subsequent Nuremberg Trials of civilians and lower-level officers are not considered here as they were conducted under the same enabling document and procedure as the first. Moreover, the subsequent prosecutions did not have the reach or juridical impact of the Nuremberg Trials. The trials in Tokyo are considered after the Nuremberg Trials. The site-specific trials that prosecuted the Russian and French collaborators and other low-level Nazi personnel are not considered as they did not arise as specific war crimes prosecutions, but rather were efforts at enforcing extant municipal law under the guise of the legal structure of the domestic jurisdiction. That is, the site-specific trials were conducted under the auspices of local authority having to do with the violation of local law. These were war crimes trials only insofar as the crimes alleged were committed during war by military personnel (Ginsburgs and Kudraivtsev 1990, pp. 16–22; Rosembaum 1993, p. 19).

In 1945, the Allies provided for the International Military Tribunal (IMT) through an agreement called the London Charter. The IMT was designed and established by the United States, Great Britain, the Soviet Union, and France and was presided over by judges from each of the four countries (Smith 1982, pp. 49–56). The framework for the prosecutions contemplated a just, fair, and wholly unobjectionable process carried out for the purposes of deterrence of future leaders in war time and retribution for those aggrieved by the Nazi campaign. On August 26, 1944, in a presidential memorandum to the secretary of war, President Franklin Roosevelt addressed the intent behind the proposed tribunal:

> The fact that they [Germany] are a defeated nation, collectively and individually, must be so impressed upon them that they will hesitate to start any new war.... The German people as a whole must have it driven home to them that the whole nation has been engaged in a lawless conspiracy against the decencies of modern civilization (Ibid., p. 21).

For the leadership of the United States, the goal of deterrence was clearly one of the primary purposes of the trials. Roosevelt and the American architects of the IMT wanted to ensure that the instigators of the last two world wars would hesitate before engaging in aggression again.

The United States secretary of state embraced the United Nations' proclamation in 1945 that "those responsible for these crimes (against humanity) shall not escape retribution" (Ibid., pp. 17–20). The premise of retribution as a goal of the trials was underscored by President Roosevelt in a statement, approved by both Winston Churchill and Josef Stalin, that declared in part, "The United Nations have made it clear that they will pursue the guilty and deliver them up in order that justice be done.... All who share the guilt will share the punishment" (Ibid., pp. 18–19).

The architects of the trials were faced with the novel and difficult question of how best to achieve the stated goals of deterrence and retribution without the prosecutions taking on the aura of summary justice. They needed to construct fair trials that would provide a venue for the dispensation of justice without giving the appearance of being little more than a lynch mob with formal rules. A suggestion was made by the Soviets that the Nazi generals be summarily executed – de-Nazification of Germany could be accomplished quickly so long as the Allies were not squeamish about large-scale executions. Despite initial support from Winston Churchill, the notion of simply slaughtering the Germans was rejected by the other Allies over concern about worldwide reaction to their treatment of those defeated in war (Ginsburgs and Kudraivtsev 1990, pp. 16–20). In September 1944, Secretary of War Stimson and Judge Advocate General Cramer had the following conversation as they discussed the appropriate framework of the trials:

> Cramer: What I want to provide against is any charges of railroading these people.
>
> Stimson: A great many people think that the question of the guilt of some of these people is already decided. I'm taking the position that they must have the substance of a trial.
>
> Cramer: I agree with you absolutely (Smith 1982, p. 26).

Secretary Stimson wrote to the president that the method of dealing with Nazi prisoners must consist of a well-defined procedure and that "such procedure must embody ... at least the rudimentary aspects of the Bill of Rights, namely, notification to the accused of the charge, the right to be heard and ... to call witnesses" (Ibid., p. 30).

The tribunal for the prosecution of the Nazis accused of war crimes was designed to further the ends of justice, retribution, and deterrence through a fair process embodied by procedural due process in the application of substantive due process. The Allies wanted to ensure that the trials would be viewed as fair by the judgment of history and by the judgment of the postwar German state. The Charter of the International Military Tribunal (IMT) was adopted on August 8, 1945 (Ibid., p. 214). The charter set forth the jurisdiction and general principles of the IMT in part as follows:

> The following acts ... are crimes within the jurisdiction of the Tribunal for which there shall be individual responsibility:
> (a) CRIMES AGAINST PEACE: namely, planning, preparing, initiation, or waging a war of aggression ...
> (b) WAR CRIMES: namely, violations of the law or the customs of war ...
> (c) CRIMES AGAINST HUMANITY: namely, murder, extermination, enslavement, deportation, and other inhumane acts committed against any civilian population (Ibid., p. 215).

The document identified with great specificity the war crimes to be considered – the substantive aspect of the prosecution – and directed the tribunal to "draw up rules for its procedure" consistent with the charter (Ibid., p. 216). Although the construction of the procedure to be used at trial was delegated to the tribunal, the charter contained an explicit provision that dictated a "Fair Trial for Defendants" in Article 16. The fair trial mandate largely adopted Stimson's argument for a rudimentary and transparent procedural due process (Ibid., pp. 217–18). The charter also provided that the judgment of the tribunal would be final with no appeal or review possible (Ibid., p. 219).

An initial consideration of the IMT suggests that the architects of the tribunal rose to the occasion and provided a venue for the fair and proper administration of justice. Still, as laudably fair as the process and substantive dimensions of the trial were, several problematic dimensions present from the inception of the idea of an international tribunal carried through the execution of the process. First, the question of jurisdiction presented a troublesome problem for the Allies. Second, enacting punitive laws after the actions the laws were designed to address had occurred was contrary to the international concept of justice, the domestic configurations of justice of the Allies (with the possible exception of the Soviet Union), and the theoretical concept of justice in the abstract.

The tribunal was created specifically to prosecute activity newly defined as criminal *after* the occurrence of that activity in a sovereign nation (Germany) where that activity had been considered legal. The legal foundation of the tribunal jurisprudence was an expanded interpretation of international common law arising out of interstate relations embodied in treaties and other agreements. In particular, the violation by the defendants of the traditional rules of war created a foundational basis for the subject matter jurisdiction while the locus of the traditionally improper activity dictated that procedural jurisdiction rested in Germany (Baird 1982, pp. 12–14; Rosembaum 1993, pp. 25–38).

Similar to the first round of defensive efforts by Charles I and by Captain Henry Wirz, the Nuremberg defendants filed a joint motion with the court that challenged the jurisdiction prior to the taking of any evidence (Benton 1955, pp. 27–30). The defense motion contained three major legal arguments arranged in separate sections of the motion. First, the defendants argued that the expansion of international common law apparently to differentiate between just and unjust wars was without precedent and, therefore, an invalid attempt at an expansion of common law. Second, the longstanding concept of *nulla poena sine lege*, that is, "no punishment without a law" was a customary bar that prohibited the application of criminal sanctions in punishment for activities declared criminal only *ex post facto*, or "after the fact." Third, the defendants set forth their objection that the Allies had created the statute that established the tribunal, the rules of law to be applied during the tribunal, the prosecutors, the judges, and the aggrieved parties (Ibid.). In essence, the defendants objected to the fact that one group filled all the roles except for that of defendant at the trial.

In the opening statement for the defendants, their counsel argued "the main juridical and fundamental problem ... concerns war as a function forbidden by international law; the breach of peace as treason perpetrated upon the world constitution" (Ibid., p. 31). In short, the defense made the initial argument that the tribunal had outlawed war only after the conclusion of the war. Each defendant individually also objected to the attempt by the tribunal to hold individuals responsible for the acts of a state in prosecuting the war (Ibid., pp. 31–75). The defense lawyers argued that even if war could be construed as a crime, only the state waging the war or committing the crime could be held responsible for those acts. The argument was straightforward: "acts of state are acts of man. Yet, they are in fact acts of state carried out by its organs and not the private acts" of individuals and the individuals should not be held accountable for these actions of the state (Ibid., p. 54). The opening by the defense counsel concluded with a concise *ex post facto* argument that suggested international law did not provide for this sort of prosecution:

> Sentences ... against individuals for breach of the peace between states would be something completely new under the aspect of law ... sentences against individuals for breach of the peace between states presupposes other laws than those in force when the actions laid before the Tribunal took place (Ibid., pp. 74–5).

The court rejected the claims of a lack of jurisdiction as well as the other dimensions of the initial defense motion to dismiss the proceedings. In response to the general objections to the proceeding raised by the motion, chief prosecutor and justice of the U.S. Supreme Court Robert Jackson stated in his opening comments:

> The Privilege of opening the first trial in history for crimes against the peace of the world imposes a grave responsibility. The wrongs which we seek to condemn and punish have been so calculated, so malignant, and so devastating that civilization cannot tolerate their being ignored, because it cannot survive their being repeated. That four great nations flushed with victory and stung with injury, stay the hand of vengeance and voluntarily submit their captive enemies to the judgment of the law is one of the most significant tributes that Power has ever paid to reason (Taylor 1992, p. 167).

Jackson addressed the unprecedented nature of the proceeding and pointed out:

> If these men are the first war leaders ... to be prosecuted in the name of the law, they are also the first to be given a chance to plead for their lives in the name of the law ....
> [T]his Tribunal, which gives them a hearing, is also the source of their only hope.... The German no less than the non-German world has accounts to settle with these defendants (Ibid., p. 168).

Jackson made a clear argument that the proceedings were in fact just and proper given the circumstances under which the tribunal was constructed. Through the trial, the leaders of the vanquished state that conducted the illegal war were provided with the opportunity to plead their case while those states that were victorious in the conflict provided a forum for the world to assert its many claims against the aggressors. The only alternative to this process would be the summary judgment and execution of the defendants suggested by the Soviets. By allowing the world to mete out both judgment and justice to the defendants, the tribunal would stand for a rule of law that would override and invalidate any future nation's claim of right to comparable aggression and brutality. The fairness of the proceeding for the defendants and their counsel was of paramount importance. Jackson acknowledged that the world would judge the trial based on how fair it was when he observed in his opening statement:

> We must never forget that the record on which we judge these defendants is the record on which history will judge us tomorrow. To pass these defendants a poisoned chalice is to put it to our lips as well. We must summon such detachment and intellectual integrity to our task that this Trial will commend itself to posterity as fulfilling humanity's aspirations to do justice (Ibid.).

That the trial had all the elements of procedural fairness other than an avenue of appeal is inarguable. The establishing charter dictated the notion of a "fair" trial and explicitly set forth the concept of fairness as a foundational dimension of the IMT. Each of the accused was presumed innocent of all stated charges unless and until the evidence presented at trial established guilt beyond a reasonable doubt. The defendants were given the same standard for conviction prevalent in many other criminal courts. Each accused individual received a full and detailed explanation of the charges in their native language. Each defendant was entitled to a full defense and vigorous representation. The defendants were given access and the services of counsel of their own choosing in order to plead their cases. Each defendant was entitled to present evidence in their own defense and to cross examine the evidence and witnesses against them. The proceedings were contemporaneously translated as they occurred into a language the accused could understand. No defendant could persuasively argue he was deprived of a fair trial to the extent a fair trial encompasses respect for the rights of the accused, a fair and full defense, and findings of guilt based on evidence (Rosembaum 1993, p. 36). The process was so clearly fair that several of the lawyers serving as defense counsel publicly stated their opinions that the trial had been fair (Ibid., fn 68).

Further, if objections to the initial jurisdiction of the court can be ignored or if the initial jurisdiction was appropriate, then the trial was also inarguably fair from a substantive due process standpoint. In other words, if the tribunal had the legal right to proceed with hearing the prosecution, the subject matter of the process and trial was appropriate. The world had never before witnessed acts of war with such a depraved magnitude and scope. The tribunal concluded:

> Defendants are charged with crimes of such immensity that the mere specific instances of criminality appear insignificant by comparison. The charge, in brief, is that of conscious participation in a nationwide government orga-nized system of cruelty and injustice ... perpetrated in the name of law.... The dagger of the assassin was concealed beneath the robe of the jurist (Ibid., p. 43).

The question of whether individuals should be held account-able for acts of state undertaken during times of war is a question inexorably linked to the question of deterrence. R. B. Perry has written:

> Had those responsible for the aggressions and inhuman-ities of the Nazi regime been allowed to go unpunished, mankind would have lost a supreme opportunity to crystal-lize in legal form a recognized and pressing moral neces-sity. The time was ripe ... to create a legal precedent for future time. Those who would have preferred exoneration, or assassination, or summary execution, were not the friends of law in principle, but the defenders of outmoded law or of the perpetuation of lawlessness (Ibid., p. 37).

An additional suggestion of the fairness of the proceedings is the fact that three of the defendants were acquitted (Persico 1994, pp. 437–9). While the acquittals alone would not be sufficient to suggest much about the trials beyond perhaps that some defendants should not have been charged, when the acquittals are considered alongside the procedural structure of the trial, the idea that some of the accused were acquitted suggests a capable defense was possible.

Though the substantive due process and the procedural due process both pass juridical muster and seem to have been fairly constructed given the limitations of a postwar environment, the goals of deterrence and retribution do not fare so well. Persico has questioned whether the trial has ever deterred one would-be aggressor (Ibid., p. 442). Neither the international prosecution of the leaders of states after wars of aggression nor holding individuals responsible for official acts of state during war has become the norm (Ibid., p. 443). Despite this observation, it may be that deterrence is not so easily measured. To determine what has not happened – and indeed why something has not happened – is quite another task from merely a determination of what has happened. In essence, that a crime did not occur because of the trials might not be clearly ascertainable. At a minimum, the tribunal has been used as a model in some instances for the prosecution of some crimes by some leaders during some conflicts.

The only truly neglected dimension of justice by the tribunal was retribution. Because the primary charges of the tribunal arose from the perpetration of a war of aggression, the more notorious dimensions of Nazi atrocities were not actually subjects of the trial. Until recently, the victims of Nazi atrocities in the death camps had little avenue of recourse. Although the sentences at the tribunal ranged from acquittal and three years in prison at the least to life in prison and execution at the most, no consideration, compensation, or remuneration was given to the victims or contemplated by the court. The victims of the Nazi regime were left to their own devices and resources to reclaim their assets and seek individual retribution through whatever avenue they could find. In the final analysis, although the balance of power was completely one-sided – so the victors could set the process to suit their needs, the tribunal effectively managed to protect the rights of the accused and set forth a fundamentally fair process. Many of the victims, indeed even many of the classes of victims, were never involved in the process in either a direct or a representative capacity (Buscher 1989, pp. 159–64; Persico 1994, pp. 437–43). That justice was incomplete from the perspectives of the victims is the unavoidable conclusion. Still, the Nuremberg Trials made dramatic improvements to the substantive due process and procedural due process dimensions of the prosecution of individuals for bad behavior during war.

From the perspective of the United States, Japan had also engaged in a war of aggression and, unlike Germany, had actually attacked the United States on its own territory. Perhaps because of the attack on Pearl Harbor or perhaps because the other Allies had more direct battle engagement with Germany, the other Allies did not share the same level of concern as the United States about war crimes allegedly committed by soldiers and civilians acting on behalf of Japan.

The Tokyo War Crimes Trial

The Nuremberg Charter, which created the basis and mechanism for prosecuting the Nazis, was the product of lengthy and complex negotiations among the Allied Powers. In stark contrast, the Tokyo Charter was an executive decree promulgated by General Douglas MacArthur at the direction of the United States Joint Chiefs of Staff with no input at all from any of the other Allies (Horowitz 1950, p. 480). Although the other Allies were not consulted or meaningfully informed of the intent to prosecute Japanese officers until after the Tokyo Charter was drafted, its heavy reliance on the Nuremberg precedent combined with a substantially lower interest on the part of the Europeans in the punishment of Japan meant this unilateral action by the United States was basically unobjectionable to the other Allies (Minear 1971, pp. 20–1). The Tokyo Charter, amended only very slightly by Great Britain and France, provided for the "just and prompt trial and punishment of the major war criminals in the Far East" (Ibid., p. 21; Brackman 1987, p. 60).

The tribunal was given jurisdiction over three specific categories of crime that reflected those addressed by the Nuremberg Trials. The Tokyo Charter provided that crimes against peace, conventional war crimes, and crimes against humanity would all be prosecuted under the broad jurisdiction of the tribunal (Roling 1993, p. 55). Unlike the Nuremberg Charter, the Tokyo Charter established that the charge of crimes against peace was a threshold charge. That is, a charge of crimes against peace was a necessary charge before any other charge could be lodged. Accordingly, only those individuals whose crimes included "crimes against peace" could be prosecuted by the tribunal (Minear 1971, p. 21).

The dictate for a "just" trial for the accused was formally assured and nominally provided for through the same types of fundamental due process guarantees constructed for the Nuremberg Trial. In particular, the charges against the defendants were provided to them in their own language. The trial was contemporaneously translated for the benefit of the defendants and their lawyers. The right of the defendants to freely choose their counsel and to participate in the construction and administration of their own defense was explicit. The defendants' right to a full and fair defense included the right to cross examine the prosecution witnesses and to call witnesses of their own to rebut the prosecution or present exculpatory evidence (Ibid., pp. 21–4; Roling 1993; p. 50). In what was perhaps a slight improvement over the Nuremberg Trials, the defendants could appeal the verdicts directly to General Douglas MacArthur in his role as supreme commander of the Allied Powers in Japan (Minear 1971, pp. 32–3).

The Tokyo Charter formally seems to provide all the trappings of procedural due process. However, the tribunal fell far short of a fair process in three important ways. First, the evidentiary standard substantially deviated from the customary rigors of criminal trials. The Tokyo Charter provided that evidence against any of the defendants could include any document "without proof of its issuance or signature" as well as diaries, letters, press reports, and sworn or unsworn out of court statements relating to the charges (Brackman 1987, p. 60). There seems to have been no document so unreliable as to render it inadmissible. Indeed, Article 13 of the charter read in part: "The tribunal shall not be bound by technical rules of evidence ... and shall admit any evidence which it deems to have probative value" (Minear 1971, p. 118). The slightest probative value outweighed any concern that could be raised about the veracity, reliability, or prejudicial nature of any of the documentary evidence. This approach of unfettered admissions of documents also seriously hampered the ability of the defense lawyers to present a proper challenge to the evidence presented. To establish a process whereby there can be almost no grounds for excluding evidence is to greatly diminish the role of defense counsel.

To grasp the impact and importance of this broadly permissive evidentiary approach established by the Tokyo Charter, there is no need to go beyond a consideration of some of the evidence admitted during the prosecution. Wartime press releases alleging atrocities written and distributed by the press secretaries of the Allies were admitted as evidence when entered by the prosecution while similar documents proffered by the defense were without exception excluded (Ibid., p. 120). The recollection of a casual conversation with a man long dead was admitted as direct evidence

(Ibid.). Correspondence allegedly written by Japanese citizens who did not testify in court was admitted with no proof of authenticity offered and no opportunity for cross examination about the authenticity or content of the letters by the defense (Ibid.). Adding insult to the evidentiary injury, once the prosecution had rested and before the defense began, the tribunal adopted the "Best Evidence Rule" (Ibid., p. 123). The "Best Evidence Rule" dictates that the "best" or most authentic evidence must be produced. For example, the person seeking to introduce a document must produce an original document instead of a copy, a map instead of a description of the map, and a witness instead of a description of what the witness may have said. Justice Pal, one of two justices to vote for acquittal on all counts, wryly noted, "in a proceeding where we had to allow the prosecution to bring in any amount of hearsay evidence, it was somewhat misplaced caution to introduce this best evidence rule particularly when it operated practically against the defense only" (Ibid., p. 122).

The second critical procedural defect was the selection and attendance policies for the jurists. The eleven justices came only from nations that actively participated in the Allied victory. The defendants had no ability to challenge the credentials of the justices or to give any input into the selection of who would oversee the process. The peculiar rule that the justices were not actually required to attend the hearings, whether for the production of evidence or for any other reason, is difficult to align with a fair process.

Two of the justices were replaced after the process had begun, apparently because they expressed concern over the lax evidentiary standards. A simple majority of the justices constituted a sufficient number present to proceed with the prosecutions and a simple majority of those present could make any decision whether or not the decision involved aspects of the trials with which the justices were familiar. Moreover, there was no requirement that the justices deliberate or consult with each other before rendering an opinion on any aspect of the proceedings. The majority opinion was drafted without any input from or debate with the dissenters. The verdicts reflected these procedural defects. Six of the justices spoke only through the majority opinion written by the presiding justice, which found all twenty-eight defendants guilty of all charges. The other justices prepared dissenting opinions that had no juridical weight or impact in order to express their objections to the majority opinion (Minear 1971, pp. 81–8, 161).

Given the close relationship between the United States and Britain and the fact that the Tokyo Charter was almost exclusively a project of the United States, it is hardly a surprise that the American and British justices did not dissent from the opinion of the court. One of the dissenters, Justice Pal of India, was the only justice with any prior international law experience. Justice Pal argued that not guilty verdicts on all counts for all defendants could be the only proper outcome because the prosecution had failed to prove its case in any dimension (Varadarajan 1998). Justice Bernard of

France likewise urged the acquittal of all defendants on all counts because the process was so thoroughly flawed that a fair trial could not be accomplished. In particular, Justice Bernard pointed out that "oral deliberations outside of all influence ... among the judges" was a guarantee of "justice" and in its absence, the verdict was invalid. Justice Roling of the Netherlands objected to the imposition of the death penalty for the nonmilitary personnel who were tried and for any crime charged against any defendant for crimes against peace. Justice Webb of Australia expressed grave concerns that, although for the Tokyo tribunal death was apparently the minimum punishment for the crime of aggressive war, no Nuremberg defendant had been sentenced to death for precisely the same charge. Justice Webb concluded "unless the Japanese accused are to be treated with less consideration than the German accused, no Japanese should be sentenced to death." Justice Webb suggested the Napoleonic tradition of exile rather than execution as an appropriate sentence and, showing some concern for the executioners as well, suggested, "it may prove revolting to hang or shoot such old men" (Brackman 1987, pp. 388–400; Minear 1971, pp. 89–93).

The third major procedural defect reflects a constant issue in postconflict war crimes tribunals: jurisdiction. Echoing the pleas of Charles I, Captain Henry Wirz, and counsel for the defendants at Nuremberg, the defense argued that the tribunal sought to impose an *ex post facto* law. Likewise, as in all the preceding cases, the court rejected the argument without much deliberation (Ibid., p. 373). Later, long after the Tokyo tribunal had done its work, Justice Roling explained the jurisdiction for the court in the following exchange:

> (Q): [Do] you think the Tokyo Court applied retroactive law?
>
> (A): Of course it did ... but retroactively in this case is not so bad as it sounds ... their claim that it would be unjust for them to have to account for the behavior was ridiculous (Roling 1993, pp. 68–9).

The Tokyo tribunal relied on Nuremberg as a precedent and adopted the Nuremberg rationale for jurisdiction. The Tokyo tribunal summarily rejected the defense's objections to the proceeding and gave no rationale for taking jurisdiction under the post hoc conditions. The refusal by the court to present even a cursory response to the jurisdiction issue raised by the defendants made the proceedings legally suspect. Moreover, the abject disregard of the foundations of jurisdiction as a predicate issue meant that the Tokyo tribunal could do little over time to move the jurisprudence of war crimes trials forward. At least at Nuremberg, the difficulty of asserting jurisdiction was acknowledged and the importance of allowing the accused a chance to present a defense was given greater weight than concerns about *ex post facto* laws. As Osiel observed with rhetorical flourish with respect to the court's legitimacy, "It is one thing to acknowledge that prosecutors have a legitimate range of dramaturgical discretion; it is quite another for them to attempt a staging of Hamlet without the prince" (Osiel 1997, p. 139).

As flawed as the procedural due process dimensions of the Tokyo tribunal may have been, the substantive due process aspects of the trials are so problematic that no procedural propriety could salvage them. Two primary defects combine to completely undermine any argument that the Tokyo tribunal involved something other than "victor's justice." First, the crimes as presented in court by the prosecution were fundamentally different than those that were the subject of the Nuremberg Trials. While waging a war of aggression had long been illegal from an international law perspective, the notion of holding individuals responsible for the acts of a state during the normal state of war was a novel and emerging concept (Hosoya 1986, pp. 45–8). Moreover, holding underlings or low-level officers and civilians responsible for the acts of state, even if those acts of state violated international norms, was a break from the claimed historical progression of the jurisprudence of war crimes trials (Ibid.). Climbing down the chain of command, as it were, to hold the most junior officers liable for the decisions of their superiors was inarguably unprecedented except for the poor example of the prosecution of Captain Henry Wirz. The large-scale atrocities and shocking strategies of planned exterminations of whole peoples by the Third Reich had no counterpart in Japan. The German invasion of Poland, without even a pretense of justification for war, had no analog in Japan. While it is true Japan conducted a traditional war and even on occasions exceeded the bounds of traditional warfare, the crimes of Japan simply were not as heinous, as broad, or as systematic as the crimes of Germany. No doubt the Korean comfort women or other victims of Japanese wrongdoing might argue the acts of the two nations were equally deserving of punishment even if the scale, scope, or range of crimes varied between the two states. Still, not one Japanese defendant was charged with ordering the mass execution of civilians, neither was one Japanese defendant shown to have conducted war in the same manner. The crimes of the Japanese that were the foundation of the Tokyo tribunal arose out of the waging of a normal war even on occasions when soldiers behaved beyond the accepted rules of engagement. Not even the forced slavery of foreign women, among the most reprehensible of the systemic acts by the Japanese forces, was part of the trial, as even those prosecuted for the infamous "Rape of Nanking" were simply charged with negligent supervision (Roling 1993, pp. 32, 47–53).

The most serious charges prosecuted by the Tokyo tribunal arose from claims of crimes of omission. That is, the primary vehicle of prosecution was the claim of failure by the defendants to prevent other individuals who were not charged with crimes from doing bad acts that might be crimes such as the torture of prisoners and the killing of survivors in submarine warfare (Ibid., pp. 74–7). One defendant who was convicted of "failure to act" was found guilty because he did not resign his commission once he realized that his efforts to prevent those around him from torturing prisoners of war was ineffective. The verdict against him stated, in part, that he should have "pressed the matter, if necessary, to the point of resigning, in order to acquit himself of a responsibility which he suspected was not being discharged" (Ibid., p. 75). This prosecution for a crime committed by someone besides the defendant was not the most egregious example of punishing one for the act of another.

Not only were the individual defendants held responsible for acts of their superiors and for negligent supervision, but also for acts of others beyond any sphere of influence of the defendants. Ultimately, the defendants were only representatives of classes of possible criminals (Brackman 1987, pp. 80–2; Minear, 1971 p. 4). That is, the twenty-eight defendants were selected from a pool of over eighty detainees designated as "Class A" prisoners. To become a member of the Class A prisoner group, one needed only be an officer of any level with some available evidence of any type against you (Ibid.). The twenty-eight faced prosecution not because their actions were worse than the fifty-four prisoners in custody who avoided prosecution or were worse than the scores of officers not charged or even detained. Rather, these defendants were chosen because, with some suggestive evidence of guilt available, given the relaxed evidentiary standards, convictions would be easier to obtain against them (Ibid.).

The arbitrary method for the determination of which individuals would become defendants leads to the next fatal flaw in substantive due process dimensions of the trials – the absence of the Japanese emperor. The prosecution revealed the depth and importance of this omission in its opening comments before the introduction of any evidence:

> Individuals are being brought to the bar of justice for the first time in history to answer personally for offenses that they have committed while acting in official capacities as chiefs of state (Brackman 1987, p. 108).

Despite this reformulation of the opening statement from the Nuremberg Trials, no chief of state was actually on trial or even mentioned during the trial. Emperor Hirohito had been the only chief of state of Japan from 1928 through 1945 and in every sense was responsible for the conduct of the state during the war. Throughout the duration of the trial and even afterward, the emperor was not charged with any crime, identified as an unindicted co-conspirator, or even implicated as a wrongdoer (Ibid.). The absence of the emperor as a defendant is a substantive defect of such magnitude that the legitimacy of the trial as a whole must be called into question. By analogy, it is hard to conceive of the Nuremberg Trials without Hitler had he lived to be prosecuted. Yasuaki has observed:

> The political character of the trial is manifest in the treatment of the emperor who under the Meiji Constitution bore ultimate responsibility for the war. The tribunal not only failed to call the Emperor to account for Japan's war

of aggression, but did not even summon him as a witness (Hosoya 1986, pp. 45–6).

Retribution and deterrence, the goals of justice, seem to have never been considered by the architects of the Tokyo tribunal. With respect to any effort at developing some level of retribution, none of the alleged victims of Japan were compensated or otherwise made whole in any fashion. The only sentence imposed by the tribunal was death and it was meted out as punishment to a representative class of convicts who may or may not have actually committed the vague actions alleged at trial. Most of the actual perpetrators of the alleged criminal activity were never prosecuted or charged. The emperor, the one man ultimately responsible for whatever misdeeds occurred in the Japanese war effort, was completely shielded from any mention throughout the entirety of the proceedings. Deterrence not only was not the stated or obvious goal of the proceedings, but the lesson for posterity from the Tokyo tribunal may be that those ultimately responsible, like the emperor, need not fear the risk of prosecution and even those who may be responsible at a lower level of command, like the Class A prisoners, are unlikely to face prosecution.

In the final analysis, the trial was nothing more than an effort to consolidate political power. The emperor retained a substantial level of popular support after the war. Had General MacArthur sought to prosecute the emperor, Macarthur would have faced a more difficult time as the leader of the occupying force. The purpose of the occupation was to restart the Japanese economy and also to inhibit any future expansionist desires and actions on the part of the ruling class. One dimension of ensuring a peaceful future for Japan and its neighbors was to create and expand an economic relationship with the United States. This strategy was consistent with the approach to Germany undertaken through the Marshall Plan as well as the broad approach to institutionalizing peaceful relations across Europe (Smith 2007). Hanging the emperor certainly would not have furthered the relation building efforts and may have damaged Japan's relationship with the United States beyond repair. Moreover, while the domestic audience in the United States at the time may not have fully appreciated the impact of the atomic bombs dropped at Hiroshima and Nagasaki, certainly the military and civilian leadership of both countries had a more profound appreciation of the impact of this first use of weapons of mass destruction.

Pursuit of the emperor – the embodiment of the divine and the political and cultural head of state – as a criminal might have simply been too much insult added to too much injury. MacArthur could not easily or effectively occupy Japan if the population was committed to open rebellion. To assuage the Japanese population, avoiding the prosecution of the emperor and other major political figures was perhaps an unavoidable compromise. Political expediency and the institutionalization of peaceful relations took priority over the pursuit of justice. Of course, if MacArthur simply wanted to build the relationship between the two countries without friction, he could have decided to avoid trials altogether. At least one tribunal judge argued that the true purpose of the trial was simply to avenge the attack on Pearl Harbor and satisfy the American public that Japan had paid for this assault (Roling 1993, pp. 78–82). If this is an accurate assessment of the motivation of the United States, then it also explains why the United States was the primary architect of the Tokyo tribunal while the Allies broadly engaged in a collaborative effort at Nuremberg. Justice Roling explained the decision to avoid a contemporaneous publication of the transcripts of the trial by noting, "I suppose that they [the United States] were perhaps a bit ashamed of what happened there" (Ibid., p. 81). When asked if the trial was "victor's justice," that is, the prosecution of the vanquished by the victors as the final element of defeat, Roling replied:

> Of course ... we were aware of the bombings and the burnings of Tokyo and Yokohama and other big cities. It was horrible, we went there for the purpose of vindicating the laws of war and yet saw every day how the allies had violated them dreadfully.... Tojo was right that in this respect Tokyo was victor's justice only. As one of the accused in the Nuremberg trial put it: "If we had won the war, there would have been another trial, in another place, for other crimes." That's quite true (Ibid., p. 87).

Charles I, Captain Wirz, Nuremberg, and Tokyo in Perspective

Charles I was tried and executed in an effort to bolster Cromwell's claim to governance. Cromwell's attempt to delegitimize the royal right to rule through prosecution depended on the construction of a flawed and untenable set of legal principles. The inability of the king to mount a defense or speak in court exposes the lack of procedural due process. The shifting laws of treason expose the lack of any substantive due process. Since, from Cromwell's perspective, royal rule had come to an end, deterrence was simply not a consideration. The claimed victim class was not even provided with the modest compensation of "being heard" in court. Still, this modest and unjust first step moved the world toward an expectation that the ruler should be ruled by law.

It is no surprise that the world did not quickly embrace the difficult prospect of a nation that has prevailed in a military conflict giving the vanquished opponent an opportunity to test the evidence of wrongdoing in a court of law. Political leaders might struggle to explain an acquittal of a notorious enemy while the prosecutions might solidify and reinvigorate the defeated military and its supporters. Nonetheless, by the time of the Civil War in the United States, the concept of law as a force that constrained rulers had begun to have genuine importance throughout the global community of states. The American Revolution moved the notion of law as the sovereign forward in the global discourse and the infallibility of rulers was no longer genuinely accepted orthodoxy.

As the Civil War ended, a war-weary nation had turned its view toward reconciliation. However, the assassination of President Lincoln raised the anger of some of the civilian and military leadership of the victorious Union and reconciliation gave way to vengeance. The fate of Captain Henry Wirz was assured. In response to the unimaginable suffering of the prisoners at Andersonville Prison and to the deaths of over thirteen thousand of those detained, the United States constructed a show trial of a mid-level officer who had no ability to ameliorate the suffering of the prisoners. The trial itself was legal farce. The charges were altered after the evidence was presented to more closely match what was presented in court. The severe prohibitions on the ability of his attorneys to be effective meant Wirz was never allowed to present a genuine defense. Perhaps most shocking, the prosecution failed to present any evidence of actual wrongdoing as alleged in the complaint or even a credible claim of the names of any actual victim. No effort was made by the prosecution to connect Wirz to the conspiracy for which he was hung. Wirz was afforded neither substantive due process nor procedural due process. The goals of the Wirz trial were limited to vengeance for the assassination of President Lincoln and an effort to implicate the civilian and military leadership of the Confederacy, especially Confederate president Jefferson Davis, in that assassination. From the perspective of the evolution and progression of war crimes tribunals, the jurisprudential contribution from the Wirz trial is that a farce will not be considered legitimate. The public and political distaste for the Wirz trial was so intense and profound that it effectively ended any further prosecutions of Confederates for war crimes during the conflict. This perhaps contributed to the groundwork of concern that Germany be dealt with fairly.

The Nuremberg Trials generally provided a broad and stringent standard of both substantive due process and procedural due process. The explicit and oft repeated assertion of the goal of deterrence to future leaders as well as those leaders who stood before the court for judgment was coupled with the repeated assertion that the victims had a right to settle their claims. In the end of course, the Nuremberg Trials did not make the victims whole, but perhaps this is an unrealistic expectation of the process. No source for a compensation fund was obviously overlooked. That is, Germany had been plundered by its leaders both morally and economically. All available resources had been squandered in the misguided war effort. Moreover, the Allies shared a common concern that the overly punitive nature of the post-World War I armistice had assisted the Nazi rise to power. The strategy of crippling the German economy after World War I had such negative consequences that few among the Allies or anywhere else in the world community wished to create a draconian restitution plan. The risk that an economic humiliation of Germany after the complete military defeat would simply cause a future recurrence of hyper-nationalism like that which led to the rise of the Nazis was too great. A substantial and comprehensive restitution plan might have undercut the intended economic rebuilding that underpinned the Marshall Plan and jeopardized the effort by the United States to rebuild Europe, including western Germany. The political constraints that pushed Allies against creating a restitution regime for the victims of the Nazis simply could not be overcome. The political realities of the need for a peaceful and prosperous Europe, including Germany, simply outweighed the need for comprehensive justice.

Despite arising more or less contemporaneously and out of the same conflict, the Tokyo trials have more in common with the trials of Charles I and Captain Henry Wirz than with the Nuremberg Trials. The substantive due process and procedural due process by the Tokyo tribunal was de jure more than de facto. While some modicums of procedural due process were provided for in the originating document, as the prosecutions progressed, there was no effort to implement formal due process, whether substantive or procedural. Deterrence was not only ignored as a goal of the process, but also given the absence of any effort at holding the emperor accountable for the crimes that were prosecuted at the trial; deterrence conceptually might have been diminished. That is, future leaders might very well look to the Tokyo Trial as sending a signal that domestic political support would translate into immunity from prosecution by the international community. Restitution was given no consideration at any time during the planning of the tribunal, the prosecution of the defendants, or as the sentences were carried out.

Despite these defects, both the Nuremberg Trials and the Tokyo trials contributed to the development of the jurisprudential lineage that was, in part, founded on the trials of both Captain Henry Wirz and Charles I. The Nuremberg Trials and the Tokyo trials set an expectation among the world populations that those who committed criminal acts in war would be held accountable, at least to some extent, after the cessation of violence (Ratner and Abrams 2001). The advent of the Cold War at the end of World War II meant that broad and direct military confrontations between the great powers of the world became less likely. While of course the potential for war between the Soviet Union and the United States and its allies was always present, the détente between the superpowers and their allies meant conflict during the Cold War would occur in different venues and in different ways than those in which the two world wars had been waged. The expectations about post-conflict judicial processes evolved in concert with the evolution of the parameters of war through the rise and fall of the Cold War. War crimes tribunals became domesticated as civil wars and civil conflicts ended. After the cessation of domestic conflict, politicians who spoke to or on behalf of the victim classes sought justice through tribunals. The criminal prosecutions after the Dirty War in Argentina, the Truth and Reconciliation process after the fall of apartheid in South Africa, and the lustration process used across the

Eastern European states after the fall of the Soviet Union are examples of the variation in domestication of war crimes trials. While the predecessors to these domestic institutions were far from perfect from the standpoint of the dispensation of justice, they paved the way for the judicial process to become a critical part of the postconflict political world.

4

Domestication of War Crimes Tribunals

Argentina, South Africa, and the Former Soviet States

As the Cold War subsided, some states moved toward resolution of their domestic political tensions through a shift toward democratized systems. Of course, how the different states managed their transitions was shaped by their unique domestic situations, institutions, and political actors. Transitional justice was an integral aspect across the spectrum of alternative approaches to the reformation of governance after authoritarianism. In this chapter, the domestication of war crimes tribunals is considered through the lens of the prosecutions arising from the Dirty War in Argentina, the Truth and Reconciliation process implemented in post-apartheid South Africa, and the widely used lustration process in the Eastern European states during the post-Soviet Union transitions. These are examples of the variations in the domestication of war crimes trials that were shaped by the earlier processes and also effected the future prosecutions.

Argentina

The Dirty War in Argentina spanned the period from 1975 through 1983. The country was governed by a military regime that ruled through the use of terror and criminal violence as official policy. This period of politics through intimidation, torture, and murder ran through the rule of successive military juntas until the installation of a popularly elected government in 1983 (Hodges 1991, pp. ix–x; Malamud-Goti 1996, pp. 3–5). The Dirty War arose as official policy once a civil government authorized the military to use any means necessary to defend the country against dissident citizens whom the government classified as subversives (Hodges 1991, p. x). This period in Argentina's history is notorious because of the remarkable and widespread use of state-sanctioned torture, assassination, and generally terroristic methods of law enforcement against not only resident aliens but also Argentine citizens. During the span of the Dirty War, over ten thousand people were tortured and killed by government officials and perhaps as many as another thirty thousand people simply disappeared (Hodges 1988, pp. 210–11; Stotzky 1993, pp. 42–3; Wynia 1992, p. 163). A tragic and lasting tribute to this claimed counter-insurgency effort by the Argentine government was the introduction into the human rights lexicon of the word *desaparecido – the disappeared one.* The word identifies citizens and foreigners taken into custody by agents of the government, in all likelihood tortured and killed, and then "disappeared" or never heard from again (Andersen 1993, pp. 2–4). Subsequently, the National Commission on the Disappearance of Persons identified 365 separate detention camps and torture facilities used during the entirety of the Dirty War (Mignone et al., 1984–1985, p. 119 at note 1). Detainees transferred out of these facilities might be dropped, either alive or dead, from a helicopter into the ocean or the Rio de la Plata or buried in some remote rural area (National Commission on the Disappearance of Persons 1984, Nunca Mas Report, pp. 223–47). The disposal of the victims was designed to render recovery of the body or identification in the event the body was recovered difficult or impossible (Mignone et al., 1984–1985, p. 121).

The architects of the Dirty War and its affiliated repression were also the instigators of the disastrous Malvinas Islands/Falklands Islands conflict with Great Britain (Malamud-Goti 1996, p. 3). The conflict with the United Kingdom over the Malvinas Islands/Falklands Islands ended with retreat and humiliation for Argentina. The embarrassment of the failed military operation combined with an inept and disastrous management of the economy so delegitimized the ruling military elite and eroded any confidence in their ability to govern that the junta relinquished control and called for national elections for president, legislators, and provincial governors (Ibid.). This election set the stage for the first prosecution in Argentina of members of the military by a civilian government. Raul R. Alfonsin, the candidate for the Radical Party, promised to prosecute and bring to justice all those acting on behalf of the government who were responsible for the gross human rights abuses that occurred under the long military rein (Mignone 1984–1985, p. 119). Raul Alfonsin was elected with an unprecedented (for a non-Peronist) fifty-two percent of the vote (Corradi 1985, p. 150).

When President Alfonsin and the elected civilian government took office in December 1983, Alfonsin requested that presidential advisors Carlos Ninos and Jaime Malamud-Goti draft enabling legislation in order to provide for the trial and punishment of those suspected of orchestrating and committing the massive violations of human rights at the heart of the Dirty War (Malamud-Goti 1996, p. 4). Malamud-Goti identified the underlying intent and goals of the prospective prosecutions as follows:

> Trials of persons accused of human rights abuses are widely proclaimed as essential to transitions from dictatorship to democracy. There are sound reasons indeed to maintain that punishment is a political tool to raise the consciousness essential to bringing about radical political change. Impartial allocations of blame to those who trample people's basic liberties ... will help restore belief in individual liberties and recreate democratic authority (Ibid., pp. 4–5).

At the outset, the claimed premise – the "impartial allocation of blame" – that served as the rationale for the trials centered on retribution delivered through proper mechanisms of substantive due process and procedural due process. The explicit purpose of the trials was to punish those people who "trampled people's basic liberties" (Ibid.). The crimes that were to be the basis of the accusations were not simply ordinary criminal acts or normal administrative functions of government. Rather, the acts were those orchestrated to fundamentally deprive people of their basic rights with no justification other than the improper preservation of political power. As the trials were planned, the acts that would subject the accused to prosecution all involved the use of the apparatus of government to commit violent criminal acts against Argentine citizens and the citizens of other nations. Procedural due process, the impartial allocation of blame, and the administration of justice in a fair manner were given high priority and privilege by the architects of the prosecutions. However, despite the commitment to meet the jurisprudential demands of procedural due process and of substantive due process, political concerns caused the purpose of the trials to move dramatically away from the ends of justice. That is, Malamud-Goti, the creator of the trials, proclaimed their political purpose as the restoration of democratic authority. Justice for the victims and for society as a whole was a secondary concern or perhaps rather a vehicle for delivery of the primary purpose of the trials: democratic consolidation. Concisely put, the trials were one important part of the strategy of Alfonsin to reestablish democracy in Argentina and secure his tenure in office (Epstein 1992, p. 179). The rationale of the trials did not originate from desires for retribution and deterrence. Justice was simply never the purpose of the prosecutions.

The notion of the trials as a political tool rather than a juridical one is clarified by an analysis of their implementation. There is no dispute that the accused were given fair trials and that both substantive due process and procedural due process were properly structured (Stotzky 1993, p. 341). Argentine philosopher and human rights activist Eduardo Rabossi noted that:

> The performance of the court was nearly perfect. Its judges acted with determination, consistency, effectiveness, and a permanent respect for the procedural forms of justice. Moreover, the substantive legal arguments ... met the very highest of international standards (Ibid.).

Some have applauded these prosecutions because they represent the first foray in Argentine history into juridical accountability at the national level for military or political elites (Peralta-Ramos and Waisman 1987, p. 104). After prosecution, five of the nine officers who ruled the three juntas from 1976 to 1982 were sentenced to terms ranging from four years to life imprisonment, although four of the defendants, the officers who were in charge of the last junta, were acquitted of all charges (Wynia 1992, p. 171).

While it may be true that these military and governmental elites were held more accountable for gross violations of law and human rights than their predecessors, the institutional arrangement for and limitations of the prosecutions served to subvert justice while presenting the appearance of full accountability. The trials actually subverted the goals of justice because of the actions taken to severely limit their scope and range prior to the initiation of the prosecutions. In particular, "The Full Stop Law" (Bill 23,492 of December 1986) and "The Due Obedience Law" (Bill 23,521 of June 1987) combined to directly undermine the capacity to prosecute those most responsible for the most egregious human rights violations. The legal process was subverted in a substantial and highly detrimental fashion. These two laws individually and together severely limited the prosecution of the military officers who were the architects and managers of the Dirty War. The first law provided a dramatically narrowed time frame in which the prosecutors could initiate an action against an individual. It limited the trials of any officer only to those cases that could be prepared for prosecution within sixty days of the passage of the law. The law was passed in December, which is a traditional holiday month in Argentina. Because the law was passed after many people had already begun their holiday leaves of absence, the functional time frame for initiation of a prosecution was even narrower than the already abbreviated sixty days provided for in the law. The second law represented an institutionalization of a "chain of command" defense to human rights violations. That is, many of the individuals who actually performed the acts that could give rise to prosecution were shielded by the limitation on lower-level officer responsibility in the Due Obedience Law. The law completely prohibited any prosecution for actions taken by any officer at the rank of lieutenant colonel or lower. Although prosecutors and judges diligently worked throughout the traditional holiday month and in fact were able to prepare 400 separate indictments against military officers within the window of the sixty-day time constraint, the Due Obedience Law, passed well after the indictments were issued, cut that number in half. Roughly half of the officers indicted were thus given explicit immunity from prosecution through the jurisdictional limitation.

Beyond the restricting legislation, President Alfonsin allowed fifty of the fifty-three generals who served at the time of his election to retire. The practical effect of this provision for sudden and mass retirement of the leaders of every branch of the military was the subsequent and unavoidable mass promotion from within the existing ranks of officers. Since the new generals were elevated from within the ranks of the junior officers who had been granted immunity through the Due Obedience Law, the new generation of leadership for the military was comprised of perpetrators of human rights violations who could never be held accountable. Thus, these low-level officers who had actually implemented the worst dimensions of the Dirty War were exempt from prosecution and also were promoted to the highest levels of control over the military (Wynia 1992, pp. 169–73). Shortly after the number of indictments was cut to 200, the Supreme Court reduced them further for technical errors and limited the number to just forty-one (Ibid.).

In the end, these limiting laws, judicial constraint, and some overlap of indictments combined to restrict actual prosecution to only fifteen generals, two admirals, and a small group of naval officers (Stotzky 1993, p. 342). The results of the trials varied dramatically from acquittals to long prison terms and many of the men convicted were subsequently pardoned or had their sentences reduced by either the executive branch or the Supreme Court (Andersen 1993, pp. 321–3). Importantly, the convicted were found guilty of relatively mundane crimes. The charges involved torture, kidnapping, rape, and murder. To be sure, each of the charges represents a horrific event for the victim and a substantial abrogation of human rights both individually and collectively. Still, there was no grand conspiracy charge, no broadly applicable charge related to planning the Dirty War, and no systemic accountability for the systemic deprivation of human rights as a governing strategy. The convicted individuals were found guilty of individual, not collective, crimes. In a sense, to isolate the violations of human rights into specific criminal acts diminishes the overall and comprehensive assault on civil society that was the Dirty War. That is, justice diminished may be justice denied.

From the beginning, the prosecution effort and the subsequent trials were unlikely to produce outcomes that served the ends of justice. Retribution was not considered as a meaningful dimension of the prosecutions. Given the elaborate efforts to shield the officer corps from prosecution, it seems clear that retribution for the bad acts was not nearly as important as protecting those responsible for them. No mechanism for redress of grievances, in any fashion, was established for either the surviving victims or their families or for the families of the deceased and disappeared. In light of the sparse number of actual prosecutions and convictions given the magnitude, scope, and impact of the Dirty War, the victims could hardly be satisfied with the retribution dimensions of the process. Indeed, the number of convictions was negligible even in relation to the modest set of original indictments or the much more abbreviated roster of indictments after the Due Obedience Law was enacted. The trials did not provide the victims and their families with any meaningful demand or delivery of retribution from the perpetrators of the Dirty War (Andersen 1993, pp. 307–12).

Deterrence was given even less consideration than retribution. Not only were most of the officers and other perpetrators protected through the jurisdictional exceptions and other limitations on prosecution, but the retirement of the old guard and promotion of the new guard rewarded some of the worst offenders. Moreover, some of the citizens who resisted the Dirty War effort, that is, members of the victim class, were also prosecuted and convicted through the same legal apparatus as those in the military. In essence, those who resisted the criminal enterprise of the government were treated as if they were the moral and legal peers of those governmental agents who presided over the mass slaughter and abuses of the Dirty War (Hodges 1988, pp. 210–11). The deterrent dimension of the trials targeted civilians as fully as it targeted the members of the military. Beyond the somewhat astonishing prosecutorial focus on civilians, the trials did what no military leader had been able to do: They united the military and restored its internal cohesion (Erro 1993, p. 145). Accordingly, rather than acting as a deterrent for future human rights abuses, these prosecutions unified the military and restored its esprit de corps as its members joined in the common defense of the Dirty War, which the military justified as a well-executed and appropriate, if brutal, counter-insurgency effort.

In 1992, then former President Alfonsin specifically discussed the notion of deterrence as a driving force behind the establishment of the trials: "Our intention was not so much to punish as to prevent, to stop what had happened from happening again, to guarantee that never again could an Argentine be taken out of his home at night and be tortured or assassinated by officials of the state apparatus" (Andersen 1993, p. 323). This lofty rhetoric is not easily reconciled with the construction and actual conduct of the trials. The limitations on prosecution and the promotion of symbolic over actual impact from the convictions suggests that Alfonsin came to care about deterrence once he found himself defending the role of the trials from the standpoint of their historical legacy. To be sure, some selection in prosecution was unavoidable given the enormous number of potential defendants. Virtually every officer and enlisted member of the armed services could have been indicted for some aspect of the Dirty War. If conspiracy charges were included in the trials, almost without exception every member of the military could have been subject to prosecution. The civilian government did not have the political or physical capacity to prosecute everyone for every crime. As Malamud-Goti commented, "to try all those responsible was plainly absurd. Directly or indirectly, thousands of officers were implicated in human rights abuse" (Malamud-Goti 1996, p. 185). While some prosecutorial discretion was inherently necessary, the government "did whatever it could to limit the prosecutions to an insignificant number of culprits" (Ibid., p. 178).

Alfonsin could perhaps have taken a more comprehensive and forceful approach to the prosecution of the violators of human rights. He might have tried to dismantle the entire institutional apparatus of the extant military as he delivered to the population a set of thorough, comprehensive, and complete human rights trials. Of course, the military would have united in opposition to such a plan and Alfonsin would have undoubtedly faced a coup and perhaps assassination. Even the modest trials Alfonsin was able to secure resulted in a more cohesive military that united in response to the perceived attack and interference in security issues from the civilian government. Likewise, if Alfonsin had given the perpetrators of the Dirty War an unambiguous, unlimited, and widely applicable pardon, he would have faced backlash from an angry civilian population that voted for him precisely because he promised to hold the military accountable for the siege that the country had endured. If he completely shielded the military from prosecution, Alfonsin would have faced a popular revolt.

Accordingly, the Alfonsin administration embraced a strategy that would maximize the civilian government's ability to maintain power and consolidate democratic and civilian control over the mechanisms of state. Specifically, the strategic approach of a lengthy investigation and the dramatic restriction of prosecutions by narrowing the scope and range of the charges through the limiting statutes allowed Alfonsin to appease some factions of the military as well as some factions of the public. The juridical tool of prosecutions for human rights violations was used primarily to consolidate civilian rule and promote the political ends of the Alfonsin government. The prosecutions were designed and implemented as mechanisms for creating a political balance between the civilian population that demanded justice for serious crimes perpetrated by the government and the military establishment that sought credit and vindication for defending the nation from radicals.

Both the public and the military had the capacity to thwart Alfonsin's agenda and undermine his governing coalition. Because he could reasonably expect reactions from the two conflicting constituencies, and therefore he reasonably feared them both, Alfonsin's options were essentially limited to a demonstration of the appearance of a judicial process and the illusion of justice to satisfy the people who voted him into office in order to hold the military accountable. While he created this legal structure for prosecuting some members of the military, he had to take care that he sufficiently shielded most of the military from any serious prosecutorial effort. For Alfonsin and Argentina, perhaps the prosecution of human rights violations served a larger purpose than justice. These trials served as a vehicle for bolstering political stability and as an institutional mark of disfavor against state-sanctioned and orchestrated violence. That the trials promoted the consolidation of democracy over satisfying the demands of justice may be problematic for the victims and those concerned with the victims. Still, Alfonsin can be credited with doing the most he could given the political realities he faced. A stable and peaceful Argentina under civilian control eventually proved attainable, in no small measure, because of the balance Alfonsin struck between justice and appeasement. An angry and reconsolidated military was simply too great a threat for Alfonsin and civilian rule for him to proceed against the perpetrators of human rights violations in broad or comprehensive terms.

The developmental path for war crimes as an expected outcome after conflict unavoidably led to domestic trials. The stark difference in the Dirty War prosecutions from their jurisprudential ancestors was that the instigator of the trials – Alfonsin – still had to contend with the instigators of the human rights violations – members of the military – as politically relevant actors even as he pursued them in court.

That is, unlike Charles I, Captain Henry Wirz, or the defendants at Nuremberg and Tokyo, the members of the military who perhaps should have been tried were not wholly deprived of political power before the initiation of the prosecutions. While Charles I still had loyal subjects and Wirz became a symbolic martyr for the defeated Southern rebellion, neither represented a functional or capable military force that could have stopped the prosecutions. Similarly, while there were no doubt loyalists to the Nazis at the time of the Nuremberg Trials, the military apparatus had been so defeated that no forceful resistance was possible. The Tokyo trials presented a shelter from liability for the emperor, but no credible argument can be made that the Japanese military structure could have overcome the Allied victory merely to stop the prosecutions. Argentina and Alfonsin were certain to face yet another military coup if, in the view of the military leadership, the trials went too far. Because there was no complete defeat of the military – perhaps an inherent dimension of a domestic conflict – there could be no complete justice.

The case of Argentina leads to a consideration of the case of South Africa. The sustaining political power of the perpetrators of human rights violations in South Africa involved economics more than brute force. While the source of the postconflict power in South Africa of the perpetrators of human rights violations differed from that in Argentina, the new leaders who steered South Africa through its transition faced a similar dilemma as that faced by Alfonsin.

The new regime did not come to or take power through such a dominating event that the elites from the old regime could be treated like powerless criminals.

The Truth and Reconciliation Commission of South Africa

The term *apartheid* refers to the systematic and multilayered segregation along racially constructed lines utilized by the minority white South African elite structure in order to maintain its domination and control over the governmental, economic, and political dimensions of the country from 1948 though 1994 (Juckes 1995, pp. 176–9 and pp. 63–87). In the wake of the civil rights movement in the United States and the expansion of civil rights throughout the industrialized segments of the world, the justification and moral foundation of apartheid began to erode with a steady increase of international and domestic disapproval of the policy. The international community expressed its disapproval first through the isolation of South Africa from the global community of cultural and sporting events. The isolating and exclusionary international sanctions spread from international athletic competitions and music and art festivals into the realm of trade and finance soon after. Domestically, opponents of apartheid engaged in a variety of resistance efforts which took a host of forms including work stoppages and strikes, nonviolent protests like those advocated by Martin Luther King, Jr. and Gandhi, and, by some opposition factions, violence (Howarth and Norval 1998).

The systematic erosion of apartheid was incremental and was opposed by most of the people in the ruling government. Each step that dismantled the separatist structure seemed to make the next step more feasible. In 1985, the ban on interracial marriage was repealed. The next year, the laws that restricted intrastate movement or migration of nonwhites, the so-called Pass Laws, were repealed. In 1989, three years after the repeal of the Pass Laws, peaceful demonstrations for the purpose of protesting apartheid were legalized for the first time. The government promised a new constitution would soon be enacted and, as a show of movement toward that goal and as a demonstration of good faith, repealed the Separate Amenities Act in 1990. This law prohibited nonwhites from using public facilities reserved for whites only.

After over thirty-two years in prison as a result of his political activity, Nelson Mandela, the deputy president of the black opposition movement African National Congress (ANC) was released in 1990. In 1991, the government repealed all the remaining laws that together constructed apartheid. The repealed laws included the Population Registration Act, which required each person to be classified into one of nine racial categories (Thompson 1995, pp. 221–47). Throughout the time period of the slow dismantling of apartheid and the explicitly racialized laws that institutionalized it, those opposed to reform engaged in a campaign against changes to the system through which they violated the human rights of those seeking reform and an end to apartheid. These violations of basic human rights were broadly spread across the population, systematically executed by multiple levels of governmental officials, and unrelenting in their application (Waldmeir 1997, pp. 22–6).

As apartheid was dismantled one law at a time, a fundamental change in the structure of government became more likely to follow and as the last vestiges of the separatist structure fell, negotiations for a constitutional change were initiated. In December 1991, nineteen political organizations sent delegates to meet with the ruling National Party in order to initiate negotiations to amend the constitution to create a more representative government (Thompson 1995, p. 247). Violence between the reformers and supporters of the status quo marred much of the early transitional period. Eventually, the government scheduled and held a white vote referendum in which voters endorsed the transition process and chose peace over continued conflict. A temporary and transitional constitution was agreed to by the representatives of the government and by the leaders of all of the parties that joined the negotiations. The interim constitution contained the explicit goal of reconciliation for the people of South Africa (Asmal, Asmal, and Roberts 1997, p. 2). The first election in which nonwhites could run for office or vote was held in April of 1994. Nelson Mandela won over sixty-two percent of the vote and was sworn in as president in May of that year (Gastrow 1995, p. 97; Juckes 1995, p. 171; Thompson 1995, pp. 254–5).

For the newly inaugurated President Mandela, reconciliation of and among his countrymen was one of the primary tasks facing the new National Unity Government. In his inaugural address to the nation, he underscored the importance of societal unification and reconciliation:

> Out of the experience of an extraordinary human disaster that lasted too long, must be born a society of which all humanity will be proud.... Never, never, and never again shall it be that this beautiful land will again experience the oppression of one by another (Thompson 1995, pp. 254–5).

The concepts of reconciliation and unification were easily operationalized. In short, President Mandela intended to move South Africa to a full embrace of a nonracial government as a multiracial country and toward an unequivocal cessation of politically driven violence (Mandela 1994, pp. 257–60 and pp. 261–8). Mandela was convinced that widespread acceptance of the new government was inextricably tied to some formal assessment of the past injustices of apartheid so that a future could be constructed that would, simply put, be more just (Asmal, Asmal, and Roberts 1997, p. 2).

Given the unusual manner in which institutional change came to South Africa, it is perhaps not unexpected that reconciliation and a focus on the just arrangement of the future societal framework took precedence over a concern about punishment of and justice for past wrongs. Apartheid ended because of persistent and unrelenting resistance and ongoing negotiations geared toward a peaceful resolution.

Change did not come to the country as a result of a military defeat or a massive economic or political collapse of the ruling government. Rather, the change altered the system without stripping the elites of all power. The existing institutions of power that structured and allowed the ruling white minority to maintain economic and political control over the majority of mixed –race and black citizens were dismantled through negotiation and resistance rather than violence and military victories.

One outcome of the negotiated nature of the system transition was that the elites under the old regime – the whites – were not wholly removed from power and influence simply because the previously oppressed groups took control of the government. That is, the group responsible for the oppression and gross violations of human rights was not eliminated from political input merely because the regime changed. Whites in South Africa were not removed from the post-transition political discourse. The ability of the newly empowered majority to consolidate the emerging democracy and hold power was not conditional on the disenfranchisement of the minority. The whites were not exiled, subjected to mass killings, or stripped of all property rights. Their possessions were not summarily seized by the new government and their property was not summarily converted to public use. They were not jailed or forced to flee the country simply for being white. Political rights of participation, including running for office and voting, were not withdrawn or constricted. The new governance model

embraced a commitment to political rights as well as property rights and it was predicated on equality among citizens
rather than merely a role reversal between those who were
oppressed and those who were the oppressors.

The fact that whites were not eliminated from the political calculus during and after the transition can no doubt
be attributed to a variety of factors. However, the central
explanation for the resulting balance of power may be
quite simple. No consideration of the transition away from
apartheid can ignore the critical role played by the economic power of whites in South Africa. The central role of
the importance of economic assets under the control of the
white minority cannot be understated. The white minority
exerted ownership and control over virtually all aspects of
the economy for over 100 years before the end of apartheid.
Control and ownership were intertwined. If the new government had chosen to present the whites in South Africa
with a future of severely restricted rights like the past had
been for those categorized as mixed-race and black in South
Africa, those whites with assets who controlled the economy
in almost every dimension would have left the country en
masse. Such a white economic flight would have depleted
South Africa of such a volume of resources that it might
have destroyed any ability of the new government to lay the
foundation for a stable economy. Along with the economic
flight, such an approach might have also caused a torrent
of emigration as whites and those who assisted in their economic and political domination might have fled rather than

face prosecution. From the standpoint of economic stability and growth, South Africa and the newly constituted government would not be able to initiate its strategy for consolidation and nation building if the whites fled with all the capital they controlled. Moreover, continued foreign direct investment was an important building block for consolidation, so the new South Africa could not run rough-shod over the old South Africa without risking a loss of confidence in the world economic community.

President Mandela faced a difficult dilemma. He had to create a viable and economically stable state while at the same time effectively providing redress for the systemic and widespread wrongs of the previous regime. Victor's vengeance was not a path open to him if he hoped to preserve the new government and institutionalize the de jure de-racialization of the power structure. Instead, reconciliation was the path available that held the most promise for success. Had the new regime attempted Nuremberg-style prosecutions, it might have led to social, economic, and ongoing political havoc that would undermine the new system. Justice could only be pursued in concert with reconciliation. He determined that the goals of justice could best be achieved through a process that would provide some sort of full and truthful disclosure about the oppressive past. For Mandela, this confessional concept inherently included a broad amnesty for the wrongdoers as a trade-off for full disclosure of the wrongs.

The enabling legislation that established the truth and reconciliation process was titled "The Promotion of National Unity and Reconciliation Act." The Act created the Truth and Reconciliation Commission, the administrative avenue for hearings, in order to provide a "useful window into apartheid and ... for arriving at justice through a clear-sighted and ethically decisive grasp of the truth about the past" (Asmal, Asmal, and Roberts 1997, p. 14). In particular, section 3(1) of the Act sets forth the broad imperative that the process should strive to establish the truth as thoroughly as possible:

> as complete a picture as possible of the causes, nature, and extent of the gross violations of human rights which were committed ... including the antecedents, circumstances, factors, and context of such violations, as well as the perspectives of the victims and the motives and perspectives of the persons responsible for the commission of the violations, by conducting investigations and holding hearings... (Ibid., p. 15).

The conceptual goal of justice as an abstract end is intertwined with the concept of "truth" as the vehicle through which the desired end is achieved. The South African truth and reconciliation process is quartered around the notion that explicating the truth about apartheid – whatever it may be – is a prerequisite to the consolidation of a peaceful post-apartheid country. While the focus on truth as the vehicle for founding reconciliation may seem orthogonal to the historic goals of justice, the constants of deterrence and retribution inherent in justice are not wholly missing from this process. Indeed, unlike the previous prosecutions, the South African structure specifically addresses retribution. In section 3(1)(c) of the Act, the commission is empowered to provide for some dimension of reparations for the victims of apartheid. The Act sets forth reparations, defined by section I(I)(xiv) of the Act, to include "any form of compensation, *ex gratia* payment, restitution, rehabilitation, or recognition" (Ibid., p. 17).

The Act creates a mandatory amnesty mechanism for those accused of perpetrating the human rights violations that were integral to the implementation of apartheid. The Act sets forth the specific requirement that the Amnesty Committee "shall" grant amnesty to any person who applies for amnesty if the members are "satisfied that" the applicant seeks amnesty for an act directly incident to and connected with some political objective associated with the official policies and that the person seeking amnesty has made "full disclosure of all relevant facts" (sec. 20; Asmal, Asmal, and Roberts 1997, p. 16). With the mandate that the Amnesty Committee grant amnesty also came the explicit authority and discretion to withhold amnesty from an unrepentant or dishonest applicant (sec. 19(4); Asmal, Asmal, and Roberts 1997, p. 17).

Kader Asmal, a former law professor at Trinity College in Dublin, minister of water affairs and forestry in President

Mandela's administration, and later minister of education as well as a member of parliament, was one of the architects of the South African Commission. Asmal explained the underlying rationale for the structure used by the South African model for human rights trials as follows:

> For reasons of principal also, the triumphalist approach of victor's justice, with its inevitable selectiveness and political opportunism, was rejected in favour of ideals of nation-building and reconciliation between the oppressors and the previously oppressed.... This rejection was consistent with the longstanding humanist ideals of the anti-apartheid resistance ... a judicial [i.e., punitive] process would have focused too much on the perpetrators to the exclusion of the victims; it would have over-individualized the horrors of apartheid ... at the expense of necessary attention to its systemic and collective evils (Asmal, Asmal, and Roberts 1997, p. 18–19).

Every indication suggests that the intent behind the language and architecture of reconciliation was authentically expressed and genuinely grounded in the firm conviction about the importance of and commitment to reconciliation. Unequivocally, the political elites within the African National Congress were convinced that a series of Nuremberg-inspired war crimes trials that focused on punishment would seriously inhibit their efforts to consolidate the new political order and would perpetuate strife (Waldmeir 1997, p. 277). These concerns about practical politics were addressed in the context of a cultural commitment to notions of forgiveness as a dimension of the desiderata of civil society. That is, in South Africa there is a broadly accepted cultural commitment to the notion of *ubuntu*, which in a very loose sense simply means that sincere apologies ought to be accepted (Ibid., pp. 276–7). This foundational attitude in the larger society as a whole made the ANC's goal of excising revenge from the formula for prosecution much more easily attainable. Because for over a century those racially categorized as white dominated every dimension, segment, and institution of the South African economy, a systematic and comprehensive extraction of revenge targeting those who perpetuated the policies of apartheid would unavoidably have resulted in a massive emigration by those targeted and almost certainly would have undermined the capacity of the ANC to successfully navigate the political transition (Ibid., pp. 271–2, 277). Those in power, white South Africans, had relinquished power. To capitulate and give up control over the mechanisms of political power amounted to an admission of wrongdoing. For those in control to hold elections that would almost certainly result in their removal from power was a broad and deep apology for the status quo. That the ANC could prevail in the elections and take the reins of power was the most comprehensive and meaningful, even profound, avenue for retribution available. The broad electoral victory and sound defeat of the status quo allowed those assuming power to be magnanimous precisely because they had won. The focus on reconciliation rather than retribution allowed the new political elites to focus on building, or rebuilding, the nation (Howarth and Norval 1998, p. 206). With the total abandonment of racialized formal laws, there was no compelling rationale for some substantial deterrence dimension to the reconciliation process. State-sanctioned and orchestrated violations of human rights by state actors like those perpetrated under apartheid were not possible under the new legal regime.

Archbishop Desmond Tutu saw *ubuntu* as not only the primary foundational principle and rationale of the Truth and Reconciliation Commission, but also as a defining characteristic of the traditional South African cultural landscape. Tutu set forth his understanding of the concept of *ubuntu* and its central cultural role in South Africa:

> We say that a human being is a human being because he belongs to a community and harmony is the essence of that community. So ubuntu actually demands that you forgive, because resentment and anger and desire for revenge undermine harmony. In our understanding, when someone doesn't forgive, we say that person does not have ubuntu. That is to say, he is not really human (Waldmeir 1997, p. 268).

From a cultural, political, and economic standpoint, for President Mandela and the other politicians that set up the plan for transitional justice, reconciliation seemed to be the only clear path for consolidation of the new system. The Act established May 1997 as the date by which an application for amnesty could be filed. Before the deadline, in excess of thirteen thousand applications for amnesty were filed with the commission (Asmal, Asmal, and Roberts 1997, pp. xiv–xv). Virtually every applicant who demonstrated remorse, repentance, and veracity was granted amnesty. Archbishop Tutu unequivocally and clearly explained why the commission chose reconciliation as the directed approach for the implementation of justice. Tutu wrote in the foreword to the Report of the Truth and Reconciliation Commission:

> There were those who believed we should follow the post World War II example of putting those guilty of gross violations of human rights on trial as the Allies did at Nuremberg. In South Africa, where we had a military stalemate, that was clearly an impossible option. Neither side in the struggle (the state nor the liberation movements) had defeated the other and hence nobody was in a position to enforce so called victor's justice (TRC Final Report, part 21 of foreword).

In the Final Report of the Truth and Reconciliation Commission, Archbishop Tutu directly addressed critics of the reconciliation approach and specifically those who criticized the amnesty aspects of the Act. Tutu's argument is that the essentially peaceful transition from massive government sanctioned and enforced repression to the de-racialized democratic system would have been impossible without the specific and broad amnesty provisions. (Ibid., part 22 of foreword). The Truth and Reconciliation Commission "has trodden the path urged on our people by the preamble to our founding Act, which called on 'the need for understanding but not for vengeance, a need for reparation but not retaliation, a need for *ubuntu* but not for victimization'" (Ibid., part 32 of foreword).

Any consideration of the substantive due process and procedural due process aspects of the hearings is bounded by the overriding concern for reconciliation. Because there was no punitive dimension, or at least anyone accused could avoid the punitive aspects of the process with minimal effort, the historical concern with substantive due process is simply less significant. The parameters of what was or was not considered a violation of human rights became less important for the accused because the redemption available through disclosure had no limits. Likewise, the procedural due process dimensions of the system were not critical since a confessional approach and full self-incrimination led to amnesty rather than execution.

In Argentina, the prosecuting government faced a still powerful military, while in South Africa the prosecuting government faced a still economically powerful minority. In both instances, those who sought to consolidate the new democracy were compelled to balance the demands of justice with the practical political reality that those responsible for massive violations of human rights could not be easily excised from the power structure of the society. Accordingly, in the absence of complete political and military victories over the perpetrators of the violations, those in charge of the transition and consolidation were forced to accommodate those who had relinquished political power.

For both Argentina and South Africa, the approach to the transitional process was the product of the need to keep the opposition from resurrecting the oppressive regime that had just failed. The countries caught up in the wave of democratization that followed the collapse of the Soviet Union faced related but quite different problems. Across Eastern Europe, the Soviet regime perpetrated gross human rights violations against the population but was also the agent of change that remained in power after the systemic alteration (Tverdova, 2011). For the satellite countries that had struggled under Soviet domination, the revolution came about because of the Soviet collapse that started in Russia. For some of these countries, the transition from authoritarianism to democracy was quick, unplanned, and essentially spontaneous.

The former Soviet states faced a novel dilemma. Because the Soviet satellite governments had been in control for so long to the exclusion of any opposition party, the capacity to run government and provide essential governmental services was concentrated in the hands of the people also responsible for maintaining the states under the Soviet direction. Although the transitions to democracy in the former Soviet states came about in an unusual manner, the problems faced in transition were not unique. The populations of these states had valid claims for justice for the years of state violation of basic human rights. For these states, there was little immediate concern that the Communist Party would resurrect itself or that Russia would attempt to compel a reconstitution of the Soviet Union. The costs of the military apparatus present in each satellite country had largely been paid for by the Soviet Union and Russia had little interest in or financial ability to continue funding these armies. The economies of these countries were highly dysfunctional. There was little risk of capital flight as the opportunity presented by the conversion to a more free market economy presented the first chance in generations for unbridled profits on investment. While the former Soviet states did not fear a resurrected military like in Argentina or fear the collapse of their economic structure like in South Africa, the very practical problem faced by those structuring the transitions had two dimensions. First, virtually every employee of the state had been involved in human rights violations or at a minimum collaboration with various police and surveillance operatives. Second, because of the ubiquitous nature of the violations, if the transitional governments prosecuted every civil servant associated with violations of rights of citizens under the Soviet regime, the new governments would simply not be able to function. That is, there would not be enough workers with governance skills and capacity for these new states to provide even the most basic administrative services.

This unusual circumstance of wholesale government involvement in not only human rights abuses but also in the transition away from authoritarianism led to an unusual permutation on war crimes trials called *lustration*.

Lustration and the Former Soviet States

The word *lustration* is derived from *lustratio* which, in Latin, means not only illumination but also purification through purging (Siklova 1996). Lustration represents one permutation of what can be thought of as truth revelation procedures (Kaminski and Nalepa 2006). That is, like the South African Truth and Reconciliation Commission, lustration served to move the countries involved toward democratic consolidation by revealing the truth behind the activities of the previous regime as a major dimension of institutions established to ensure transitional justice. The process by which lustration is accomplished often looks very similar to a traditional criminal proceeding in a traditional court setting (Posner and Vermeule 2004). Accordingly, the process may face many of the traditional problems of retroactive justice (Ibid.). Although the lustration process has only been utilized in post-communist Europe, it is quite similar in some critical ways to the truth and reconciliation process that originated in South Africa but more recently has also been utilized in Latin America and southeast Asia (e.g., Haynor 2001; Rotberg and Thompson 2002; Skaar, Gloppen, and Suhrke 2005). The most obvious difference between the lustration processes that spread across the former Soviet states and the previous trials and tribunals is that lustration is developed as a dimension of the labor code rather than the criminal justice code (Kaminski and Nalepa 2006, pp. 384–5). While lustration may result in a variety of punishments, the most important aspect of the lustration system is that it acts as a mechanism for a determination of disqualification from eligibility to work for the government. The new government thus achieves some substantial ability to acquire legitimacy by avoiding, as much as possible, association with the previous illegitimate regime.

The lustration variation on the reconciliation process arises in part because of three specific dimensions of the post-communist transitions. First, the concern with collaboration with the former authoritarian governments arises in part because of the unique intelligence structures of those communist regimes. Citizens were not only encouraged but also expected to actively assist the intelligence apparatus at the central control of each of the communist governments. The substantial involvement of average citizens with the intelligence gathering process was a singular characteristic of these communist states. Second, the transitional concerns in these countries were informed not only by an effort to account for the injustices of the past, but also to reestablish legitimate government broadly construed. The only claim to legitimacy that could be made by the Soviet satellite states, beyond claims arising out of force, was the widespread acceptance and recognition of them by the United States and the balance of the global community (Ibid., p. 391). The restoration of the rule of law was critical for those political actors involved with orchestrating the transition (McAdams 1997). Third, in part because the regimes existed apart from legitimate legal foundations of government, the act of collaboration with the police through acting as an informant against your fellow citizens was not an illegal act. In the absence of the parameters of legally proscribed behavior, the acts of informing and collaborating are simply more attenuated from the traditional acts of violence that concern the historical accounting of human rights violations and war crimes generally. That is, the acts that collectively and individually deprived people of their rights, at least with respect to collaborative and informant acts, were so diffused and so widespread that the identification of these acts as the proximate cause of specific acts of violence or human rights deprivation was much more difficult.

Lustration represents an end point in the evolution of the domestic oriented structure of war crimes trials. The approach of truth revelation for the purposes of constructing the new bureaucratic capacity moves away from the initial goals of justice and focuses more acutely on the transitional purpose of the process. The processes by which lustration was accomplished normally encompassed a modicum of procedural due process that included the ability to challenge the evidence against the subject of the lustration hearing and an appeal process, whereby an applicant could have a disqualification from office overturned (Kaminski and Nalepa 2006). Some in the international community have been critical of the lustration process because it presents a determination of collective guilt premised on an individual's status as a member of an organization (Ellis 1997, p. 182). This questionable dimension of lustration is reminiscent of the approach of the Tokyo trials, where defendants were chosen as representatives of classes of potential criminals.

Still, despite the substantive due process issue of status alone creating the possibility of prosecution, the lustration process as a whole was directed toward the disqualification of individuals from holding governmental office based on what can be broadly understood as a past history of abuse of similar governmental powers. Perhaps the most interesting dimension of the lustration process is the fact that the goals of justice, retribution, and deterrence seem to be given a prominent role in the process. Similar to the South African case, the human rights violations were so widespread and were committed by so many individuals that the emerging government had no capacity to provide any retribution beyond establishing the truth. However, the revealed truth of the past was the cornerstone for reestablishing the rule of law and constructing a new guarantee of the institutional protection of basic rights (Dimitrijevic 2006). While the post-Soviet states struggled to consolidate their proto-democracies, the lustration process served as a clear and unambiguous public commitment to deter future actions by future governments that would replicate the improper behavior of the communist regimes.

To be clear, reflective of the variety of ways in which Soviet domination ended, lustration was implemented along a spectrum of modality. That is, because the transitions away from the Soviet-controlled government varied, it is no surprise that the severity of the lustration also varied. East Germany and the Czech Republic saw the relatively rapid collapse of relatively brutal regimes while Poland and Hungary introduced lustration after more or less negotiated transitions. Regardless of whether the lustration process in question was immediate, broadly applicable, and severe in consequence or whether it was a more modest endeavor undertaken with less haste, the process served to consolidate the democratic transition. Indeed, the states successfully "lustrated" have evolved into advanced democracies while those former Soviet states that are "non-lustrated" have struggled with democratic consolidation (Fein 2005, p. 205).

Domestic war crimes trials have become a standard aspect of civil transitions from authoritarian regimes to democratic ones. The dictates of procedural due process have been institutionalized in that the accused have been allowed to mount defenses and appeal adverse outcomes. While concerns about substantive due process have lingered through this evolution, including the ongoing question of whether laws may proscribe acts retroactively and the extent to which individuals should be held accountable for acts of state, in a general sense, prosecutions are pursued only for extraordinary conduct that goes beyond the normal legitimate use of government power. These endogenous or domestic processes are shaped by the political fortunes of those political actors who are in control of the transition away from the prior regime and charged with consolidation of the new structure. Accordingly, prosecution in the domestic realm has been bounded by the military, economic, or political strength of those who might be accused. The collapse of the Soviet state led to these broad and often simultaneous transitions across Eastern Europe (May and Milton 2005). The end of the USSR also meant an end to the Cold War, which created an opportunity for cross-national cooperation driven by concerns other than the contestation among the superpowers. In this context, the concept of war crimes was exported to new conflicts by the international community. For the first time, parties that were not directly involved in conflict constructed war crimes tribunals for the purposes of prosecuting defendants who had done no direct harm to the architects of the trials. The international community stood as neither victor nor victim and presented a vehicle for the dispensation of justice unadulterated by involvement in the conflict.

5

Third-Party War Crimes Tribunals

The ICTY and the ICTR

The collapse of the Soviet state led to broad and often simultaneous transitions across Eastern Europe (May and Milton 2005). The end of the USSR also meant an end to the Cold War, which created an opportunity for cross-national cooperation driven by concerns other than the contestation among the superpowers. It is in this context that the concept of war crimes was exported to new conflicts by the international community. For the first time, parties not directly involved in conflict constructed war crimes tribunals for the purposes of prosecuting defendants who had done no direct harm to the architects of the trials. The international community stood as neither victor nor victim and presented a vehicle for the dispensation of justice unadulterated by involvement in the conflict. The former Yugoslav states and Rwanda are the best examples of this step in the development of war crimes trials.

The Former Yugoslav States

The verb *to balkanize* or the noun *balkanization* are common terms in the political world as well as among the general public. These words are used to suggest deconstruction of a society or organization along ethnic or group demarcations that leads to actual or metaphoric tragedy (Bugajski 1996, p. 115; Sowell 1994, p. 31). This recognition by the global community of the transformation of the name of a geographic region into a shorthand description for violent ethnic-oriented conflict is a strong suggestion of the nature and scope of the societal violence brought about by the struggle for power in Bosnia. Serbians, Croatians, and enclaves of Muslims have struggled for self-governance and political control in an area of the world often dominated by economically and politically powerful states from outside the immediate region.

The victorious Allied powers created Yugoslavia after World War I out of political expediency and convenience. The negotiated boundaries of the state were not arrived at through careful and close consultation with the occupants of the territory, but rather apart from the concerns of most of the population that would be affected. From the time the Yugoslav boundaries were first drawn, the Serbian-controlled government was in perpetual conflict with the

Croat minority that aspired to independence (Barria and Roper 2005, p. 3). Like much of Europe, the region suffered violence and bloodshed as a result of occupation by the Nazis and the ubiquitous impact of World War II. The Serbian-controlled military forces in the region targeted Croats and Bosnian Muslims, and Serbs were murdered in Nazi concentration camps along with Jews and other victims of the regime (Ibid.). The end of World War II saw the imposition of the brutal and repressive authoritarian regime of Marshal Tito. The factions of Yugoslavia were kept from direct engagement with each other through the establishment of Tito's police state. The authoritarian structure managed to maintain peace, or at least the absence of open and armed conflict, among the factions until Tito met his demise in 1980. After the collapse of the authoritarian regime, dissolution of the country of Yugoslavia seemed to be the destiny for the region. The path that lay ahead for a post-Tito Yugoslavia ran through a torrent of violence, brutality, and civil war that carried with it massive and widespread violations of human rights.

Slobodan Milosevic took control of the government after organizing the overthrow of President Ivan Stambolic in 1989. Although Serbian nationalism as a tool of political power was suppressed under Tito's authoritarian rule, beginning in 1991, Milosevic's hyperbolic rhetoric and aggressive style of Serbian nationalism led to and inspired a rolling sequence of violent succession efforts and armed conflicts. From 1991 through 1995, the violent clashes between the different ethnic enclaves led to more than one hundred and seventy-four thousand people injured and more than one hundred and forty-five thousand deaths in Bosnia-Herzegovina (Crnobrnja 1996). Throughout 1991, the provinces of Macedonia, Slovenia, Croatia, and Bosnia successively asserted independence from the state of Yugoslavia. The declarations of Macedonia and Slovenia were met with little resistance from the Serbian-controlled central government. However, the government responded to the Croatian secession with force. In December 1991, Serbian forces invaded Croatia under the auspices of assuring protection for Serbs that resided in Croatia from Franjo Tudjman's newly created Croatian government (Barria and Roper 2005 pp. 3–4). In Bosnia, the Serbian population was larger than in Croatia and, in conjunction with the Serbian army from Belgrade, Serbs in Bosnia rebelled against the push for independence. The global community's concern about the overall situation and destabilizing environment in Yugoslavia led to an increased international diplomatic presence. The international community pressured the parties involved in the conflicts and pushed through a series of cease fire agreements that quickly failed. As the intensity of conflicts began to increase, the United Nations began to report and investigate claims of ethnic cleansing operations undertaken by the Serbian military and quasi-military forces. After there could no longer be any doubt that Serbian forces were in fact engaging in widespread violations of human rights, including ethnic cleansing, in 1993, the

United Nations Security Council created a free-standing ad hoc tribunal for the purposes of the criminal prosecution of war crimes committed in the former Yugoslav states. For the first time, a third party that was neither victor nor victim established a forum for the prosecution of war crimes. The ad hoc tribunal was named the International Criminal Tribunal for the former Yugoslavia (ICTY).

The United States and its NATO allies pressured the Serbian, the Bosnian, and the Croatian governments to agree to the terms of the Dayton Peace Accords in 1995. The Dayton Peace Accords presented a brokered end to the conflict that nonetheless left much unresolved (Petrovcic 1995). Throughout the period of negotiation, the goal of the international community was an end to the Bosnian war but without proper attention to the political problems inherent in the process of the dissolution of Yugoslavia (Wieseltier 1996, p. 192). The United States was the target of a great deal of criticism because it sought stability and an end to the combat without regard to the process that had led to war or the acts of the parties during the span of the violence. Wieseltier (Ibid.) argued:

> The United States waited to intervene against genocide until a change in the balance of power made its intervention less of a leap. In August of 1995, Croatia conquered Krajina and completed an ethnic cleansing of its Serbs. This established Croatia as a strategic counterweight to Serbia, and made the ethnic boundaries of the region seem more like political boundaries.... The atrocities of the

> Croatians were expedient atrocities ... the Croatian victory
> has become the premise of the Bosnian peace process....
> The deal the United States is promoting is a ratification of
> the results of genocide, not a repeal of them.

The premise of resolution embodied by the Dayton Peace
Accords was a geographic dissolution based upon ethnic den-
sity. The shortfall of the plan was that it simply drew lines
favorable to the groups that were most powerful in an area
and it did not in any substantive way address the underlying power distribution issues that led to the violence or the
manner in which the contestation over territory had been
fought. The plan has been referred to by Francis Boyle, the
attorney for Bosnia before the World Court and legal advi-
sor to the president of Bosnia, as a "nihilistic carve-up of
Bosnia" (Boyle 1996, p. 1). In essence, the United States, the
European Union, Russia, and the United Nations imposed
the agreement on the parties to the conflict and forced them
to submit to a cleavage of the territory at stake. The resolution of the conflict was imposed by these powerful states and
the United Nations in order to reduce the burden of externalities of the war, including refugee flows and economic
disruption, rather than to resolve the disagreements among
the parties. From Boyle's perspective, "Bosnia was sacrificed
on the altar of Great Power politics to the Machiavellian god
of expedience" (Ibid.).

Two years after its creation, the ICTY took custody of
its first defendants in 1995. The trials began in 1996 with

the capacity to charge the accused with the commission of four distinct crimes: "grave breaches of the 1949 Geneva Conventions, violations of the laws or customs of war, genocide, and crimes against humanity" (Yacoubian 2003, p. 11). The initial efforts by the ICTY were unremarkable because of the lack of activity.

In response to the Serbian army's initiation of a campaign of genocide against ethnic Albanians in Kosovo in 1998, the jurisdiction of the tribunal was expanded. The inauspicious beginnings were marked by a complete absence of defendants for the first two years and then a failure to detain or charge any high-ranking officials until 1999 (Barria and Roper 2005, p. 21). By 1999, millions of Albanian refugees fled the country because of the disruption and violence. Eventually, after more unsuccessful peace negotiations after the Dayton Accord, NATO air strikes led to a retreat of the Serbian forces (Ibid., p. 5). Shortly after the retreat, perhaps because of it, Slobodan Milosevic began to lose control of his government and power began to shift away from him. Vladimir Kostunica defeated Milosevic in the 2000 presidential election. When Milosevic attempted to throw out the election results, a popular uprising against this effort forced him out of office (Bass 2000, p. 93). Over the objection of the newly installed President Kostunica, in 2001, Serbian prime minister Zoran Djindjic allowed the extradition of Slobodan Milosevic to The Hague to face charges before the ICTY (Ibid., p. 94).

After several unsuccessful attempts on Djindjic's life, Serbian nationals ultimately assassinated Prime Minister Djindjic in March 2003, in part as retaliation for his extradition of Milosevic. The nationalist Serbians, those who supported Milosevic in any event, used Milosevic's extradition and impending trial as a focal point for the expression of generalized opposition to pro-Western policies and domestic reformist approaches to politics (Ibid.). The government responded to the assassination and political mobilization in support of Milosevic with a broad suppression or crackdown on the remaining dimensions of the coalition that supported Milosevic and his government. Thousands were detained and arrested and forty-five people were charged with crimes that arose out of or were related to the assassination of Djindjic. One European diplomat framed the crackdown as a positive response to the political violence: "[T]hey are dealing with organized crime in a manner we could not have dreamt of two months ago." (Dahl 2003, par. 10).

Milosevic was originally indicted in 1999 for war crimes committed in Kosovo. Eventually, the charges against him were enhanced to include prosecution for similar acts in Croatia as well as for genocide in Bosnia. The indictment of Milosevic encompassed activities engaged in between 1991 and 1999 in Bosnia and Herzegovina, Croatia, and Kosovo. He was charged with sixty-six separate counts that included genocide, war crimes, and crimes against humanity (Bass 2003). The trial of Milosevic began on February 12, 2002. The prosecution presented almost 300 witnesses, more than five thousand separate exhibits, and took over two years. Milosevic, who had a degree in law, served as architect of his defense strategy (Jorgenson 2004, p. 711). The charges had survived a defense motion to dismiss for lack of evidence and the prosecution was approximately forty hours away from resting its case when Milosevic died of heart failure on March 18, 2006 (icty.org/sections/TheCases/KeyFigures 2010, p. 9).

Since it became active in 1999, the ICTY has prosecuted many upper-level officials from the Milosevic government. By June 2010, the tribunal had indicted 161 people for a range of charges that arose out of the "serious violations of international humanitarian law committed in the territory of Yugloslavia" (Ibid., p. 1). Sixty-two individuals from fifty separate cases have been sentenced while twelve defendants were acquitted in nine separate cases (Ibid., p. 4). Twenty indictments were withdrawn and ten defendants died before they were transferred to The Hague, while six defendants died during or while awaiting trial (Ibid., p. 9). Eighteen defendants are involved in the nine active cases at the trial level and sixteen defendants in the four cases actively before the Appeals Chamber (Ibid., p. 1). Additional indictments could also exist, however; the prosecutor has the authority to present sealed indictments if a determination is made that a public indictment might increase the chances that the suspect will evade arrest (Barria and Roper 2005).

Taken as a whole, the ICTY proceedings at The Hague seem to deliver justice to the accused because both the procedural due process and substantive due process dimensions of the institutional arrangement are soundly constructed. Specifically, there can be no serious argument that the accused are not entitled to a full and fair defense. The evidence and procedure codes rival any in the world and the defense lawyers are skilled and professionally trained (see, e.g., icty.org/sections/LegalLibrary/Defence 2010). Likewise, the prosecutors are held to strict rules of evidence and the other aspects of what makes a trial fair. Both parties have the capacity to appeal an adverse trial court ruling to the Appeals Chamber and both prosecutors and defendants have successfully appealed. The Dayton Accords included an express agreement by Serbia, Croatia, and Bosnia, the states that are home to the defendants, to extradite any of their indicted citizens to the ICTY. Although prosecutions through the ICTY remain controversial to many of the citizens of the former Yugoslav states, the office of the prosecutor has been successful by any measure of prosecuting the accused. For instance, only two of those indicted so far are not yet in custody (icty.org/sections/TheCases/KeyFigures 2010, p. 3). The ICTY, taken as a whole, has performed well in its delivery of procedural due process and substantive due process. It has also focused on deterrence and retribution, at least as much as is feasible.

Although of course virtually every trial could be more efficiently and fairly run, even if not quite perfect, the procedural due process aspects of the ICTY compares very favorably to other modern tribunals. That the defendants facing prosecution before the court have not only the right to counsel of their choosing but also the right to a sound appellate process puts the ICTY among the best of the tribunals. The glaring defect of the tribunals is the issue of timely prosecution. The importance of expeditiously prosecuting the defendants and an efficient process for the trials was explicitly confirmed through the resolution that created the tribunal. However, the early lack of funding at the outset of the creation of the ICTY lengthened the process so much that the average time for a single trial exceeded three years (Barria and Roper 2005).These long delays in prosecution may not only undermine the value of the process for the victim class, but might also compromise, at least for some trials, the integrity of the evidentiary standards of the proceedings. Specifically, the long delays can create a problem, although perhaps not insurmountable, because so much of the evidence against the defendants depends upon the memories of witnesses, which become somewhat less reliable as time passes. Although Milosevic, the most important and high-profile of those brought before the tribunal or associated with the conflict generally, died before the process could run its course regarding his crimes, while the case was proceeding, the court was lauded. For instance, *The Economist* urged that "Once the trial is over, he and his supporters will find it hard to argue that he did not get a fair hearing" (Lesson 2003).

From a substantive due process standpoint, the ICTY is also properly constituted. The four foundational charges upon which the indictments could be founded are grave breaches of the 1949 Geneva Conventions, violations of the laws or customs of war, genocide, and crimes against humanity. Each was explicitly set forth in the charter that established the tribunal. Moreover, at least since 1999, the tribunal focused on prosecuting officials as highly ranked as possible. The ICTY also has prosecuted non-Serbian defendants accused of the same types of war crimes committed by the Serb defendants. The court has also indicted and convicted Croats and Bosnian Muslims, and Kosovar Albanians may soon be on the way (icty.org/sections/TheCases/KeyFigures 2010). This effective prosecution of those accused of war crimes regardless of the side of the conflict the defendant was on is a critical progression here that cannot be understated. While perhaps a prosecutorial approach that covers all sides of a conflict should be expected as a result of a third-party imposition of the process, this more uniform treatment of the parties helps to validate not only the substantive due process aspect of the trials, but it also promotes the deterrence effect of the tribunal.

While it is surely the case that the impact of efforts at deterrence beyond those directly affected by the war crimes trials may be called into question, the proceedings of the ICTY have made a substantial contribution to the furtherance of deterrence as an aspect of the desiderata of these types of trials. The prosecutions targeted not only those among the Serbian ranks who committed criminal acts but also pursued Muslims and Croats for committing similar criminal acts while engaged in the conflict. Additionally, the distribution of the proportion of prosecutions across these ethnic cleavages, at least conceptually, reflects the relative degree of responsibility for the chaotic violence. That is, Serbs, who were most responsible for the mass violations of human rights, were also prosecuted more often than the others. Perhaps the most important contribution by the ICTY to the jurisprudence of deterrence is the fact that Slobodan Milosevic was prosecuted. The prosecution of the domestically and internationally identifiable and acknowledged head of state is a first for modern tribunals. A further aspect of the ICTY that has promoted the premise of deterrence as a rationale for the tribunals has been the nature of the targeted prosecutions. That is, the prosecutorial approach has been to actively seek out the specific officials that ordered or directed the genocidal acts that occurred. Those who were actually responsible from a chain of command perspective are the targets of prosecution. This pointed attempt to prosecute those with the most authority over, and therefore the most responsibility for, the bad acts in question provides a prospective warning that the earlier modern trials, like those in Tokyo and Argentina, did not send. Specifically, those in command will not be safe from prosecution. Still, the message has been muted by the plea bargains that have been struck. If one can bargain away atrocities and reach an accord with prosecutors, then the deterrent effect hoped for through prosecution at the highest levels may very well be fatally undermined.

Although the ICTY has accomplished a great deal from a prosecutorial standpoint and has furthered the development of the jurisprudence of justice, several aspects of the process fall short of the ideal and have been shaped by concerns over politics rather than the interests of justice. The ICTY was slow to initiate many prosecutions at first in large part because of a lack of funding. Once it was institutionally capable of conducting prosecutions and providing full defenses, it was still essentially incapable of providing for substantial measures of retribution. While those convicted before the tribunal have faced significant penalties, the ICTY has made no effort to bring the victims of the Yugoslav tragedies to any approximation of the *status quo ante*. That is, there has been no effort to repair the damage done and make the victims whole. Of course, the resolutions that established the ICTY, as well as the Rwanda tribunal, were primarily concerned with stopping the ongoing violence and the massive violations of human rights. Neither one of the UN Security Council resolutions that created the two tribunal structures identified or delineated retribution or reparations as a rationale or goal of the newly created institutions (Yacoubian 1998, par. 18). The perpetrators of the atrocities in the former Yugoslav states have not been compelled to make their victims whole by either the tribunal or the domestic governments. For instance, although more than a million people were displaced from their homes, no recourse has been provided to them (Barria and Roper 2005, p. 24). No wrongful death compensation fund has been established for the families of the victims and no compensation has been provided for the survivors of torture or rape (Engle 2005; Haddad 2010). That the victims of the atrocities have not been provided with an avenue of redress for their specific injuries indicates that justice through the ICTY is an incomplete endeavor. Although both the procedural due process and the substantive due process dimensions of the ICTY are well-constructed and deterrence was a significant goal of the entire endeavor, because the international community failed to demand or provide recompense for these victims, the ICTY has fallen short of delivering justice.

The role of politics and political consolidation here, as in every previous set of tribunals, is critical. For the ICTY, it seems that the consolidation of political power is observationally equivalent with many dimensions of the pursuit of justice. Although the outcome of the conflict was a strong force in the shaping of the trials, the stake of the international community in a peaceful Balkan region overwhelmed the domestic politics. That is, because the outcome of the conflict was determined in large part by the international community, the amount of victor's justice dealt out was limited. Since none of the parties to the dispute were in control of the ICTY, it could not be used to promote one side of the conflict over the other. The international involvement in the conflict led to the specific political outcome, which had an impact on the tribunals in at least two important dimensions. First, the political outcome can best be understood as a stalemate or a draw. Every group involved in the belligerence suffered heavy casualties and no group could claim to be the unambiguous victor at the end of the hostilities. Because there were atrocities on all sides and no clear victor, the defendants who found themselves prosecuted at the ICTY came from every side of the hostilities. Without a victor, there simply can be no victor's justice.

Second, although there unambiguously was no clear winner, Serbia without question was the clear loser. The Croatians and the Bosnians both sought and achieved independence. The goal for Serbia under the guidance of Milosevic was to keep control of Croatia and Bosnia as provinces and to ethnically cleanse non-Serb citizens from the territory. Thanks to the international intervention, Serbia only achieved a portion of that goal. The international community, on the other hand, consolidated power – in particular the power to claim, if not a monopoly over the prosecution of war crimes, at least the right to proceed with prosecution where desired. Accordingly, the prosecutions at the ICTY are only victor's justice to the extent that the victors are those running The Hague.

Most of the defendants prosecuted through the ICTY have been Serbian. These trials have not been unjust. After all, their structure and processes seem to be driven by concerns about legal appropriateness and a balanced sense of fairness for the accused. Still, political necessity is the foundation upon which the ICTY was built. The political imperative that underpins the ICTY is that the United Nations sought validation for its international role as peacekeeper and neutral arbiter through these prosecutions. The ICTY was also the first half of the proving grounds for the efficacy of third-party international prosecution efforts and the necessity of the International Criminal Court. Whether the conflict in the former Yugoslav states is viewed as ending in a tie or as a victory by the international community over Milosevic's vision of a greater Serbian empire, or even if those two frames of the outcome are seen as complements rather than rivals, the war crimes trials process supports the argument that concerns about political consolidation after the war in Yugoslavia had a direct impact on the manner in which justice was pursued. Those most concerned with prosecuting the massive violations of human rights in the former Yugoslav states did not have a tangible stake in the final outcome of the ongoing power struggle so long as the violence ended.

The International Commission on the Balkans put this situation in this context:

> The central controversy over the punishment of war crimes is whether peace and justice are contradictory or complementary ... peace must take precedence over justice.... Bosnia in 1996 is not Germany in 1945, the victors are not judging the vanquished. Instead, compromises are being made, some of them distasteful (Tindemans 1996, pp. 90–1).

The strength of the ethnic identities for the citizens across the Balkans has led to a widespread conceptualization of individual rights as derivatives of group rights (Rubin 1996, pp. 61–3). The problematic outcome for conflict resolution across the region that arises from this conceptualization of individual rights as grounded in group rights is that an infringement on the rights of an individual is interpreted by that person's group as a transgression of similar magnitude against the group. For the former Yugoslav states, none of the parties in the conflict were capable of easily achieving either an unequivocal political or military victory. Moreover, none of the parties in the conflict were averse to the use of widespread human rights violations in order to pursue their political or military objectives. Accordingly, while it might be true that for the former Yugoslav states, the third-party prosecutions for human rights violations failed to persuade the belligerent parties that the conduct during the conflict was wrongful, the ICTY did help establish and promote the development of an international norm of prosecution for these kinds of acts and an international right of the international community to intervene. In the final analysis, the international norms dimensions of the ICTY were more important than party-specific conflict resolution and any effort at redress of party-specific wrongs.

While the ICTY was initially slow to act and somewhat inefficient when trials began, that it existed at all when the violence in Rwanda erupted paved the way for the creation of the International Criminal Tribunal for Rwanda (ICTR). In most ways, both from a procedural due process and substantive due process standpoint, the ICTR was a clone of the

ICTY. Still, perhaps because the conflicts were so different both in execution and in the manner in which they ended, the outcomes of the two efforts at prosecution were substantially different.

Rwanda

The Tutsi and the Hutu are the two culturally and politically dominant ethnic groups in Rwanda (Khiddu-Makubuya 1994, pp. 143–4). The other major ethnic group, the Twa, makes up less than one percent of the population, consists largely of economically marginal artisans and hunters, and has never been in contention for political control in Rwanda (Watson 1991, p. 2). So although there are others in the country, the conflict in and the politics of Rwanda entail the contest between the Tutsi and the Hutu. Somewhat reminiscent of the situation in South Africa, despite the fact that about ninety percent of the population in Rwanda identifies as Hutu, for hundreds of years since the colonial period, the minority Tutsi group has held firm control over the government. This minority control over the institutions of state has been maintained through a domination of the Hutu and the Twa that has included political violence and civil oppression of every stripe. The civil war that started in 1959 ended after over two years with the fall of the Tutsi monarchy in 1961 (Ibid., pp. 155–6). Rwanda achieved independence from Belgium the next year in 1962. For Rwanda, the colonial legacy is one of constructed group identity forged and delineated by the oppression by the group favored by the colonists over the vast majority of the balance of the citizenry (Newbury 1988, p. 207). With this imposed governing structure came a norm of the use and manipulation of the power and capacity of the state to secure advantages for the Tutsi as the dominant or politically powerful group (Ibid., p. 208). In fact, the construction of these ethnic cleavages may have occurred because of the distribution of political power rather than any actual genetic or cultural differences between the groups. Indeed, Newbury makes the case that:

> [F]or Rwanda, it would be more accurate to argue that Tuutsi [sic] chiefs, through their use and abuse of power, created Hutu consciousness.... It was in fact oppression in its many different forms that brought about the cohesion among Hutu that contributed to the revolution and its outcome (Ibid., p. 209).

The long history of political domination of the Hutu by the Tutsi and the rigid delineation of the group identities against a backdrop of continuous scarcity of most resources set the stage for the devolution of Rwandan political culture into violent tragedy (Prunier 1995, p. 354). Throughout the modern era, Rwanda has been a densely populated country by African standards with roughly 256 people per square kilometer (Watson 1991, p. 16). More than one-third of the population of Rwanda is comprised of subsistence-level farmers who farm on tiny parcels of less than half a hectare (Ibid.). Rwanda suffers from a perpetual food supply deficit that, when combined with a relatively high population growth rate of about three percent annually, has led to an average daily caloric intake of a "grossly inadequate" 1,400 calories (Ibid.). Within the context of an oppressive historical record of communal violence used as a mechanism for political control and perpetual and severe competition among members of the population for the basic necessities of life, the United Nations established the International Criminal Tribunal for Rwanda (Security Counsel Resolution 955, 8 Nov. 1994) (Prunier 1995, pp. 354–5).

Between the beginning of April and the end of June 1994, well over five hundred thousand and perhaps as many as one million Tutsi and moderate Hutu were tortured and killed by Hutu extremists in a genocidal rampage (Doctors Without Borders 1995, p. 3). This widespread murder of masses of people was the reaction by the Hutu extremists to a con-sociational or power sharing transitional government developed and brokered by the United Nations. The sheer brutality and volume of violence that occurred as a result of the Hutu elite's opposition to the proposed power sharing arrangement led to not only the execution of about one-sixth of the entire population of the country, but also created an enormous and unprecedented flow of refugees (Ibid., p. 4). Within forty-eight hours of the onslaught of violence, well over two hundred thousand refugees fled Rwanda and spread into neighboring Tanzania for sanctuary (Ibid., pp. 3–4). Even moderate Hutu were slaughtered. To be deemed a moderate Hutu, one need only oppose the slaughter of the

Tutsi or support the power sharing arrangement and peace plan devised by the United Nations (Ibid., pp. 3–4). The conflict came to an unsteady end when the army of exiled Tutsi, called the Rwandan Patriotic Front, defeated the Hutu forces engaged in the slaughter (Daly 2002, p. 355). The end of the violence led to a repatriation of Tutsi so that, despite the hundreds of thousands of murders, the Tutsi population returned to about fifteen percent of the total population of the country (Des Forges 1999).

The United Nations may have been compelled to respond to the slaughter simply because the number of civilian victims was enormous and the violence was so shocking that to ignore the conflict would undermine its moral authority to become involved in any other conflict. It could also simply be that the United Nations could not allow Rwanda to utterly ignore the governing settlement put forth as a peace accord. Whatever the motivations, the United Nations created a judicial body to prosecute those accused of wrongdoing during the violent rampage. The body was given the overly wordy title of *"International Criminal Tribunal for the Prosecution of Persons Responsible for Genocide and other Serious Violations of International Humanitarian Law Committed in the Territory of Rwanda and Rwandan citizens responsible for Genocide and other such violations committed in the territory of neighboring States between January 1, 1994 and December 31, 1994"* (Security Counsel Resolution 955, 8 Nov. 1994, p. 1). It has since become commonly referred to as the International Criminal Tribunal for Rwanda or ICTR.

The ICTR builds upon the structure of the ICTY and is an exemplary model of procedural due process. In a real sense, the ICTR represents the culmination of responses to virtually every criticism involving procedural due process ever made about any of the previous war crimes trials. For example, through Rule 44, the ICTR explicitly provided for the appointment of defense counsel and gave the defendants wide latitude in the selection of the defense team. Rules 45 and 55 created a strict set of regulations about the issuance and process of arrest warrants. Critics of the ICTR will gain no traction in the realm of procedural due process. The trials have been fairly constructed by any matrix that could be utilized.

The substantive due process dimensions of the ICTR are also above reproach and were constructed with equal concern for past critiques of other trials as the procedural due process dimensions. The jurisdiction of the ICTR, as set forth in Rule 2, covers genocide, torture, sexual assault, and "other serious violations" of humanitarian law (Rule 2). Those who assert that the ICTR is skewed toward punishing the Hutu claim that the limitation on jurisdiction of the ICTR to calendar year 1994 only unduly restricts the potential for prosecution of the actions of the Tutsi (International Tribunal for Rwanda, Africa 2000 1996, pp. 7–12). The thrust of the criticism is that only Hutu can be held accountable at the ICTR for the atrocities committed in Rwanda (Ibid.). To embrace this jurisdictional limitation as a major failing and affront to justice requires an unsupportable assumption. The international community would have to accept as equals the mass atrocities committed by the Hutu during the 1994 rampages with previous, much less violent, efforts by the Tutsi at political contestation for whatever time period the Hutu apologists deem appropriate.

Even if somehow the proposition that the ICTR metes out unequal treatment for the Hutu and the Tutsi could be accepted, the more significant defect of the ICTR is to be found in its paralysis and inaction. According to the fifteenth annual *Report of the International Criminal Tribunal for Rwanda,* the completion strategy for the tribunal contemplates an end to trial-level prosecutions by the end of 2011 and a completion of any outstanding appeals by the end of 2013 (Byron 2010, p. 3). The ICTR has, through July of 2010, convicted thirty-six defendants with nine more convictions pending a decision from the appellate process (ICTR 2010, Status of Cases). Eight defendants have been acquitted and two defendants died before trial. Twenty-one cases are in progress and two have not yet begun. Two cases were transferred to French domestic courts and two defendants were released after the prosecutor withdrew their indictments. Seven defendants were released after serving out their prison sentences and ten people under indictment remain at large. In all, the ICTR has dealt with ninety defendants. To put that number in proper context, at the end of the violence, at one point as many as one hundred thousand Rwandans were in jail awaiting prosecution for their actions during the genocidal campaign (Brannigan and Jones 2009).

The ICTR has no capacity to conduct trials on the same scale as the atrocities that were committed. The criticism of the tribunal by Hutu apologists, among others, really went no further than a critique of the institutional design. In other words, criticism of the ICTR is limited to expressing an exception to the design rather than the actual outcomes because the court has done so little. If the tribunal could somehow actually hold those accused accountable at a scale that approximates the scale of the violence, then perhaps concern over the one-sided prosecutorial approach might be worthy of serious consideration. When the ICTR looked to perhaps be on the verge of a substantial number of prosecutions, one commentator argued:

> Proving "genocide" in the Rwandan courts is the justice meted out to the losers of Rwanda's civil war by the victors. Proving "genocide" through an international tribunal ... is justice which reflects the power relationship between the west and the rest (International Tribunal for Rwanda, Africa 2000, 1996, pp. 13–14).

While the prosecutions in the ICTR have been models of procedural due process and substantive due process, the relatively small of number of prosecutions given the magnitude of the violence suggests that deterrence and retribution are secondary concerns. The inability of the international community to fully prosecute or process the accused from Rwanda presented a difficult dilemma but also in the end presented an opportunity for innovation. If the international community had not intervened, violent conflict between the Hutu and the Tutsi would likely have continued until the Tutsi were completely eliminated from Rwanda either through exile or death. The international and scholarly communities have maintained that unless justice is delivered – that is, unless those who committed the atrocities are held accountable for them – the contestation between Hutu and Tutsi over control of Rwanda and its resources is very likely to turn violent again (Prunier 1995, p. 355). This legacy of violent conflict is especially likely to lead to a recurrence given the abject scarcity of resources and broad poverty. In short, the struggle for power in Rwanda is equivalent to a struggle for survival (Ibid.).

In 2000, the Rwandan government instituted a domestic structure to deliver transitional justice to its citizenry (Amnesty International 2002; Rettig 2008, p. 30). This unconventional and ambitious step was taken partly in response to the slow start at the ICTR and no doubt partly in order to exert domestic control over the process that had been taken over by the international community. This domestic transitional justice system was constructed under the ambit of the traditional, both pre- and post-colonial, dispute resolution system called *gacaca* (ga-CHA-cha) (Rettig 2008, p. 30). The purpose of the post-conflict *gacaca* process, or technically the *inkiko gacaca* or the *gacaca* courts, is to reintegrate the massive number of detainees into their communities so long as representatives of those communities are convinced that the accused in question are remorseful about the crimes committed and have been fully truthful and candid about those crimes (Aghion 2002; Rettig 2008, p. 30). The structure of the *gacaca* system is straightforward. The term loosely translates into English as "justice on the grass" (Reyntjens 1990). The historical system consisted of local officials sitting in judgment over the resolution of property disputes, disputes over inheritance, or allegations of theft (Ibid.). A person who was found liable under this system would not only pay restitution to the aggrieved individual but also would provide the community with some token of atonement such as alcohol for communal consumption (Rettig 2008, p. 30).

The laws that established the *gacaca* structure as the mechanism for moving the society past the genocide as well as the massive detentions that arose after the cessation of violence offer some modicum of leniency but support a punitive aspect of sentencing absent from the historical *gacaca* (Brannigan and Jones 2009; Sarkin 2001). Specifically, failure to cooperate can lead to a substantial prison sentence while full cooperation can cut the term in half. The mitigated sentences include a substantial public service dimension (Rettig 2008, p. 31). The *gacaca* structure has seemingly been shaped by the international community's sensibilities about procedural due process and substantive due process. There are three levels to *gacaca* including the cell level, the sector level, and the appellate level. The cell level acts as an evidentiary clearinghouse where evidence against the accused is assessed and the accused are categorized according to the severity of the allegations against them. Over one hundred and twenty-five thousand Rwandans are now the elected judges or *inyangamugayo* in one of the three levels of court who control the *gacaca* process (Ibid.). The judges undergo a scant three days of training but otherwise there are no special requirements other than the prohibition against involvement by those involved in the genocide. The trials may be as short as an hour or as long as several days and normally involve groups of defendants accused of related acts. There is no prosecutor or defense counsel. Rather, the president of the tribunal, analogous to a chair of a committee, presides over the trial and controls the flow of evidence and defendants may not choose to remain silent. All testimony is given under oath. The resolution of any given case is driven in part by the participation of the crowd that gathers to hear and respond to the evidence. The panel of judges, which typically has five members, meets in private to render a judgment. Appeals are limited and rarely successful. A critical jurisdictional aspect of the *gacaca* system is that violence against members of the Hutu majority by the Tutsi members of the Rwandan Patriotic Front are not covered, while property crimes by Hutu against Tutsi are (Waldorf 2006).

Rwanda presents a picture of the two extremes of possible locales and structures for postconflict trials. The genocide was simultaneously addressed at the international level by states and individuals that were not stakeholders in the conflict and at the domestic level by members of the communities in which the violence occurred. The international arbiters of justice were neither victors nor victims so perhaps they could dispense justice fairly and evenly. However, the ICTR had no capacity to actually address the atrocities in a comprehensive way because of the scale of the violations of human rights. While the local effort seems more likely to provide what has been termed "mass justice for mass atrocity" (Ibid.), the domestic effort faced a resource challenge very similar to the international one. Specifically, there is no capacity to offer a full trial-like structure to the accused. It is possible that as many as one million Rwandans are directly implicated in the violence. This poor country could not afford fully developed Western-style trials even if the political will was present to conduct them. Indeed, it is difficult to imagine even the wealthiest nations managing what amounts to a simultaneous prosecution of that volume of their citizens.

While each of the trials or tribunals assessed so far has been bounded by the political or economic strength of the parties to the conflict that led to the transitional justice period, Rwanda presents an extreme version of the limitations of the capacity to prosecute. The scope of the limitation of the ICTR was not immediately obvious as the scope of the civilian involvement in the genocide was not obvious when the ICTR was created. In simple terms, the mass atrocity in Rwanda was of such magnitude that no tribunal structure could have easily provided all the rudimentary elements of justice. The involvement in wrongdoing was so widespread that Rwanda was doomed to achieve an imperfect justice under the best possible scenario. Given the limitations on resources available, it is remarkable any transitional process was possible in Rwanda. Both the ICTY and the ICTR were forays into an institutionalized international venue for the resolution of claims of genocide and other gross violations of human rights that paved the way for the establishment of the International Criminal Court (ICC). The ICTY and the ICTR encompassed nearly identical comprehensive codes for prosecution, conduct of the trial, the provision for a defense, and all of the trappings of procedural due process and substantive due process. Since these international tribunals were trial runs, so to speak, for the ICC, the problems faced by both the ICTY and the ICTR in execution of the dispensation of justice were not yet obvious as the international community moved toward adoption of the Rome Statute, which would establish the ICC. The evolution of war crimes tribunals at this point, without question, had solidified in a commitment to procedural due process and to substantive due process. However, the proper formal structure to ensure fairness may be a necessary condition for justice to be the product of the trials, but it is not sufficient. In the next chapter, the institutionalization and globalization of war crimes tribunals at the international level becomes solidified through the creation and development of the International Criminal Court.

6

Globalization of War Crimes Tribunals through the International Criminal Court

Once third parties had claimed the right or obligation to pursue transitional justice, a global institution for the purposes of prosecuting the worst abusers of human rights was the natural next step in the evolution of war crimes trials. However, this perhaps obvious next step for war crimes tri als presented serious challenges to the sovereignty of states. The institution had to be constructed to accomplish its goals without creating a perpetual threat to the very states upon which it would rely not only for funding and operational concerns, but also cooperation from a prosecutorial stance.

The International Criminal Court holds a unique place in the evolution of war crimes tribunals, not only because it is the first permanent and independent criminal court dedicated to prosecuting gross abuses of human rights, but also because it is the first war crimes tribunal since the modern

era of war crimes trials began with the Nuremberg prosecutions of the Nazis that has been opposed by the United
States. Indeed, not only has the United States declined to
become a party to the treaty or to participate in the administration of the International Criminal Court (ICC), it has
actively attempted to undermine the court. Because of this
oddity of the historical path of war crimes trials, this chapter is organized slightly differently than the previous ones.
After a description of the creation of the ICC, which also
addresses the procedural due process and substantive due
process dimensions of its legal architecture, the stated rationale for the opposition of the United States is thoroughly
examined as well as the reasons that this rationale cannot
be sincere. Then, the structural limitations on the reach of
the ICC are discussed, followed by a consideration of the
activities of the court since its inception.

The terms of the Rome Statute of the International
Criminal Court (ICC) were agreed to on July 17, 1998. This
agreement was drafted by a special United Nations diplomatic conference charged with the creation of a standing
international human rights tribunal. The introductory language contained in the preamble to the statute sets forth
the purposes of the effort as the creation and establishment
of a tribunal that is both independent and permanent with
criminal jurisdiction over gross violations of human rights
violations and crimes that are of serious concern to the members of the international community. The treaty reached the
required threshold of adoption by 120 states on July 17, 1998

and by July 1, 2002 the necessary sixty states had ratified it. The ICC became an institutionalized fixture in the international community as the first treaty-based, permanent, independent, international court devoted to the prosecution of war crimes and related activities. The ICC has been given specific grants of jurisdiction over the following crimes committed by states or individuals: crimes of genocide, crimes against humanity, war crimes, and the crime of aggression (Rome Statute, Preamble, Article 5).

Whether an independent and permanent criminal court for these types of crimes could or should exist has been debated at least since the war crimes prosecutions in Nuremburg and Tokyo after World War II (UN General Assembly Resolution 260, 9 Dec. 1948). Although the role and merit of the court continues to be the subject of international debate, it has been institutionalized and is in fact operating as a standing criminal tribunal for these specific categories of crimes. The benefit of the ICC as a standing tribunal rather than continuing an ad hoc approach to the creation of this sort of tribunal only as circumstances dictate is that the ends of justice are served because a standing tribunal might eliminate selective prosecutions and perhaps an established court could maintain a predictable and speedy process.

One of the mainstream arguments in favor of the standing tribunal is that an institutionalized structure such as the ICC is a critical necessity in order for the protection of international human rights to advance and for the further development of international norms against the sorts of terrible acts that might be prosecuted through the ICC (Neier 1998, pp. 252–60). Those opposed to the creation and institutionalization of a standing criminal tribunal argue such an institution threatens and undermines the sovereignty of nations, inevitably would be manipulated for political purposes, and faces procedural difficulties that make the proper dispensation of justice through such a tribunal unworkable. Justice may also be better served through ad hoc tribunals that can be and have been tailored to the specific conflict situations that give rise to the need for transitional justice. Many who favor a standing tribunal as well as many who prefer the ad hoc system maintain that each of these rival approaches provides the best way for the international community to provide for deterrence and retribution. The debate between the advocates of ad hoc tribunals and the advocates of a standing one assumes that human rights tribunals are effective and direct instruments of justice rather than primarily instruments of power and political consolidation. The ICC represents the institutionalization of these types of tribunals and now is sufficiently seasoned to assess whether the permanent court avoids the impact of political pressures as hoped or whether the institutionalization itself was shaped by political constraints.

The International Criminal Court has been constructed with elaborate codes of conduct for both the prosecutors and the defense bar. The rules of evidence and procedure rival any criminal justice system in the world. Procedural due

process and substantive due process have been institutionalized to ensure fairness for the accused. Retribution is a
key element in the dispensation of justice as victims of the
crimes prosecuted there may apply for restitution.

The first annual "Report of the International Criminal
Court" presents a concise and unambiguous description of
the institution when it describes the court as:

> ... an independent, treaty-based, permanent judicial insti-
> tution with jurisdiction over persons for the most serious
> crimes of international concern, namely genocide, crimes
> against humanity and war crimes By punishing individuals
> who commit these crimes, the Court is intended to contrib-
> ute to the deterrence of such crimes as well as to interna-
> tional peace and security and respect for international
> justice. The Court is complementary to national jurisdic-
> tions and its Statutes and Rules of Procedure and Evidence
> guarantee fair, public trials consistent with internationally
> recognized human rights (ICC 2005, A/60/177, p. 2).

Despite these laudable and positive dimensions of the structure of the ICC, it nonetheless has been designed to present
a morality play which prosecutes some of the weakest political actors in the world while shielding from prosecution
those states responsible for the creation and perpetuation of
the court. In short, the ICC is designed to prosecute weak
states while insulating the powerful states that created it.

The institutionalization of a permanent war crimes tribunal through the International Criminal Court was heralded

by many as a significant step forward in the furtherance of robust international criminal law jurisprudence. Not only did the new court fully embrace a thorough provision of procedural due process and substantive due process as fixed aspects of the juridical process, it also moved the international community toward greater acceptance of an idea of universal jurisdiction for some especially heinous crimes. The mandate of the ICC seems broad and comprehensive. The court has been widely embraced by the international community. The United States joined China, Iraq, Libya, Yemen, Qatar, and Israel as the only seven states to vote against the treaty (Smith and Smith 2006). Given the broad support garnered by the treaty and subsequently the court, the ICC offered great promise for the development of jurisprudence regarding the trial and punishment for violations of international criminal law.

The near universal adoption of the ICC by those states that are identified as belonging to the developed world presents the question as to why a sovereign state would voluntarily bind its own hands, surrender a bit of its sovereignty, and choose to subject its state agents to extra-territorial liability and the potential for punishment by the international community. An explanation for this behavior could likely be constructed that would be grounded in appeals to justice and respect for the rule of law. However, reliance on notions of a morally grounded state, state altruism, or a voluntary surrender of sovereignty might present a needlessly complex explanation. Instead, there is a more straightforward and parsimonious explanation that more completely captures the political logic that informs the broad adoption of the ICC. Concisely put, the states that were instrumental in the construction of this institution, the signatory states to the treaty and those who ratified it, have no fear of the institution. The constituent states face no risk at all that their agents or their personnel could face prosecution before the ICC or be charged by a prosecutor. The institutional design of the court sets firm safeguards soundly in place that ensure only the weakest states could ever face the indictment or the prosecution of their personnel.

As a side concern, if the interpretation of these limitations on the court is accurate, then the question might be raised as to what forms the basis of the determined opposition of the United States government to the court. In other words, if in fact developed nations like the United States need not fear prosecution in front of the ICC, then there should be some discernable explanation for why so many policymakers and politicians in the United States are so strongly committed to undermining the ICC and so strongly opposed to any cooperation by the United States in the creation or administration of the court. Recent scholarship has demonstrated that opposition among policy and political elites in the United States can be credited to the electoral logic of the institutional design of the Senate (Smith and Smith 2006; Smith and Smith 2009).

This argument that an electoral disconnection is at the root of the opposition of the United States to the court is germane to the consideration of the overall evolution of war crimes tribunals because it is necessary to understand this opposition in order to assess the role of political concerns in the design and development of the court. From the outset of the creation of the treaty that gave rise to the court, the hostility of political elites in the United States toward the court has been persistent, unwavering, and adamant. Although President Clinton signed the Rome Statute in the last month of his presidency, it was never brought up for ratification in the Senate and when George W. Bush assumed the presidency, his administration moved to quickly "unsign" the Rome Statute in early 2002.

The opposition to the court from policymakers in the United States usually is predicated, generally speaking, on some expressed concern that diplomatic, policy, or, most important, military personnel acting on behalf of the United States will be brought before the international court and unfairly or unjustly subjected to prosecution before a highly politicized tribunal. For instance, the former undersecretary of state for political affairs, Marc Grossman, claimed the United States "must insure that our soldiers and government officials are not exposed to the prospect of politicized prosecutions and investigations" (Becker 2002). A related claim upon which opposition is grounded is that the court can even abridge the sovereignty of nonratifying states and the structural independence of the court means that the existence of the court undercuts the authority and scope of power of the United Nations Security Council (Arnold 2003).

The claimed fear of politically driven prosecutions of members of the armed services of the United States, the central core of this resistance, is, simply put, not sincere. While no doubt some senators might oppose involvement in the court because of some genuine principle, opposition from senators who oppose the court has been shown to be because of strategic electoral reasons (Smith and Smith 2006; Smith and Smith 2009). In short, they are afraid of an electoral admonishment from voters. Because the court has a severe jurisdictional constraint in the form of complementarity, and the United States has entered into over 100 bilateral immunity agreements (BIAs) and status of forces agreements (SOFAs), which proscribe any possibility for the prosecution of the personnel from the United States, members of the armed forces of the United States as well as civilians acting on its behalf, simply put, cannot be prosecuted by the court. These institutional barriers to prosecution also protect each of the developed states that negotiated the original treaty and created the court. Although these institutional barriers are practically speaking insurmountable hurdles to the prosecution of any citizen of the United States, members of the Senate, the ratifying body, have kept up a relentless and strident opposition to the treaty and have in the most belligerent manner available thwarted ratification. The diplomatic sensibilities of the United States might have persuaded policymakers to engage in "cheap talk" and take the moral high road through support of the ICC. This would have allowed the United States to exert some influence over the organization without facing a real risk of prosecution. Instead, the Senate has publicly opposed the court, undermined it with some specific actions addressed later in this chapter, and avoided taking any action to ratify the Rome Treaty or even to reject it. A straightforward case could be made that the United States ought to join and promote the court in order to promote its own policies and punish those around the globe who are committing atrocities or acting in a manner inconsistent with the desires of the United States. Generally speaking, international organizations, including the court, serve the purposes of but do not constrain the interests of the states that are the most powerful (Mearsheimer 1994).

One explanation for the hostility of the United States toward the court is grounded in a general hesitation to cede even modest amounts of the power of national sovereignty to some international organization because of concern about politically driven mistreatment. However, this standard explanation is less than persuasive given the sanctioning capacity of the World Trade Organization and the dispute resolution mechanisms of economically oriented international organizations such as NAFTA and CAFTA. This traditional explanation of an overriding concern about sovereignty has been undermined by the administration of President George W. Bush. The Bush State Department and Department of Justice gave unambiguous and strong support to the World Court or the International Court of Justice (ICJ). The ICJ determined the state of Texas violated the rights afforded Jose Ernesto Medellin, a Mexican national charged with and convicted of murder, under international protocol, when it declined to allow him to exercise his right to contact the Mexican consulate upon his arrest. The protocol at issue is provided by the Vienna Convention of Consular Relations of 1963 (see generally, Montgomery 2005, p. 5A). The issue of hostility by the United States toward the ICC in light of an absence of hostility toward other international organizations including other international courts critically informs the political dynamics that underpin the creation of the ICC.

The extant literature accounts for the opposition of the United States through an explication of the institutional structure of the United States Senate and the resulting electoral logic for each member of the Senate (Smith and Smith 2006; Smith and Smith 2009). Every senator is risk averse and will avoid providing a potentially inflammatory issue, like giving an international court criminal jurisdiction over military personnel, to their rivals for their seats. Senate incumbents generally are safe bets for reelection unless they make a major policy blunder or behave badly. Because military spending and the geographic origin for the all-volunteer forces are spread approximately uniformly throughout each state, all senators see the issue of how they treat the troops and the military generally as ever present on their electoral horizons. Accordingly, the basis of the hostility of the United States to the ICC is found in the electoral logic faced by every senator instead of some profound and thoughtful concern about the actual prosecutions that might be conducted by the court (Smith and Smith 2006; Smith and Smith 2009).

If opposition to the ICC in the United States is explained by foundational electoral logic, it is also the road to insight as to why allies of the United States that might be comparably situated internationally have signed onto and promoted the court. States such as Canada, the United Kingdom, Germany, Australia, and Poland, as well as every other member of NATO, have fully embraced the court. In this context, a comparably situated state is simply one that, on a regular basis, provides personnel to support international peacekeeping efforts. Because these allies of the United States are engaged in the international realm of peacekeeping in a similar capacity as the United States, they all are faced with a similar potential and risk of politically motivated prosecutions. That is, if the United States might be vulnerable to such a prosecution, so would all of the other nations that regularly participate in peacekeeping missions around the world. In short, before a full understanding of the dynamics that led to the International Criminal Court can be developed, the political logic behind the conflict between the opposition of the United States and the support of all the other Western states needs to be clarified.

Two streams of research seek to explain the resistance of the United States to the court. One approach is concerned with the very broad jurisdictional mandate for the court and is especially concerned with the court's jurisdiction over the citizens of states not party to the treaty. Those concerned with the exercise by the court of jurisdiction over those who have not consented to the jurisdiction assert that the United States should resist this remarkable expansion of power (Ailslieger 1999; Morris 2001; Scheffer 1999a, 1999b; Scheffer 2001). The response to this argument is that the jurisdiction of the court as created by the Rome Statute is simply a reflection of sound and longstanding principles in international law and that the United States could best serve its own interests through ratification (Scharf 2001). The other primary explanation for the opposition of the United States focuses on the dynamics of international politics. This explanation finds the foundation of the opposition of the United States to the ICC in the realm of the United Nations Security Council.

In essence, because the Security Council gives the United States such a prominent platform for and substantial levels of control over the pursuit of international criminal pros ecutions, the structure for the International Criminal Court is likely to provide a comparatively diminished role for the United States and the United States opposes trading more for less (Ralph 2005; Schabas 2004). Both of these categorical arguments assume that personnel acting on behalf of the United States would be subject to politically motivated prosecutions before the ICC. An expanding body of work in the scholarly international relations literature places the origin of foreign policy preferences soundly within the scope of domestic politics (Fearon 1994; Martin 2000; Milner

1997; Raustiala 1997). This understanding of foreign policy choices as in part driven by domestic audience costs likely accounts for the opposition of the United States to the ICC (Smith and Smith 2006, Smith and Smith 2009).

The approaches that explain the opposition of the United States through a reliance on the breadth of jurisdiction of the court assume that the scope of prosecutorial jurisdiction is incredibly broad and is unrivaled in history (Morris 2001). If the scope of jurisdiction of the ICC is compared to those of the other globally based courts like the Tribunal of the Law of the Sea, the International Court of Justice (ICJ), or the World Trade Organization's Dispute Settlement System, the ICC seems to have much greater latitude in its prosecutorial domain (Donnelly 1986). For example, the ICJ can only exercise jurisdiction when the state involved has explicitly and unambiguously consented to allow the involvement of the ICJ. Specifically, contentious jurisdiction before the ICJ can be invoked three ways: the parties can be subject to jurisdiction through a compromissory clause, they can make a declaration under the optional clause, or they can execute a specific agreement for a particular dispute (Ailslieger 1999, p. 87; Morris 2001, pp. 19–22). Accordingly, the ICJ relies upon a consent-based model of jurisdiction while the chief prosecutor of the International Criminal Court exercises authority without any reliance at all on consent (Morris 2001, p. 20).

Under the provisions of authority in Article 12 of the Rome Statute, the chief prosecutor can exercise jurisdiction over the citizens or nationals of states not party to the treaty so long as those individuals are accused of the commission of crimes within the territory of a state that is in fact party to the treaty. This jurisdiction over the citizens of nonparty states has been controversial in some quarters (Morris 2001). The crux of the argument against this broad jurisdictional reach is that neither delegated universal jurisdiction nor territorial jurisdiction, the two traditional sources of jurisdiction, provides an avenue for the construction of jurisdictional authority over nonparty citizens by the court (Ibid.). Although a delegated universal jurisdiction theory could be used to argue that, since some states employ concepts of universal jurisdiction in order to domestically prosecute defendants accused of the types of crimes against humanity that are the focus of the ICC, customary international law permits the grant to or assumption of universal jurisdiction by the court. The critique of this approach is that it fails to account for the critical difference between a state assertion of universal jurisdiction and a nongovernmental international organization asserting a comparable right to prosecute (Ibid., p. 43). Likewise, there is no prior analog or precedent to the establishment of territorial jurisdiction as the foundation for the exercise of jurisdiction by a global court over the personnel of states that have not consented to jurisdiction and are not a participant in the creation of the court (Ibid., p. 47). In short, the jurisdictional reach of the ICC, which gives authority to the chief prosecutor to assert jurisdiction over the citizens of states that are not parties to the treaty or constituent members of the court, goes well beyond the basic fundaments of international law principles of jurisdiction (Ibid., p. 66).

The primary negotiator for the United States at the Rome Conference and the subsequent ambassador at large for the United States for War Crimes Issues, David Scheffer, is an advocate for the argument that the issue of broad jurisdiction for the court is a sufficiently serious one that should preclude participation in the court or ratification of the treaty by the United States (Scheffer 1999a; Scheffer 1999b; Scheffer 2001). Indeed, Scheffer considers the broad power of the court to investigate the citizens and personnel of states that have not consented to jurisdiction as "the single most fundamental flaw in the Rome Treaty that makes it impossible for the United States to sign" (England 2001; Scheffer 1999b; Scharf 2001). Scheffer's position is that the United States has no real option but to oppose the court given the broad claim of what seems to be universal jurisdiction:

> The U.S. legal position [during the Clinton administration] was that customary international law does not yet entitle a state, whether as a Party or as a non-Party to the ICC Treaty, to delegate to a treaty-based International Criminal Court its own domestic authority to bring to justice individuals who commit crimes on its sovereign territory or otherwise under the principle of universal jurisdiction, without first obtaining the consent of that individual's state of nationality either through ratification of the Rome Treaty or by

special consent, or without a referral of the situation by the Security Council (Scheffer 2001, p. 65).

Of course, there are those who do not accept Scheffer's characterization and posit the counterargument that because nonparty states could be subjected to the jurisdictional reach of the court, the United States is better served through ratification of the Rome Statute so that it could wield more influence over any prosecutions that might arise (Gallarotti and Preis 1999, p. 53; Scharf 2001; Van de Kieft 2002, p. 2367; van de Vyver 2001, p. 796). Moreover, and critical for the analysis here, the complementarity aspects and provisions of the treaty dictate that unless there is a total collapse of the domestic legal system as well as a total collapse of the military justice system, the ICC could never actually exercise jurisdiction over American service personnel (Sadat-Wexler 1999, p. 244).

Scheffer and others dismiss the idea that complementarity as a jurisdictional constraint is sufficiently sturdy to act as a barrier to prosecution that would protect the personnel of the United States from prosecution (Bolton 2001; Gurule 2001; Scheffer 1999). These critics argue that the language of Article 12 could be construed as enabling the court to exert jurisdiction whenever personnel acting on behalf of the United States are accused of one of the material offenses within the purview of the court within the territorial domain of a party state. The United States proposed a different version of Article 12 that would have proscribed this type of jurisdiction and also mandated acquiescence of jurisdiction by the state of citizenship of the defendant (Leigh 2001; Scheffer 1999, p. 20). Scheffer pointed out the importance of the issue in unambiguous terms: "The United States made compromises throughout the Rome process, but we always emphasized that the issue of jurisdiction had to be resolved satisfactorily or else the entire treaty and the integrity of the Court would be imperiled" (Scheffer 1999, p. 17). This objection can be thought of as a claim that Article 12 confers upon the court what is equivalent to universal jurisdiction because of the absence of a requirement of consent to jurisdiction by the state whose personnel could be prosecuted. Scheffer further makes the argument that if only the opt-out clause that was in the initial institutional design drafted by the International Law Commission in 1994 had not been removed from the Rome Statute, the United States more likely than not would have supported the court. The opt-out clause provided a mechanism for states to object to and override the jurisdiction of the court regarding crimes against humanity and war crimes but not genocide (Ibid., p. 19).

Scheffer's argument could be summed as a suggestion that only parties to a treaty ought to be bound by the terms of that treaty (Ibid., p. 18). This argument, that the functional existence of universal jurisdiction justifies the opposition of the United States, is undercut not only by the institutional design of complementarity, but also by the multiple bilateral immunity agreements and status of forces agreements entered into between the United States and most of the countries that have signed the treaty. Even though some of the member states of the European Union have declined to execute bilateral immunity agreements (BIA) with the United States, the extant NATO Status of Forces Agreement (1951) makes these new BIAs redundant safeguards for covered personnel (Baxter 1958; Draper 1951). This rationale for the opposition by the United States to the court is widely considered to be insincere (Scharf 2001). The first line of evidence that indicates this rationale for opposition is insincere comes from the bargaining posture assumed by the United States while in Rome to negotiate the treaty (Ibid., p. 77). If in fact the United States had sincere concerns and was strongly opposed to some form of universal jurisdiction for the ICC over war crimes, crimes against humanity, and genocide, it would have presented a challenge to the jurisdictional structure for those crimes during the negotiations at the Rome conference. Instead:

> No one at the Rome Diplomatic Conference disputed that the core crimes within the ICC's jurisdiction – genocide, crimes against humanity, and war crimes – were crimes of universal jurisdiction under customary international law (Ibid.).

Although the United States did submit a proposal that suggested an alternate structure for jurisdiction, the alternate would still have allowed universal jurisdiction for genocide but required consent of the home state of the accused for prosecution of war crimes or crimes against humanity that fell short of genocide. Germany and Korea also proposed similar alternative jurisdictional structures, but otherwise there was broad consensus at the conference to embrace the universal jurisdiction as ultimately enacted (Kirsch and Holmes 1999, p. 5). The proposal of alternate jurisdiction presented by the United States demonstrates a willingness to acknowledge and accept universal jurisdiction and therefore undermines Scheffer's claim that the United States finds universal jurisdiction too expansive of a power for the court (Scharf 2001, pp. 77–8). More evidence that this claim is insincere can be found in the other tribunals in Yugoslavia, Rwanda, and Sierra Leone, which all have universal jurisdiction, including potentially over citizens from the United States, with no objection from the United States (Schabas 2004, p. 710).

The primary alternative explanation for the opposition of the United States to the ICC is that it is driven by concern over a diminished role in international politics. That is, if the potential role of the United States on the ICC is compared to its actual position on the United Nations Security Council, it is clear that there is no scenario wherein the United States could wield as much influence in the court as it does on the council. Because, along with the United Kingdom, China, France, and Russia, the United States is one of only five permanent members of the Security Council, the United States possesses a strong veto capability over any action taken by the Security Council. While membership on the Security

Council rotates to all United Nations member states and fifteen new states join the council each year as fifteen cycle off, the permanent members like the United States maintain the capacity to veto any proposal deemed hostile to their own interests or the interest of their allies. No state, including the United States if it were a participant, has any special privilege that dictates or shapes the actions of the court or prosecutor. The influence of the United States would be no greater and no less than any other of the participant states. Thus, the argument is that the United States should oppose any new institution that limits its capability or capacity to serve its own interests whenever necessary (Ralph 2005). Of course the politics behind war crimes tribunals have also been shaped by the politically powerful states, so it is not clear that this argument is any more useful in explaining the opposition of the United States than the argument about overly broad jurisdiction (Rudolph 2001).

The original proposal that delineated the relationship between the court and the Security Council prepared by the United Nations International Law Commission (ILC) was acceptable to the United States (Schabas 2004, United Nations 1994). There, the chief prosecutor of the ICC was not allowed to pursue allegations of threats, breaches of the peace, or acts of aggression that were under active consideration or were before the Security Council unless the Security Council allowed the court to proceed (United Nations 1994, Art 23[3]). If this version of the article had been incorporated into the adopted version of the Rome Statute, the ICC would have institutionally been a functional subordinate of the Security Council with a limited power to proceed with prosecution only when granted express permission by the Security Council or tacit permission through no action. The Clinton administration seems likely to have embraced the court under this stricture:

> The ILC's final draft statute for the ICC addressed many of the U.S. objectives and constituted, in our opinion, a good starting point for far more detailed and comprehensive discussions. Though not identical to U.S. positions, the ILC draft recognized that the Security Council should determine whether cases ... should be considered by the ICC, that the Security Council must act before any alleged crime of aggression could be prosecuted against an individual and that the prosecutor should act only in cases referred either by a state party to the treaty or by the Council (Scheffer 1999, p. 13, also see Lippman 1997).

However, the delegates to the Rome Convention did not share this vision of the court as an extension of and subordinate to the Security Council. The adopted version of the relevant portion of the treaty, Article 16, sets forth the relationship between the court and the council. The court has a broad mandate and wide authority to initiate and advance investigations, free of oversight by or interference from the Security Council, although the Security Council has the ability to intervene through a resolution in some circumstances (El Zeidy 2002; Schabas 2004, p. 716). Schabas succinctly explains:

[T]he Rome Statute was an attempt to effect indirectly what could not be done directly, namely reform of the United Nations and amendment of the Charter. This unprecedented challenge to the Security Council accounts for the antagonism of the United States (Schabas 2004, p. 720).

This view explains the opposition of the United States through the lens of realist concerns. That is, since the United States has so much more control in the Security Council than it could ever aspire to have at the court, it will never support the court (Ralph 2005, pp. 41–2).

Both of these approaches, the overly broad jurisdiction argument and the diminished role in international prosecutions argument, overlook the role of domestic audience costs as the foundation for the opposition. Recent scholarship has demonstrated that the electoral logic of senators can account for this opposition (Smith and Smith 2006; Smith and Smith 2009). This approach considers the preferences of the state not as merely the product of a unitary actor, but rather as a function of the underlying electoral logic of the policymakers in the United States.

The role and impact of domestic politics and the affiliated domestic audience costs that arise from those politics on foreign policy has taken center stage across many issue areas in the scholarship that addresses international relations. The domestic concerns and political pressures have been instrumental in the explanation of a wide range of issues as varied as the adoption of international environmental agreements and the absence of violent conflict or war among democratic societies (Maoz and Russett 1993; Russett 1996). Raustiala (1997), for example, finds the source of the hostility of the United States toward the Convention on Biological Diversity in domestic politics through specifically considering the relationship between the branches of government, the pressure exerted by interest groups, as well as the political and electoral incentives of the politicians involved. The concept of the democratic peace in international security has been well studied (Bueno de Mesquita et al. 1999; Maoz and Russett 1993; Russett 1996; Schultz 1999; Zacher and Matthews 1995). The basic premise that informs this approach is that domestic political forces shape the actions and preferences of the policymakers who structure foreign policy (Milner 1997). At least in some quarters, the influence of domestic political concerns in shaping foreign policy is underappreciated (Martin 2000, p. 13).

The members of Congress in the United States influence the executive, the nominal head of foreign policy, in a variety of both formal and informal ways (Martin 2000). Because Congress can undermine the implementation of any agreement, even when the president and those under him negotiate executive agreements, which provide for no formal role in construction for senators, presidents try to anticipate and accommodate likely congressional reactions (Martin 2000, p. 79). The realms of international trade and overall foreign policy are not immune from the influence of domestic political concerns. Because the costs to be paid to domestic political audiences in a democracy have to be considered as a negative cost for any leader who backs down during an international crisis, democratic states are more likely to signal their actual intentions in a more unambiguous fashion than authoritarians (Fearon 1994, p. 581). This insight about the costs to democratic leaders arising from foreign policy concerns has been the foundation of explanations about the democratic peace, which is one of the most significant, persistent, and robust findings in international security (Bueno de Mesquita et al. 1999; Maoz and Russett 1993; Russett 1996; Schultz 1999; Zacher and Matthews 1995). Democracies are not somehow immune to conflict; indeed, democratic states are just about as prone to violent conflict as nondemocracies (Maoz and Russett 1996, p. 624). Rather, over the last 200 years, democracies simply put, have almost never waged armed conflict with other democracies (Ibid.). Interest groups and other domestic political actors likewise play a significant role in the construction of the trade policy of the United States (Baldwin and McGee 1998; Grossman and Helpman 1994).

This concern with domestic audience costs explains the opposition of the United States to the ICC (Smith and Smith 2006; Smith and Smith 2009). Supporters such as Sadat-Wexler (1999), Leigh (2001), and Latore (2002) and opponents like Scheffer (1999) accept that the ICC has the ability to be a valuable and positive institution in the promotion of global human rights norms and, as a corollary, peace. Despite the potential for the ability of the court to promote this positive policy, there is a disconnect between the rhetoric of the United States which expresses solid support for global human rights and in particular international justice, but is a strong opponent of the ICC (Ralph 2005; Schabas 2004; van de Vyver 2001). This account explains opposition as driven by an electoral disconnect between the policy that is most beneficial to the state and the political pressures that dictate a different outcome. The preferred policy outcome fails over nothing more than the electoral calculus of the elected policymakers (Smith and Smith 2006; Smith and Smith 2009). The argument is supported by the former ambassador at large for war crimes issues who, in a moment of candor, said, "Any arrangement by which a U.N.-sponsored tribunal could assert jurisdiction to prosecute Americans would be political poison in Congress" (Lippman 1997, p. A16). As has been demonstrated elsewhere, the electoral incentive structure for politicians in the United States accounts for the opposition (Smith and Smith 2006; Smith and Smith 2009). Placing the issues of overly broad jurisdiction and questions of diminished authority for the Security Council in the proper context – frames that obscure the actual basis of the opposition of the United States – allows a more nuanced consideration of the jurisdictional structure of the ICC and in particular the issue of complementarity.

The purpose of the Rome Statute, as set forth in the preamble, is to establish a permanent tribunal independent of the control of any given state and that maintains jurisdiction over gross violations of human rights that are "the most serious crimes of concern to the international community."

The court has a specific grant of jurisdiction to prosecute crimes of genocide, war crimes, crimes against humanity, and the crime of state aggression (Rome Statute, Preamble, Article 5). The chief prosecutor of the ICC has the ability to exercise the jurisdiction of the court through the initiation and pursuit of investigations. The chief prosecutor has the authority, under two conditions, to exercise jurisdiction and may proceed under either.

The first condition that allows the chief prosecutor to initiate an investigation and bring charges is when the crime occurred in a territory of a ratifying state (Article 12.a). The second circumstance under which the chief prosecutor could proceed is when the accused is a national or citizen of a ratifying state (Article 12.b). Under Article 5, the jurisdiction of the court extends over the four specific categories of crimes.

Complementarity, as structured by the Rome Statute, specifically limits the scope of jurisdiction of the chief prosecutor. In Article 1 of the Rome Statute, there is an unambiguous restriction that states that the court "shall be complementary to national criminal jurisdictions." This restriction means that so long as a state has the capacity to initiate an investigation and pursue a prosecution of a violation of the specific crimes for which the ICC has jurisdiction, then the prosecutor has no ability to move the case into the jurisdiction of the court. In short, because the jurisdiction of the court is secondary, or complementary, to the jurisdictions of the states, it cannot assume jurisdiction as a venue of first resort. Although there is a conceptual dictate that the state in question must be willing as well as able to prosecute the defendants who might be subjected to process at the ICC, there is an absence of statutory definition or description of the threshold activities which determine what acts are necessary in order to constitute a determination that a state is "willing to prosecute." That is, a ratifying state apparently must make an overt and clear statement of refusal to prosecute or must be wholly incapable of investigation regarding any claims of prohibited activities before the chief prosecutor has the right to open an investigation. The jurisdictional constraint of complementarity is a strict limitation on the scope of actions of the office of the chief prosecutor and an unambiguous institutionalization of deference to the domestic or national courts of the nations that constructed the court.

Article 17 does permit the chief prosecutor to assess the legitimacy of criminal investigations and prosecutions at the state level and to claim jurisdiction over a case if it is prolonged or delayed without good cause or if the national institutions seem to be protecting the accused and shielding the suspects from prosecution. (Rome Statute, Article 17, a, b, c). However, in light of the length of time the ICC has taken to initiate prosecutions, and given the extended periods before prosecutions were pursued in both the ICTY and the ICTR, it is difficult to determine the matrix by which "needless delay" could be measured. Further, the treaty makes no attempt to articulate what might be counted as a sufficiently rigorous investigation or prosecution. In fact, the treaty is silent even regarding definitions of the manner and extent of punishment meted out for the crimes that fall within the ambit of the jurisdiction of the court. The construction of the punitive dimension of the process is solely within the discretion of the prosecuting state. Examples of how this might manifest itself in a problematic fashion are easy to imagine. Suppose a British soldier is discharged without a jail term or any other punishment for killing several unarmed, seriously wounded, and unconscious Iraqis. Even if this act could be construed as falling under the substantive jurisdictional scope of the authority of the ICC, the soldier could not face additional prosecution before the court even though the punishment is nothing more than an involuntary separation from service.

There is a nominal reservation of authority by the chief prosecutor to assess or evaluate the legitimacy of any germane domestic criminal investigation or prosecution. However, practically speaking, the potential for the chief prosecutor to exercise this oversight authority is problematic. Each of the party states, that is, every one of the countries that has ratified the treaty, has in place a functional code of military justice that dictates the manner in which service personnel are disciplined and otherwise held accountable for unlawful acts. Each of the party states also has a fully functioning domestic or municipal system for the investigation and prosecution of criminal acts. Since each one of these countries not only has a municipal criminal code and a system in place to pursue prosecutions, but also has a fully functional military code of justice and conduct, there could be no referral for prosecution or investigation of military personnel of the signing states because jurisdiction could not be validly taken unless there was a complete collapse of both avenues of domestic prosecution capacity or an unambiguous declaration by the state that neither investigation nor prosecution would occur.

Furthermore, the court exercises jurisdiction only over individuals and not over states. This jurisdictional constraint not only distinguishes the ICC from other international tribunals like the ICJ, it also reinforces the secondary or complementary nature of the prosecutions in the ICC (Danner 2003, Tan 2004). In spite of the nominally broad power granted to the chief prosecutor, the scope of impact of the jurisdictional constraint of complementarity means that the actual authority over where jurisdiction begins and ends for the court is within the discretion of the member states and their domestic or national courts rather than that of the chief prosecutor.

Two additional ways in which the jurisdiction of the ICC is limited are important to consider before an examination of the court's activities since its inception can be put in context. Both Bilateral Immunity Agreements and Status of Forces Agreements act to severely restrict the range of situations in which the court could interject itself for the purposes of initiating an investigation or a prosecution.

The Rome Statute contemplates and provides for the creation of a broad exception to jurisdiction under Article 98. This portion of the treaty specifically restricts extradition by the ICC of any accused person from a state if there are other legal obligations of that state that create a conflict in obligations under international law (Rome Statute, Article 98 sections 1–2). That is, if a state would be required to surrender custody to the ICC and that state was also obligated under international law to decline to surrender custody, the Rome Statute makes the claims of the ICC subordinate to any other obligation in international law. The United States negotiated and entered into the first Bilateral Immunity Agreement, also referred to as Article 98 Agreements, in August of 2002 with Romania. Since then, more than 100 other nations have entered into bilateral immunity agreements with the United States. A complete listing of various BIAs, including the parties to the agreements and the content of the agreements, is available through the American Nongovernmental Organization Coalition for the International Criminal Court (amicc.org/usinfo/administration_policy_BIAs.html). The upshot of the BIAs is they provide a prohibition on extradition to the court of the service personnel of the party states to the agreements.

One controversial aspect of the BIAs beyond the severe limitation on jurisdictional capacity they represent for the court is the manner in which the United States persuaded other countries to commit. In conjunction with the passage of the law, titled the American Service Members' Protection Act, in July of 2003, the United States announced that all future military aid for its allies would be conditional on the execution by those recipient states of bilateral immunity agreements (Becker 2002). Although waivers of this restriction were ultimately offered by the United States to twenty-two states that had not entered into a bilateral immunity agreement, those states also had not yet ratified the Rome Statute. For states unwilling to enter into a BIA with the United States and that also ratified the Rome Statute, the United States withheld about $6.2 million in previously committed direct military aid in 2004.

The United States has not limited its efforts to undermine the ICC to these dyadic relationships. The United States has also created severe limitations on the scope of jurisdiction of the court through the Security Council of the United Nations. Specifically, the United States has manipulated the Security Council as a venue through which Status of Forces Agreements (SOFAs) have been altered to further limit any possibility of jurisdiction of the court over personnel from the United States involved in United Nations peacekeeping missions. For example, the United States sought permanent broad immunity from the possibility of investigation by or prosecution by the ICC for all involved personnel as a condition for supporting the ongoing mandate of the United Nations Mission in Bosnia. Supporters of the court were outraged at this demand and the secretary general of the United Nations, Kofi Annan, sent a strongly worded letter to Colin Powell, then the secretary of state for the United States. The thrust of Annan's complaint to Powell was that acquiescence to the demands of the United States would risk creating a de facto alteration to the text of the Rome Statute and would severely undermine the legitimacy of the Rome Statute as well as the credibility of the Security Council (Smith and Smith 2009, p. 38).

Eventually the Security Council structured a compromise, Resolution 1422, that satisfied the demands of the United States while at least nominally ameliorating the concerns of the international community. Resolution 1422 granted blanket immunity to the United States for any personnel involved in UN peacekeeping operations for a period of one year, with the potential for successive one-year renewals of the immunity. This broad immunity for peacekeepers from the United States from the jurisdiction of the court was continued through a renewal of the resolution in July 2003. By June 2004, the United States had executed so many SOFAs that there was no longer a need to seek a renewal of the resolution. Of course, given the dictates of complementarity and the expansive reach of both the Bilateral Immunity Agreements and the SOFAs, any immunity procured for personnel of the United States through the Security Council resolution process is a redundant protection from the reach of the court. Indeed, little was given up by the United States when it declined to renew the resolution-based blanket immunity beyond the ability of policymakers to show to some swath of voters or other domestic audience their emphatic opposition to the court (Allen 2002; Kyl 2004; Lauria 2004). In short, the source of the opposition of the United States to the court can be found in electoral concerns rather than some concern the prosecutors will act out of political motivations or about some reduction of sovereign power. The electoral logic that makes this opposition intractable, if predictable, is revealed through an examination of the institutional structure of the House of Representatives as well as the Senate.

While the Senate has exclusive authority over the ratification of treaties, including this one, the institutional characteristics of the House of Representatives also informs this discussion because of the impact the House had on the Senate's approach to the ICC. The lobbying and appropriation process for defense dollars or patronage causes the allocation of the funding to be broadly diffused across House districts (Derouen and Heo 2000; Mayer 1991, pp. 158–74; Ray 1981). The local payoff for defense spending goes beyond the provision of jobs and the creation of economic activity spurred by manufacturing alone (Hooker and Knetter 1997; Nincic and Cusack 1979). In fact, the employment of personnel by the military is arguably the primary benefit of military expenditures in any given district (Arnold 1979, pp. 95, 119; Menkin 2004; Sasaki 1963). The Department of Defense employs millions of people across all fifty states. The budget process that leads to a diffusion of military budget expenditures across House districts organically leads to a diffusion of spending across every state. Because spending associated with the defense budget is so diffuse, every state has a substantial amount of military patronage whether through employment, production of goods, or often, both. Thus every senator has a great deal of defense spending within his or her geographic area of electoral concern. Therefore, each senator has some significant swath of constituents concerned about defense issues and defense spending. These topics are salient to these voters in terms that go beyond the bounds of simple patriotism or security. In brief, every senator has a specific constituency with a direct economic concern about military patronage (Clotfelter 1970). The electoral dynamics suggested here regarding the saliency and diffusion of defense-related issues is reinforced by the volunteer ranks of the military. All fifty states are source states for the military personnel in the all-volunteer forces. Two more brief observations inform the argument about the electoral source of opposition to the ICC. Because one-third of the senators stand for reelection every election cycle and senate incumbents have a tremendous advantage, senators tend to be risk adverse and do not seek out potentially incendiary issues that might disadvantage them in their next election (Ansolabehere and Snyder 2002; Collier and Munger 1994; Gelman and King 1990; Highton 2000). Senate support for the court, whether institutional or individual, would be easy for rivals to portray as support for the prosecution of military personnel of the United States by the international community. The shades of nuance necessary to explain complementarity as a rebuttal are not likely talking points to be utilized in the heat of a campaign where low-level rationality and simple communication strategies are favored (Popkin 1991). When President George W. Bush ran for reelection in 2004, he often responded to questions and critiques about the Iraq war from Democratic candidate Senator John Kerry with a declaration that the United States would never ask for a permission slip from foreign interests before it acted as it saw fit to protect itself. This line invariably resulted in raucous applause and assent. Accordingly, any policy that can be easily framed or perceived as requesting permission from abroad for the actions of the United States military or that might be seen as subjecting the personnel of the United States military to politically driven prosecutions by any other state or organization is a politically risky and unlikely position for either challengers or incumbents.

The broad and comprehensive jurisdictional limitations contained in the Rome Statute mean that the states that embraced the treaty, and those like the United States that have sought to undermine it, have no reason to fear that their personnel could ever be subjected to investigation or prosecuted by the court. In particular, the restriction of complementarity dictates that the court cannot operate as a primary venue for any country with a military or civil or criminal justice code that could function through a domestic court system. Furthermore, the widely executed and comprehensive Bilateral Immunity Agreements and Status of Forces Agreements prohibit the investigation or prosecution of any personnel of any of the states party to these agreements. Prosecution of a covered individual is simply not possible. Any concerns or assertions that somehow an out of control or rogue chief prosecutor with some political agenda could investigate and indict the service personnel of the states that constructed the court should be fully alleviated by these broad, ubiquitous, and unambiguous limitations on the jurisdiction of the court. The court simply has no capacity to assert jurisdiction over the states that created it. So long as the commission of the crimes prohibited by the Rome Statute are committed by individuals from or actually in states that are able to prosecute, whether in civilian municipal courts or through a military court of justice, the court simply may not exercise jurisdiction.

The Rome Statute unequivocally makes the court a supplemental and secondary system. The complementarity provisions (Rome Statute, Articles 1 and 17) mean that the court has no capacity to act as a rival of or peer to domestic legal structures. This inability to act as a court of initial jurisdiction, when combined with the widespread adoption of BIAs and SOFAs, suggests that, although the International Criminal Court has institutionalized important concerns over substantive due process and procedural due process, it has done so with such limitations on the potential to exercise jurisdiction that most of the states in the world could never find their personnel before the court. Indeed, this multifaceted constraint on the jurisdiction of the court suggests that it might just have as well been named the International Criminal Court for sub-Saharan Africa.

Since the court began operations in July of 2002, it has, in the parlance of the annual reports on activity prepared for the United Nations, "been seized of five situations" (International Criminal Court 2010, p. 2). The court is actively prosecuting defendants from the conflicts in Uganda, the Democratic Republic of the Congo, the Central African Republic, and Darfur, the Sudan (Ibid.). While the investigation regarding Darfur, the Sudan was referred to the court by the United Nations Security Council, the other three investigations were all initiated by the states themselves (International Criminal Court 2006, p. 1). Specifically, the Uganda investigation was the first and began when Yoweri Museveni, the president of Uganda, requested the court initiate an investigation of the actions of the Lord's Resistance Army (LRA) in December of 2003. The next year, in April of 2004, the president of the Democratic Republic of the Congo requested the chief prosecutor open an investigation of crimes within his state. In January of 2005, the chief prosecutor was asked by the government of the Central African Republic to open an investigation there. The chief prosecutor is also conducting an investigation of crimes against humanity committed in Kenya between 2005 and 2009 (International Criminal Court 2010, p. 2). Preliminary investigations, which are information gathering efforts rather than prosecutorial efforts, can be triggered by any complaint sent to the chief prosecutor by any party.

Currently, preliminary investigations involving conflicts in Palestine, Georgia, Colombia, Guinea, and Afghanistan seem destined to fall short of full investigations or indictments because of complementarity or the lack of cooperation from the involved state while the preliminary investigation into actions in the Cote d'Ivoire might well move toward a full investigation (Ibid., p. 2, pp. 13–18).

The investigations and prosecutions that have been initiated as a result of the conflicts in Uganda, the Democratic Republic of the Congo, the Central African Republic, and Darfur, the Sudan have resulted in a variety of convictions and acquittals. In all, since the first arrest warrants were issued in October of 2005, thousands of witnesses have testified or assisted the chief prosecutor in the investigative phases. While the number of convictions is modest compared to the ICTY and the ICTR, tens compared to hundreds, the court has made steady progress with the cases and matters before it.

As would be expected given the institutional design of the court, the substantive due process aspects and the procedural due process aspects of both the investigations and the prosecutions meet or exceed the standards of international justice. Moreover, the court specifically concerns itself with the participation of the aggrieved in the process (International Criminal Court, *Registry Facts and Figures* 2010, pp. 3–5). In particular, victims participate as witnesses and there is an express attempt by the court to structure reparations whenever appropriate for the victims of the convicted. An especially noteworthy advancement is the construction of a witness protection plan for those who testify or otherwise assist in the prosecutions (Ibid., pp. 4–5). This institutionalized structure for witness protection emerged from a similar protection plan in the ad hoc tribunals as well as the Special Court for Sierra Leone.

The actions of the court to date and the foreseeable trajectory of its activities suggest that there should be little concern that the chief prosecutor will initiate a politically driven investigation. The hands of the prosecutor are tightly bound by the limitations on jurisdiction and jurisdiction has to be clearly established in order for a trial to actually begin. Establishing jurisdiction before the court is not easy to do and is especially difficult if a suspect seeks refuge in a state that might pursue or actually pursues a domestic investigation. To date, despite annual resources that exceed one hundred million euros and a staff of almost 1,000, the court has only claimed jurisdiction where a state has initiated an investigation or where the United Nations has referred the matter.

At this point, not only do the broad jurisdictional restrictions of complementarity, bolstered by the multiple and various BIAs and SOFAs, undermine the meme of a politically active rogue chief prosecutor acting as a threat to established democracies, but the actual experience of the court also demonstrates that this is a fabricated concern. Moreover, in light of the recent War on Terror and the accompanying belligerence in Afghanistan and Iraq, the notion that, regardless of the jurisdictional constraints, the court presents a threat or might assert jurisdiction over the personnel of the United States or any of its allies seems completely unfounded. The war in Afghanistan, the invasion of Iraq in general, and the scandal arising out of the Abu Ghraib prison mistreatment specifically, in addition to the questionably legal detentions of individuals at the United States Naval Station in Guantanamo Bay Cuba, GTMO or Gitmo in the vernacular, each provide a multifaceted opportunity for a politically oriented chief prosecutor to try and manipulate the court for political purposes, yet no prosecutions or investigations have been initiated. If the court does not attempt to reign in or punish the Western democracies when they are mounting aggressive war around the world, there seems to be few if any scenarios where a politically driven prosecution would be initiated.

While the argument could be made that the court is incapable of asserting jurisdiction because the United States did not ratify the Rome Statute, since the jurisdictional constraints are so broad, any assumption that a politically activated rogue prosecutor will ignore these limitations on jurisdiction post-ratification should suggest that the same prosecutor would ignore the restrictions before ratification. In other words, the claim that political concerns will drive a chief prosecutor to initiate an action regardless of the jurisdictional constraints is seriously undermined by the absence of political indictments despite the court having access to ample resources during a period of controversial acts of state that might lead to such indictments. Not only has the chief prosecutor never attempted to assert jurisdiction in any marginal or questionable case, but the office of the chief prosecutor has not actually initiated any apparently politically motivated investigations because no case of any sort has actually been initiated by the chief prosecutor. Perhaps the case could be made that the referring states have targeted their politically unruly rivals for power, but the notion of the president of Uganda manipulating the court is something quite different than the idea of a flawed institution.

The role of the United Nations Security Council in limiting the court is the final limitation on jurisdiction that ought to be considered. The court is limited in any ability to launch an agenda separate from that of the international community because the United Nations Security Council can proscribe involvement of the ICC in any given conflict. For instance, the United States almost succeeded in avoiding jurisdiction for the ICC over those accused of crimes in Darfur, the Sudan. The other member states of the Security Council united against the effort and argued that the court was the only "logical place" for the Darfur trials to be held (Hoge 2005). The United States also attempted in December 2004 to block a resolution, supported by European states with membership on the Security Council, asking the chief prosecutor to initiate an investigation into the use of child soldiers by the three parties in conflict in Burundi. A referral was requested by the government of Burundi in light of the deaths in August 2004 of 150 Congolese refugees (Zagaris 2005). The point is that the Security Council has the prerogative to keep virtually any matter out of the scope of concern of the chief prosecutor.

The broad expectation from the international legal community is that "the majority of prosecutions for international crimes are expected to take place in domestic courts" (Akande 2004). Accordingly, that the court has limited jurisdiction is not an inherently damning characteristic. Although the court may be limited in jurisdictional reach and may have been structured by the powerful states for the purposes of policing some regions of the world where violence might be part of the political culture, it still has been a tremendously important step in the evolution of war crimes tribunals. These limitations on the overall value of the court should not completely overshadow the larger context and importance of its creation and operation. The European states have fully embraced the ICC and been its most vocal advocates. The United Kingdom, for instance, which ratified the Rome Statute in October of 2001, congratulated twelve states that ratified it in April of 2002. Jack Straw, the British foreign secretary, placed the establishment of the court in context:

> This is an historic day for international justice and for the human rights of every citizen in the world.... This government has always been an enthusiastic supporter of the Court. It is our belief that the global rule of law is stronger than the local rule of tyrants (Global News Wire 2002).

The argument here has two streams. First, the jurisdictional constraints on the ICC are so severe that the court seems destined to primarily institutionalize show trials through the prosecutions of individuals from politically weak states. However, while the court could perhaps do more and do it more broadly, the trials it does conduct are done quite well. The expectations in the international community regarding the substantive due process and procedural due process aspects of transitional justice have been institutionalized through the ICC. Moreover, it is the source of substantial progress in the areas of deterrence and retribution as guiding principles behind the dispensation of justice. The court has created an unprecedented role in the prosecution for the victims of atrocities and has also established a substantial structure for reparations and witness protection. Still, despite an era of perpetual violent conflict since the inception of the court, the court has relatively modest activities with prosecutions arising exclusively out of conflict in sub-Saharan Africa. No inquiry has ever been suggested by the chief prosecutor or anyone affiliated with the ICC as a result of any activities associated with the wars in Afghanistan or Iraq or any behavior arising out of the War on Terror. Just as it was designed to do, the stricture of complementarity has been a complete barrier to any investigation by the chief prosecutor of any actions by the developed nations that created the court.

Whatever the initial intent regarding the jurisdictional constraints of the ICC, it has developed into a permanent venue for the international criminal prosecutions of weak states and the political actors within those weak states. Just as substantive due process and procedural due process reached maturation, even if limited in scope, in the international sphere through the ICC, the most powerful states in the world, those who developed the modern version of the war crimes tribunal, co-opted the institutional structure of the tribunals. The response of the United States and its allies to the terrorist attack of September 11, 2001 included the invasion of both Afghanistan and Iraq and the detention of a broad range of individuals from a variety of countries. From the outset, those who structured a response to the 9/11 attacks indicated their intent to hold war crimes tribunals across the range of conflicts. In the next chapter, the manner in which the evolved concept of a war crime tribunal was co-opted by the administration of President George W. Bush for the purposes of promotion of the multifront war effort demonstrates the reversion of war crimes from a vehicle of abstract justice to a mechanism for political prosecutions.

7

The Fall of War Crimes Tribunals

Afghanistan, Iraq, and the War
on Terror

Shortly before 9:00 in the morning on September 11, 2001,
terrorists flew a commandeered commercial airplane into
the North Tower building of the World Trade Center in New
York City. Roughly twenty minutes later, a second hijacked
airplane exploded into the South Tower and within an
hour, a third airplane crashed into the Pentagon building
in Washington, DC. Shortly after that, a fourth airplane
wrecked in Somerset County, Pennsylvania, brought down
by passengers on the plane who fought back against the terrorists who had seized control. By mid-afternoon, the twin
towers of the World Trade Center had collapsed and by the
end of the day, one additional building collapsed, followed
by a fourth on September 12. The government of the United
States responded to this unprecedented terrorist attack in
a variety of ways. Airports were immediately closed from

coast to coast as the country became a "no-fly zone" and by the end of October Congress passed and the president signed into law the USA Patriot Act, which gave the federal government a host of new investigative tools perhaps at the cost of some civil liberties (Shortell and Smith 2005, p. 173).

In response to the attacks, President George W. Bush announced the start of the War on Terror and made the following declarations:

> Our war on terror begins with Al Quaida, but it does not end there. It will not end until every terrorist group of global reach has been found, stopped, and defeated ... we will pursue nations that provide safe haven to terrorism. Every nation, in every region, now has a decision to make. Either you are with us or you are with the terrorists (Bush 2001a).

Within weeks, the initiation of the War on Terror had led to the arrests and incarceration of alleged terrorists in thirty-eight countries and the launch of an invasion of Afghanistan named Operation Enduring Freedom (Bush 2001b). The military operation in Afghanistan began on October 7 with a host of missile strikes launched from air, land, and sea by the United States and its allies (Ibid.). The initiation of the War on Terror and the subsequent invasion of Afghanistan were accompanied by what might be termed the institutionalization of the War on Terror through the creation of an expansive bureaucracy, the Office of Homeland Security

(Bush 2001a). Subsequently, as part of the larger effort of the War on Terror, the United States and its allies expanded military operations that were in place as a result of United Nations sanctions against Iraq through the invasion of Iraq on March 20, 2003 and the toppling of the regime of Saddam Hussein.

While these two actual wars in Afghanistan and Iraq are sometimes thought of as completely separate endeavors, they are inextricably tied together through their connections to the metaphorical War on Terror. The War on Terror was the rationale for the initiation of both wars and also has shaped the way in which at least some dimensions of the two wars have been waged. Of particular interest here, the broad claim of a War on Terror has been used as the analytical foundation for the manner in which those detained as a result of the wars have been treated. Specifically, the construction and design of war crimes tribunals arising out of the three discrete conflict arenas, Afghanistan, Iraq, and global terrorism, share a common origin and purpose. This chapter begins with a consideration of the trials, held in Iraq, of former president Saddam Hussein as well as the members of the Ba'athist Party government and military that ruled the country before the war. Then, the war crimes trials that have arisen specifically out of the conflict in Afghanistan are considered. Finally, the war crimes trials that have arisen as a result of the more ephemeral War on Terror are addressed followed by a discussion of detainees from the War on Terror who have not been tried.

Iraq

The nominal rationale for the invasion of Iraq was not only the claim that Iraq supported terrorism, but also that it had and intended to use weapons of mass destruction and, in particular, nuclear weapons. President Bush claimed that the objective of Operation Iraqi Freedom was "to disarm Iraq of weapons of mass destruction, to end Saddam Hussein's support for terrorism, and to free the Iraqi people" (Bush 2003). Some of the traditionally close allies of the United States such as the United Kingdom, Italy, and Poland, as ardent supporters of the War on Terror, all had ratified the Rome Statute and also contributed troops to the Iraq invasion. The Polish government was unambiguous in its support for action in Iraq and declared, "We are ready to use a Polish contingent in the international coalition to contribute to making Iraq comply with the U.N. resolutions.... It's clear that the problem of existing weapons of mass destruction is a fact" (White House Press Release 2003).

Although the Ba'athist government fell within weeks of the initiation of military action, Saddam Hussein evaded capture by the occupying force for almost nine months. Even though Hussein was not yet in custody, the newly formed Iraqi government, in conjunction with the international force and in particular the United States, took a host of actions to demonstrate it was not only in control of the country, but also that it intended to hold the Ba'athist elite responsible for any criminal activity that occurred under the previous regime. The new order in Iraq brought with it a flurry of legislative activity that included the creation of a tribunal for war crimes and other atrocities committed by high-ranking officials of the previous regime, including Saddam Hussein. The Statute of the Iraqi Special Tribunal was signed into law on December 10, 2003. It created the Iraqi Special Tribunal, which is also sometimes referred to as the Supreme Iraqi Criminal Tribunal or the Iraqi High Tribunal. Three days after the creation of the Iraqi Special Tribunal, Hussein was taken into custody by military personnel of the United States on December 13, 2003. His trial for war crimes and other crimes against humanity began almost two years later on October 19, 2005.

The Iraqi Special Tribunal was created to provide for the prosecution of Hussein and other Ba'athist leaders for genocide, crimes against humanity, war crimes, and violations of some domestic laws for acts that occurred between July 17, 1968 and May 1, 2003 (Coalitional Provisional Authority 2003, Art. 1, Art. 38). The Iraqi Special Tribunal became the primary venue for the dispensation of justice in regards to the manner and mechanisms of governance utilized by the Ba'athist regime. Articles 11 through 14 provide the definitions of the actions deemed criminal behavior under the substantive due process dimensions of the Iraqi Special Tribunal (Ibid., Art. 11–14). Saddam Hussein was not the only defendant but, as head of state and as the personalized target of the military intervention by the United States, was the primary focus of the process (Bush 2003). Conspicuous in its absence is any crime or activity arising out of the initial justification for the invasion, which was the development or deployment of weapons of mass destruction. Rather, the crimes identified generally fall within the range of topics that have historically been prosecuted through war crimes tribunals. In general terms, the scope of crimes covered by the Iraqi Special Tribunal means that it was designed only to prosecute the roughly forty former members of the Ba'athist government identified as "most wanted fugitives" on the unusual deck of Iraqi fugitive playing cards issued as part of the war propaganda effort by the United States (Scharf 2004).

The definition of genocide for purposes of the Iraqi Special Tribunal is taken from the Convention on the Prevention and Punishment of the Crime of Genocide, which the pre-Ba'athist government of Iraq ratified in January of 1959 (Coalitional Provisional Authority 2003, Art. 11). The definitions of crimes against humanity include the standard definitional fare of murder, extermination, enslavement, forcible deportations, torture, sexual crimes, group persecution, "enforced disappearances," and other inhumane acts that cause grave suffering or injury (Ibid., Art. 12). The definitions of war crimes were taken from the Geneva Conventions of August 12, 1949 and broadly defined international law (Ibid., Art. 13). The last category of covered crimes were outliers from the standpoint of the historical path of war crimes trials and uniquely applicable to Iraq. This category included domestic prohibitions on the threat of force against other Arab countries, abuse of the judiciary, and the squandering of public resources (Ibid., Art. 14). Article 15 of the Statute for the Iraqi Special Tribunal made individuals who committed the crimes listed in Articles 11 through 14 criminally responsible for those acts and stripped away any claim of immunity that might be made because the individual was acting on behalf of the state (Ibid., Art. 15).

Apart from the oddities of the provisions for prosecuting aggression toward Arab states in particular, there is nothing especially remarkable about the substantive due process aspects of the Iraqi Special Tribunal. The covered crimes are consistent with the array of activities covered by war crimes tribunals from Charles I forward and certainly are in line with the crimes covered by the Nuremberg Trials. Of course, the crimes covered by the Iraqi Special Tribunal were almost completely unrelated to the predicate cause of the conflict that gave rise to the tribunal or to the manner in which that conflict was conducted. So while the schedule of crimes in the abstract seems reasonable, the premise of the prosecutions was wholly unrelated not only to the premise of the invasion, but also to the conduct of conflict. The war crimes in question were not affiliated in any meaningful sense with the war in question. Accordingly, once the substantive due process characteristics of the Iraqi Special Tribunal are put into the context that gave rise to them, there is a substantial disconnect between the rationale for the war, the actions of the parties during the war, and the foundation for the actual prosecutions.

This initially troubling dimension of a rationale disconnect for the Iraqi Special Tribunal from a substantive due process standpoint is perhaps the least serious deficiency. The procedural due process provisions of the Iraqi Special Tribunal, much like the substantive due process provisions, at first glance seem reasonably designed to provide for a fair trial. However, a closer examination raises serious questions about whether the procedural dimensions of the tribunal can be reconciled with any concept of a just process. The right to a fair defense mounted by competent counsel is a fundamental dimension of procedural due process. The absence or presence of this right to counsel has been a perpetually controversial aspect of war crimes tribunals. For the Iraqi Special Tribunal, a formal right to counsel was undermined in a variety of ways. First and most bluntly, defense counsel members were often killed. Saadoun al-Janabi, the lead attorney for Awad al-Bander, was kidnapped on October 20, 2005 and found murdered the next day (Associated Press 2006, p. 6). Al-Bander was a co-defendant with Hussein and had been the chief justice under the former regime. The vehicle carrying defense lawyers Adel al-Zubeidi and Thamir al-Khuzaie, both representing former vice president Taha Yassin Ramadan and Hussein's half-brother Barzan al-Tikriti, was attacked by armed men on November 8, 2005 (Ibid.). Al-Khuzaie was gravely wounded and al-Zubeidi was killed. Defense attorney Khamas al-Obeidi was kidnapped from his home on June 21, 2006 and murdered shortly thereafter (Ibid.). These sorts of problems of course likely could have been avoided had the trial been relocated to either the ICC or even to a special tribunal set up at The Hague or elsewhere.

In a similar vein to the constant personal peril and absence of security for the defense counsel, the presiding judges faced professional peril and an absence of job security if they showed an inclination to rule in favor of Hussein at all. The Iraqi Special Tribunal allowed for the removal of any judge for any reason. The Iraqi president, in conjunction with any two vice presidents, can remove a judge upon the recommendation of the Council of Ministers. Even this minimal procedural hurdle was ignored in January of 2006 when Chief Judge Amin was removed from his post for being too soft in dealing with Hussein and the other defendants (Kami 2006; Peterson 2007, p. 285). In September of 2006, Chief Justice Abdullah al-Amiri was removed after he merely stated that Hussein was not a dictator (Oppel 2006). The apparent lack of independence for the judges must be assessed in the light of the idea that any expectation of judicial job security was dependant upon a focus on "the wishes and goals of the Iraqi government, the Americans, and the British" (Peterson 2007, p. 285).

There were other substantial defects regarding court personnel. The occupying force was responsible for the selection of the judges (Packer 2006, p. 29). The United States and its allies took control of the entire process, including not only the selection but also the training for the judges, regardless of the fact that no aspect of the prosecutions arose from the purpose of the invasion. Many of the judges were allowed to conceal their identities and judge through a veil of anonymity (Peterson 2007, p. 285). These serious flaws in the procedural due process structure of the court were probably sufficient to deny the defendants a fair trial. These flaws were not, however, the only procedural due process defects. The evidentiary standards harkened back to those used in the Tokyo trials. A chamber, the five-judge panel charged with conducting the trial of any prosecution, was empowered to admit "any relevant evidence which it deems to have probative value" and it "may" exclude evidence for lack of credibility or undue prejudice (The Statute of the Iraqi Special Tribunal, Rules of Procedure and Evidence Rule 79). The identity of witnesses and those who claimed to be victims could be, and in fact often were, concealed (Ibid., Sec. 8, Art. 21, 22), and testimony could be taken by telephone or any other means (Iraqi Special Tribunal Rules of Procedure and Evidence Rule 80). There was an express declaration that the crimes referenced in Articles 11 through 14 would not be subject to or limited by any claim of any statute of limitations (The Statute of the Iraqi Special Tribunal Sec. 6, Art. 17). The punishment for any crime which had no counterpart under the 1969 criminal code of Iraq was determined on an ad hoc basis by the Trial Chambers (Ibid., Sec. 8, Art. 24). In other words, for many of the charges, the judges could mete out whatever punishment they chose at any time during the process. No specific penalty was identified for the specific crimes punished by the Iraqi Special Tribunal other than the crime of aggression toward Arab states and the squandering of public assets.

The failures of the Iraqi Special Tribunal to follow the boundaries of the norms for a just proceeding in both the substantive due process dimension and the procedural due process dimension suggest it has more in common with the early efforts such as the trial of Charles I or the prosecution of Captain Henry Wirz than it has with the more recent sets of tribunals. Much like those early trials, the Iraqi Special Tribunal did not provide a vehicle for deterrence or retribution in any meaningful sense. On November 5, 2006, Chief Justice Raouf Abdel-Rahman pronounced Saddam Hussein guilty of a variety of charges. Hussein was sentenced to death by hanging for the willful killing of civilians in Dujail and he was sentenced to a variety of moot multiyear sentences for a host of other crimes ranging from torture to "inhumane acts" (Peterson 2007, p. 257). Hussein responded as expected, with defiance and a charge that the judges were "puppets" and "servants of the occupiers" (Burns and Semple 2006).

The notion of deterrence is simply not an integral aspect of the Iraqi Special Tribunal because the court is so strictly limited in time and scope. There is no avenue available through which current high-ranking officials in Iraq could ever be brought before this tribunal. Once again, had the trials somehow been processed through the International Criminal Court, they might have served as a deterring exemplar for those in Iraq to avoid future massive violations of human rights, but the trials were held in a venue designed to prosecute and convict specific politicians. The trials were not demonstrations of a generalizable code of justice, but rather of a targeted effort to eliminate specific political elites who had lost power. The goal of deterrence could perhaps have been promoted generally through these trials to try and discourage those outside of Iraq from engaging in gross violations of human rights, but again, because of the narrowly tailored jurisdiction, there seems to be no exportable lesson from the trials beyond the idea that those who lose wars are killed. Finally, with respect to retribution, the Statute of the Iraqi Special Tribunal makes no provision for retribution in any form (Amnesty International 2005).

Accordingly, the Iraqi Special Tribunal was narrowly designed to prosecute and execute one specific set of political elites to ensure they did not return to power. There was no regard for the international criminal jurisprudence embodied in the International Criminal Court or its modern predecessors. The Iraqi Special Tribunal was derived from jurisprudence of Charles I, the Wirz trial, and the Tokyo trials without the evolved development of actual concern for justice. There was a token construction of substantive due process and procedural due process protections designed to ensure that the goal of the tribunal – the de-Ba'athification of Iraq – was accomplished. The Bush administration dismantled almost 500 years of developed jurisprudence since the war crimes trial of Charles I in the nine months between when the occupying allies toppled the government of Saddam Hussein and when they constructed the tribunal for his prosecution. As if planned by the Bush administration, a multifaceted attack on the concept of war crimes trials followed and tracked the multifaceted War on Terror.

Afghanistan and the War on Terror

Unlike in Iraq, the conflict in Afghanistan actually began as a direct response to the terrorism of 9/11. Some members of a loosely organized set of oppositionist groups across the Middle East known as Al Quaida had allied with the loosely organized ruling group in Afghanistan known as the Taliban. The Taliban came to power in some parts of Afghanistan as a result of the nonexistence of a functional central state government. The Taliban is in essence the administrative branch of very conservative Islamic religious leaders who maintained or imposed traditional political and social constraints across Afghanistan driven through a decentralized theocracy. Al Quaida is the umbrella name for a variety of groups that seek political change across the Middle East. While nominally, many of the demands of Al Quaida are consistent with the goals of the Taliban, the Taliban are geographically limited to Afghanistan while Al Quaida originates with Saudi citizens who are unhappy with, among other things, the close connection between the Saudi government and the United States. The goals of Al Quaida are somewhat difficult to precisely determine because of the decentralized nature of the group. That is, since there is not a hierarchical structure, it is difficult to determine the preferences of the entity with certainty. However, there are some common objectives that, even if not all-inclusive, are suggestive of the goals of the group. The complaints of those who claim to speak for Al Quaida involve two major issues. First, the absence of sufficient piety and commitment to a specific theological framework in government across the Middle East is a perpetual source of complaint. Second, the relationship between the Western powers, especially the United States, and the elites of the oil producing countries, especially the United Arab Emirates, leads to a series of perpetual complaints that oil is sold at too low of a price to the West. These two issues lead to a host of other complaints, for instance, that troops from the United States were stationed on sacred ground after repelling the Iraqi invasion of Kuwait. Regardless of why those involved in the Taliban and those involved in Al Quaida found common ground, the fact is they did. The Taliban allowed Al Quaida access to a variety of training facilities in Afghanistan.

On November 13, 2001, shortly after the 9/11 attacks in September and the initiation of the war in Afghanistan in October, President George W. Bush issued a military order that provided for the trial of persons detained pursuant to the War on Terror or the conflict in Afghanistan (Bush 2001c). Two elements of this military order are

especially noteworthy. First, the order sets forth the following rationale:

> e) To Protect the United States and its citizens, and for the
> effective conduct of military operations and prevention of
> terrorist attacks, it is necessary for individuals subject to
> this order pursuant to section 2 hereof to be detained, and
> when tried, to be tried for violations of war and other appli-
> cable laws by military tribunal (Ibid., p. 1).

This is a noteworthy aspect of the military order because
it sets out the intention by the government of the United
States to pursue those engaged in Afghanistan as war criminals. Moreover, it establishes the foundation for a claim of
anticipatory justice, so to speak. That is, the prevention of
a terrorist act is set forth as a rationale for not only detention, but also the actual prosecution of an individual for a
war crime for acts that have not yet happened. While there
may be some merit in punishing prospective bad behavior,
this order represents the first step in that direction taken
under the auspices of war crimes tribunals. Additionally,
perhaps because of recognition of the difficult evidentiary
road ahead, the order specifically eliminated the standard
rules of evidence before any tribunal had been seated or initiated any proceeding. The order provided that:

> f) Given the danger to the safety of the United States and
> the nature of international terrorism, and to the extent
> provided by and under this order, I find ... that it is not

practicable to apply in military commissions under this order the principles of law and rules of evidence generally recognized in the trial of criminal cases in the United States district courts (Ibid., p. 1).

The order provided express authority to the secretary of defense for the creation of military commissions to act as both a trier of fact and as a trier of law and to mete out whatever punishment the commissions deemed appropriate, including the death penalty (Ibid., p. 1–3). Additional dimensions of the order set out the parameters under which the government intended to construct both the procedural due process and substantive due process aspects of the trials. The order specifically deprived any of the detainees from claiming a right to proceed in any other venue:

Sec 7 (b) of the order states:

with respect to any individual subject to this order – (1) military tribunals shall have exclusive jurisdiction with respect to offenses by the individual; and, (2) the individual shall not be privileged to seek any remedy or maintain any proceeding, directly or indirectly, or to have any such remedy or proceeding sought on the individual's behalf in (i) any court of the United States, or any State thereof, (ii) any court of any foreign nation, or (iii) any international tribunal (Ibid., pp. 4–5).

The order not only proscribed the possibility of jurisdiction in any other venue, it also affirmatively declared that no detainee could claim any substantive or procedural right, benefit, or privilege as a result of the order (Ibid., p. 5). The order does not actually delineate the specific crimes that are going to be the foundation of the contemplated trials. Indeed, it simply identifies the substantive basis for the trials as "individuals acting alone and in concert involved in international terrorism" and that the trials are necessary "for the effective conduct of military operations' prevention of terrorist attacks" (Ibid., p. 1). In short, the order provides that any act deemed to be supportive of terrorism, as defined by the secretary of defense or the president, could be the basis for a trial nominally referred to as a war crimes trial. There is no development or construction of the substantive due process aspects of these trials as initially contemplated by the administration of President Bush. Any action deemed supportive of terrorism could be prosecuted by these commissions. Who might be charged under the order is set out with a great deal more specificity than what crimes might subject those individuals to prosecution. The order identifies as subject to the order any noncitizen of the United States the president determines:

(i) is or was a member of the organization known as al Quaida;

(ii) has engaged in, aided or abetted, or conspired to commit, acts of international terrorism, or acts in preparation therefore, that have caused, threaten to cause, or have as their aim to cause injury to or adverse effects on the United States, its citizens, national security, foreign policy, or economy, or;

(iii) has knowingly harbored one or more individuals described (above) (Ibid., pp. 1–2).

In essence, any act deemed in any way in furtherance of "international terrorism" as defined by George W. Bush could subject an individual to prosecution in front of one of these military commissions. There is simply no clear delineation or effort at even a minimal definition of the acts that could subject an individual to prosecution. The substantive due process architecture of the order gives the president unbridled discretion to allow the crimes to be defined by fiat.

As sparse as the attention to substantive due process was, the procedural due process dimensions of this initial design are indefensible. The right to appeal is limited to a direct appeal to the secretary of defense or the president (Ibid., p. 2). Only two-thirds of those sitting in judgment need be persuaded in order for a defendant to be convicted and of course, any evidence could be admitted if the presiding officer determined it had probative value. Any disclosure of the activity of the commissions could happen in secret proceedings. The secretary of defense was given broad authority and discretion regarding every dimension of the process and could change the process without oversight beyond that of the office of the president.

There is no provision or concern with retribution or deterrence in any aspect of the original design of these tribunals beyond the broad notion that enemies of the United States will face a difficult time. Any message of deterrence of terrorism is more likely to be found in the invasion of Afghanistan rather than in the meager commission proceedings. Even if pressures for deterrence somehow are conveyed through these commissions, it is difficult to conceptualize how people in a comparable position to those on the suicide mission of 9/11 could be deterred. If someone is willing to die as a result of some course of action, it is a hard to imagine that the intent to carry out that action might be altered because of the fear of punishment.

Four months after the attack of 9/11 and two months after the order by President Bush that provided for military commissions, the first 774 prisoners arrived in Guantanamo Bay, Cuba to be housed in a detention facility, originally called Camp X-ray, located on the United States Naval Base there (Worthington 2007, p. xii). Almost 1,000 men and boys have been detained at the prison at Guantanamo Bay (AP 2009). The facility at Guantanamo Bay was chosen because it is arguably beyond the reach of the courts in the United States. By placing the detainees there, the Bush administration could claim that no rights flowed to the prisoners from the United States constitution or criminal code. This line of argument complemented the claims that no dimension of the Geneva Conventions applied to these detainees and that, because they were alleged to be terrorists, they were in a legal limbo. They were not soldiers and they were not civilians. They could not seek legal protections from any international agreements or from the domestic law of the United States. Rather, these detainees were a new category of prisoner that the United States termed "unlawful enemy combatants" (Wolfowitz 2004). Vice President Dick Cheney summed up this new category of prisoner in a straightforward manner: "They don't deserve to be treated as a prisoner of war. They don't deserve the same guarantees and safeguards that would be used for an American citizen going through the normal judicial process" (Worthington 2007, p. 126). Secretary of Defense Donald Rumsfeld was even more blunt than the vice president when he said: "They will be handled not as prisoners of war, because they're not, but as unlawful combatants. Technically, unlawful combatants do not have any rights under the Geneva Convention" (Reuters 2002). An interesting implication that has yet to be resolved is whether this created status, if adopted and recognized internationally, would also apply to the personnel of the private security contractors hired by the United States to provide a host of tasks previously done by the military (Barnes 2007).

The actual hearings that have occurred, so far, have been as unstructured and idiosyncratic as the initial design of the commissions allowed. Although there is a requirement that the prosecutors and the defense counsel engage in discovery, whereby each side discloses the evidence to be presented, the vague institutional design fails to obligate the prosecution to disclose any aspect of the evidence with sufficient time available to allow the defense team to investigate or test the evidence. The prosecution is under no obligation to allow the defense lawyers a chance for any pretrial interviews of witnesses slated to testify for the prosecution. The prosecutors are allowed to use classified evidence that is shielded from the defendant and his lawyers. The identity of witnesses, those who interrogate witnesses and defendants, and informants may all be concealed from the defendants and the defense teams. As one of the defense counsel, Navy Lt. Commander William Kuebler complained, "This is a process that's not designed to be fair; it's designed to produce convictions" (Williams 2007).

Of the almost 1,000 men and boys detained, over 640 have been transferred, released, or are awaiting release (Associated Press 2009). These men and boys have been deemed to be no longer a threat or often never a threat to the United States. Many of the detainees were taken into custody as a result of the $5000 bounty offered by the United States for anyone allegedly involved with the Taliban, Al Quaida, or terrorism in general. More than 200 of the prisoners in Guantanamo Bay were initially detained because bounty hunters turned them over in order to collect the $5000 reward offered (Williams 2007). Because the threshold for an allegation that would justify arrest was very low and the bounty hunters only needed to fill out an affidavit, it is unclear how many of those detained through the bounty system were actually involved in terrorism or any belligerence (Worthington 2007, pp. 111–21). The affidavits provided by the bounty hunters, which were the foundation of detention for these individuals, were deemed classified by the United States and are unavailable for examination by defense counsel (Williams 2007). The release without charge of over sixty percent of the detainees is perhaps a predictable outcome given the detention for hire approach taken. The unjust outcome for these prisoners is staggering in its magnitude. After years of isolation and detention without charge, they are simply released, having been reclassified as a paradoxically named "non-enemy combatant" (Wolfowitz 2004, pp. 3–4).

Of all of the detainees, fewer than seventy-five have been deemed viable candidates for prosecution (Associated Press 2009). This means that over ninety percent of those people that have been detained have not and will not be prosecuted for any crime. This fact stands in stark contrast to the overheated rhetoric from members of the Bush administration when the first detainees arrived at Guantanamo Bay. Marine Brigadier General Mike Lehnert, the officer in charge of the facility, claimed that "These (prisoners) represent the worst elements of al-Qaeda and the Taliban. We asked for the worst guys first" (Worthington 2007, p. 127). When Secretary of Defense Donald Rumsfeld toured the prison at Guantanamo Bay, he claimed the people detained there were "among the most dangerous, best-trained, vicious killers on the face of the earth" (Ibid.).

The efforts at constructing a façade of judicial propriety around the detention facility at Guantanamo Bay actually revealed the almost complete absence of a concern about justice. This presentation of a concern about justice as little more than window dressing for a military action is underscored by the fact that the legal basis for holding a majority of the detainees at the facility was to be found in the "Authorization for the Use of Military Force" (Ratner and Ray 2004). This joint resolution was passed by both houses of Congress on September 18, 2001 and gave express authority to the president to exercise all necessary and proper force against anyone deemed by the president to have been involved in any aspect of the 9/11 terrorism or in assisting those involved in any way. This broad grant of authority combined with the creation of the idea of "non-enemy combatants" meant that normal notions of judicial structure were to give way to military concerns.

The Bush administration had at least four options for conducting prosecutions of anyone thought to have committed some act that would justify prosecution in front of a war crimes tribunal. Those accused of grave crimes affiliated with terrorism, including the attacks of 9/11, might simply have been charged in federal court under the auspices of the federal criminal law. The administration successfully prosecuted John Walker Lindh in that venue for his actions in Afghanistan. Lindh was dubbed "the American Taliban" and categorized as an enemy combatant although he was little more than a foot soldier who volunteered with a group loyal to the Taliban. He was charged with ten counts in February of 2002 and eventually pled guilty to one charge of serving the Taliban and one charge of carrying a weapon (Worthington 2007, p. 262). The difficulty of proceeding in the federal court system was of course that the evidentiary code might have made convictions difficult to obtain. Perhaps even more important, the overwhelming majority of detainees for whom the United States had no inculpating evidence beyond the affidavits of bounty hunters would likely have prevailed on habeas corpus claims and the government would have been ordered to release them from custody well before any trial.

The administration could have proceeded against any of the detainees actually suspected of committing a war crime through the normal channels prescribed in the military code of justice. The problem with any utilization of the extant military system is that the accused are allowed a robust defense. While the evidentiary rules are relaxed compared to the federal court system, the prosecution must still demonstrate the existence of reliable evidence that establishes guilt. Any burden of proof may have been too large of a hurdle for the prosecutors of the Guatanamo detainees.

The United States could have asked that the United Nations Security Council establish an ad hoc tribunal like those set up for the situation in Rwanda or the former Yugoslav states. Finally, if none of these other venues seemed appropriate, the United States could have petitioned the International Criminal Court to take jurisdiction. The Bush administration never considered turning the process over to an international tribunal. Instead, the policy of the United States was structured to maintain absolute political control over the process.

By creating a new legal status, unlawful enemy combatant, and constructing the detention center in a location beyond the jurisdictional reach of municipal or international court systems, the Bush administration was able to present a public claim of the provision of just as much justice as the "terrorists" deserved. Political concerns regarding how the domestic audience would interpret the events arising out of the detentions in Guantanamo seem to have outweighed any concern about justice or security. Eventually, members of the administration admitted what was obvious from the volume of prisoners ultimately released. In the end, no major figures from the Taliban or Al Quaida were actually detained in the prison at Guantanamo Bay (Ibid., pp. 128–9).

Three final aspects of the detentions at Guantanamo Bay and the War on Terror demonstrate the damage done to the development of the jurisprudence of war crimes tribunals by the Bush administration. A group of individuals detained in Afghanistan in 2001 is referred to by their ethnic identity of the Uighers. The Uighers (WEE-gerz) are Turkic-speaking Chinese nationals who are Muslim. Most Uighers are Sunni Muslims. There are about nine million Uighers in the oil-rich Xinjiang province in China. The Uighers have resisted rule by the Han Chinese and have long objected to the control over the oil resources located there. In the mid-1990s, waves of occasionally violent protests across the cities of Xinjiang were met with strong suppression efforts by the central government. Many Uighers fled to Afghanistan and Pakistan to escape this wave of oppression by the Chinese government. In 2002, about thirty Uighers living in Afghanistan and Pakistan were taken into custody by the United States. They were turned over to military personnel of the United States by bounty hunters from Pakistan and were shortly thereafter transferred to the prison at Guantanamo Bay. Almost immediately upon their arrival, the Uighers were determined by the authorities from the United States to pose no security threat to the United States or any other country. However, the Chinese government considers the Uighers who fled the country in the 1990s to be terrorists. If the United States simply returned the Uighers to China, the strong expectation is they would be persecuted and might possibly be killed.

Over a period of eight years, many of the initially detained Uighers were freed – or at least released from prison in Guantanamo and relocated to a few countries around the world. The latest freed were relocated to Palau, an island nation in the Pacific Ocean (Johnston 2009). Although the Uighers that were released to Palau had no prior connections there, a local Muslim community agreed to assist in the transition. The transfer of prisoners to Palau meant seven Uighers continued to be detained a decade after they were wrongfully imprisoned and a decade after the government of the United States determined they did not present a security threat. Although a federal district judge ordered that the Uighers be released into the United States in October of 2008, the court of appeals overturned that ruling in February 2009. The Supreme Court took up the case in the fall of 2009, one month before the latest relocation, for the purpose of determining whether the district courts have the authority to order the release of detainees determined by the government to be no threat to security.

On March 1, 2010, citing a change in the material facts that gave rise to the case, the Supreme Court dismissed *Kiyemba v. Obama* (08–1234), the appeal filed on behalf of the Uighers, because some of them had been given the opportunity to relocate (MSNBC 2010). The Supreme Court decision let the Obama Justice Department dodge a challenging argument before the Supreme Court about whether the district courts have the power to order the release of detainees into the territory of the United States. The case has broader implications beyond the plight of the Uighers because it could have determined whether the other Guantanamo detainees have the right to pursue relief through the federal courts. Although there had previously been a determination through *Rasul v. Bush* and *Hamdi v. Rumsfeld* that both foreign detainees and citizen detainees could seek habeas corpus relief and challenge the basis for their detentions, there has not yet been a determination that the courts could actually provide a remedy, such as ordering the release of a prisoner. Pointing to the change in circumstances of the prisoners, that some of the Uighers had now been offered their freedom, the justices of the Supreme Court dismissed the appeal in an unsigned opinion just three weeks before oral arguments were scheduled.

Regardless of what ultimately happens to the Uighers or the other detainees in the Guantanamo Bay facility, the damage inflicted by the Bush administration throughout the first decade of the War on Terror on the development of the jurisprudence of war crimes tribunals is staggering. Barack Obama was sworn in as president and successor to George W. Bush in January of 2009. Although he had pledged to close the prison facility at Guantanamo Bay by the end of 2010, the Obama administration has altered very few of the policies implemented by the Bush administration with respect to the detainees and the prison is still in operation. Indeed, the Obama administration has institutionalized some dimensions of the system for handling the detainees that are antithetical to any real commitment to the administration of justice. The manner in which the War on Terror, as waged in Afghanistan and Iraq and administered in the United States and at the facility at Guantanamo Bay, has undermined the development of substantive due process and procedural due process with respect to war crimes tribunals is perhaps best illustrated by the claim that the Unites States has the right to detain individuals indefinitely without charge or the provision of any administrative or legal avenue through which a detainee could challenge the lawfulness of the detention.

On March 7, 2011, President Obama signed an executive order that provides for a continuation of the indefinite detention of many of the detainees that remain prisoners of the United States at Guantanamo Bay. Since the order contains a provision for the periodic review of the basis for the detention, this policy may open the possibility of release if somehow the circumstances under which a detainee is held change; the order certainly solidifies long-term indefinite detention without charge as an indisputable dimension of the Obama administration's policy for the Guantanamo detainees (Obama 2011). The order maintains executive and military control over the review process. The review process will focus on the necessity of continued detention but not engage questions of the lawfulness of the detention. In short, the United States has determined that it has the ability and the right to indefinitely imprison individuals without charging them with a crime or providing them with any trial process under which they could challenge the detention. This development means that more detainees face the possibility of detainment for life without ever being charged with a crime. Like Bush before him, Obama finds the authority to use indefinite detention in the authorization for the use of military force passed simultaneously by both houses of Congress in response to the 9/11 terrorist attacks in 2001. Currently, forty-eight prisoners that have not been charged with any specific crime are administratively scheduled for indefinite detention (Linzer 2010).

The idea that the United States knowingly imprisons individuals, the Uighers and all of those detainees eventually released, that are unquestionably no threat to the security of the country combined with the notion that indefinite detentions are to be institutionalized, represents a substantial diminution of the concept of war crimes trials as a vehicle for the delivery of justice. The actions of the United States toward those perceived to be its enemies and those who are merely innocents caught up as collateral victims are not the only avenue through which the War on Terror has diminished the development of war crimes trials jurisprudence. The treatment by the United States of its own personnel has also taken a toll on the integrity of the concept of war crimes trials. Indeed, it seems as if even the military justice system in the United States has been undermined by the War on Terror (Solis 2007). The Abu Ghraib prison in Iraq became infamous in 2003 when photographs of military personnel from the United States abusing the Iraqis held prisoner there were provided to news outlets. The violations of normal protocols included sexually oriented humiliations, physical abuse that rose to the level of torture, intimidation with attack dogs, threats of death, actual deaths, and a host of other bad acts (Serrano 2007). The photographs depicted smiling soldiers posing with sometimes nude detainees held in painful or humiliating positions or propped up like trophies from an animal hunt. While thirteen people ultimately faced charges before military courts over the abuses at Abu Ghraib, only one of those defendants was an officer. Lt. Colonel Steven Jordan was accused of dereliction of duty, cruelty and maltreatment of prisoners, and failure to train and supervise soldiers (Dishneau 2007). Lt. Colonel Jordan repeatedly claimed he was not responsible for the use of the improper interrogation techniques at Abu Ghraib and that he was not in charge of the facility when the abuses occurred. After three years of litigation, the military court agreed with Lt. Colonel Jordon and he was acquitted of all charges except for one. He was found guilty of disobeying an order because he had been instructed not to contact any other soldiers about the investigation into Abu Ghraib and he in fact had several conversations with others about it (Ibid.).

In April 2006, Marine Corps Sgt. Lawrence G. Hutchins III, a squad leader, persuaded seven men under his command to kidnap and kill a middle-aged Iraqi man. The purpose of this murder was to "send a message to insurgents to stop attacking Marines in the Hamandiya area" near Baghdad (Perry 2007b). The unarmed victim was taken from his bed in the middle of the night, marched down the street about 1,000 yards, and shot by the marines eleven times. After he was killed, the marines placed a shovel and an assault rifle by the corpse to give the appearance that the man was in the process of planting a roadside improvised explosive device (Perry 2007a). Sgt. Hutchins was convicted of conspiracy to commit murder and breaking into the house, but not pre-meditated murder. The other defendants were released upon conviction after being sentenced to time served or were sentenced to very short prison terms. Sgt. Hutchins, convicted of the most serious crimes and the only one sentenced to a lengthy prison term, was freed from prison after his conviction was overturned on appeal in 2010 (*U.S. v Hutchins III*, Docket # 200800393, April 22, 2010). The winning appeal by Hutchins was based on a claim that he was not given his appropriate rights to counsel because members of his original defense team retired from the Marines without first properly withdrawing from his case.

One more case against the military personnel of the United States bears discussion. An incident in 2005 in Haditha, Iraq, in which marines killed twenty-four unarmed civilians, including women and children, resulted in charges for war crimes filed against eight marines, including two officers. The witnesses to the killings claimed that the marines were angry over the death of one of their own, Lance Cpl. Miguel "TJ" Terrazas, who was killed by a roadside bomb, and that they killed the Iraqi citizens as revenge for his death. However, since the charges were first brought, six of the defendants have sought and obtained a dismissal of all charges against them and one was acquitted at his court martial (Whitcomb 2008). The only remaining defendant is the alleged leader of the massacre, Staff Sgt. Frank Wuterich. The prosecution of Wuterich is on hold pending the resolution of his appeal, based on the Hutchins decision, that he should not be prosecuted because of a deprivation of full rights to counsel (Ibid.).

Just at the moment the international community had institutionalized, however imperfectly, a permanent and independent venue for the prosecution of war crimes trials, the Bush administration charted a course in response to terrorism that pulled the jurisprudence of war crimes back to its origins. The post-9/11 allegations of war crimes and the mechanisms established to prosecute those allegations were a reversion of war crimes jurisprudence to nothing more than a product of the exercise of political and military power. The War on Terror led to widespread allegations of war crimes and many detentions of individuals arising out of those allegations, but few prosecutions and convictions. The notion of indefinite detention without charge wholly undermines any pretense of substantive due process. Procedural due process fares no better under this scenario since the minimalist process that has been contemplated, an occasional determination by the president and his personnel regarding whether detention continues to be necessary, provides to the detained neither rights nor remedies for potential violations of any conceptual or actual rights.

The detainees are subject to continued imprisonment at the whim of the administration and have absolutely no avenue of judicial recourse to challenge these detentions. No retribution has been sought from these detainees for any of the acts that gave rise to the invasion of Afghanistan. This could simply be a function of the overall lack of process regarding the detainees. It could also be that no retribution can be meaningfully sought until after some establishment of guilt and some allocation of responsibility have occurred. Since so many of the detainees have simply been released without charge, there can be little ability to create the necessary nexus between the actions that lead to an assignation of guilt and the responsibility to the victims to ameliorate the impact of the actions that led to the determination of guilt. The detainees have not been found guilty or even accused of any actions upon which some mechanism for retribution could be predicated. Accordingly, there is no dimension of actual retribution arising out of the allegations of war crimes that arose as a dimension of the War on Terror. The goal of deterrence has suffered under the War on Terror as much as the goal of retribution. Not only has the War on Terror undermined the international concept of deterrence, but the light treatment by the United States of its own personnel for serious breaches of the law of war has undermined the domestic concept of the rule of law with respect to military justice.

8

Conclusion

The arc of development of the jurisprudence of war crimes trials has taken a clear path from the initial need to justify the killing of Charles I. The first forays into the prosecution of political leaders as a result of the acts committed by them or undertaken at their command during conflict were remarkable first steps toward state accountability for behavior during war. The jurisprudence that was the foundation upon which war crimes trials could be constructed was simply a premise that those who enforce the law should also be held accountable to the law.

As the jurisprudence of war crimes tribunals developed with each conflict and the subsequent determination after the conflict ended as to the treatment to be meted out to war criminals, any effort at delivering justice and providing accountability for the misdeeds of war was limited by the political needs and the capacity of the winners on the battlefield or at the ballot box. War crimes trials have served to publicly display the norms and the expectations of the international community regarding the scope of acceptable behavior during conflict. However, these public displays of the machinations of justice are conducted by the victorious. The victors proceed with trials without any fear of facing prosecution since those winning nations are also responsible for the creation or operation of the tribunals. When taken either individually or considered as a whole, these tribunals seem to be undertaken in order to accomplish political con-solidation rather than to ensure a proper dispensation of justice. The international community moved the concept of war crimes tribunals along a path of jurisprudential devel-opment that meant each successive iteration moved closer to delivering an instrument for the dispensation of justice. Although these tribunals were far from perfect, there was substantial value in even the flawed war crimes trials. Even if not every person who commits crimes during war is held accountable for those acts and even if the states that are the most powerful in the world are not held accountable and insulate their personnel from any meaningful prose-cution, the trials and tribunals have more often than not seemingly assisted in the avoidance of additional conflict. Regrettably, the circumstances that brought about the War on Terror led the George W. Bush administration, Bush II, to revert to political consolidation and expediency as the primary, perhaps sole, function of the tribunals. The slow rise stands in stark contrast to this rapid fall of the integrity of war crimes trials.

The first attempts to prosecute civilian and military leaders before some type of judicial tribunal that would impose punishment for the violation of law originate with the inauspicious show trial of Charles I of England. He was executed after a show trial put on by his political rival Oliver Cromwell. Cromwell could not undermine the right of the king to rule, but if the king were accountable to the law and violated the law, then Cromwell could justify the execution. Captain Henry Wirz may have been the last casualty of the Civil War in the United States. Wirz, commandant of an undersupplied and overcrowded Confederate prison, was also executed by the victors in war after a very public show trial that provided nothing in the way of procedural due process or substantive due process. When the victorious Allies decided to conduct the Nuremberg Trials after World War II, the preference for an actual fair process of prosecution set in a legitimate forum where law could be impartially administered won out over these early models of victor's justice that were little more than summary prosecution of the losing side of a war.

The promising movement toward justice as a guiding principle of postconflict judicial processes did not progress through the Tokyo trials. In fact, the group of symbolic trials for low-level Japanese officers who may have committed no crime was a short-lived reversion to purely political trials. Since the Nuremberg Trials, and perhaps despite the

Tokyo trials, the international community now expects that the perpetrators of war crimes and other gross violations of human rights be held accountable before a judicial body, even if on an ad hoc basis, as part of the normal process of conflict resolution. The bad acts that lead to prosecution during conflict have been variously called crimes against humanity, gross violations of human rights, or war crimes. The ad hoc prosecutions since the Nuremberg Trials created a sound jurisprudence of prosecution that has progressed, developed, and evolved with each successive series of prosecutions, trials, or tribunals. Unlike the International Criminal Court, the permanent court established under the Rome Statute, the ad hoc prosecutions before it each took a specific form to meet the needs of the parties at the time. The ad hoc trials or tribunals varied in the scope of the crimes covered and, as a result, varied considerably in the range of substantive due process provided as well as the procedural rules established. The shared purpose of the ad hoc tribunals, almost without exception, is the establishment or reimplementation of the rule of law and a just accounting for the crimes that occurred.

Also without exception, the ad hoc trials have been constructed, at least from a de jure standpoint, to redress serious violations of human rights as a fundamental dimension and element of the restoration of the rule of law and to the provision of justice once a conflict has ended. The trials have been conducted both domestically and through international forums. The structure of the prosecutions has been built on a notion of the prosecution of individuals who acted contrary to the internationally accepted norms of proper conduct during conflict. These individuals are usually prosecuted for acting on behalf of a government during conflict. Usually, some improper behavior by the agents of government against civilians, especially some wrongful use of force, is a necessary element to the crimes that are the subject of the prosecution. Importantly, the actions that lead to these prosecutions of agents of government are the type of criminal acts that categorically are claimed to be universally unacceptable. These categories of actions that are covered by the range of universally abhorrent or unacceptable acts have been catalogued from that first indictment of Charles I through every successive set of war crimes tribunals including those crimes listed in the Rome Statute that led to the creation of the International Criminal Court and the indictment of Saddam Hussein and the prosecution of the War on Terror.

The creation of the International Criminal Court was motivated in part by a desire to establish predictability for the parameters of prosecution and to provide some efficiency in the ongoing administration of justice for this category of crime. Specifically, the institutionalization of the court could have reduced claims of selective justice in prosecution and diminished the often idiosyncratic operation of the ad hoc trials. The International Criminal Court also presented a venue through which the concept of universal jurisdiction could continue to evolve and solidify as an internationally accepted norm. That is, the International Criminal Court brought hope that some particularly awful crimes would be acknowledged to be so terrible that a global jurisdiction would create a foundation upon which to pursue prosecution against the perpetrators of those crimes regardless of the geographic location of the crimes or the accused.

The fundamental question considered here through the historical evolution and development of war crimes tribunals in their various forms is whether human rights tribunals, ad hoc or standing, promote and are the product of concerns about justice or are they more likely to simply be a manifestation of normal political processes and efforts to consolidate political power. It seems that human rights trials generally are political in nature even when they also serve juridical purposes. There has been little systematic and generalizable analysis of the concept of war crimes tribunals in part because the trials are formed after some particularly egregious level of violent conflict or oppression. The trials also do not reach fruition until at least some of the accused perpetrators of that violence or oppression have been defeated and taken into custody by the victor. Those who stand before such tribunals are rarely sympathetic figures so the treatment of the accused is rarely of primary concern to the watching world. Of course, because the accused in any given war crimes tribunal will complain of political motivations behind the prosecutions and a fundamental absence of fairness in the process, the complaints of the accused are often disregarded by the international community. Since the notion that defendants could be systemic critics without first being driven by self-interest seems implausible, seldom have the complaints of the accused been given much attention and accordingly there is little contemporaneous discussion of whether any given trial is primarily an exercise in politics or justice.

The cases examined here demonstrate that the purpose of the tribunals has been the consolidation of political power, often through the appeasement of some specific factions. The role of political consolidation in the construction of these tribunals was revealed through considering the degree to which justice was promoted through the specific operational rules of the trials. The scope of the commitment to justice in each of the various tribunals was gauged through an analysis of the substantive due process and procedural due process aspects of each institutional setup. The matrix used here to assess the evolution, development, and implementation of the war crimes trials is a simple and generalizable conceptualization of justice as the product of substantive due process and procedural due process with the dual goals of deterrence and retribution. This configuration is straightforward and parsimonious. Any shortfall in the construction of the substantive due process aspects of a trial means the accused has not been fairly treated regarding the content of the charges and the claims prosecuted. When the procedural due process aspects of the tribunal are inadequate to ensure that the evidence against the defendant is fully and adequately tested, then a robust defense cannot be presented. Deterrence is a critical goal because both the actual defendants on trial and any other people in situations similar to the defendants before they were put on trial should be discouraged from engaging in acts in the future comparable to those that led to the charges. Retribution is a critical goal for justice because the specific victims of the crimes as well as society as a whole should be and are entitled to be placed into a position of *status quo ante*, or the same condition they were in before the criminal acts that led to the prosecutions occurred.

Whether the trials are primarily concerned with justice as defined here or are primarily vehicles of political concerns can only be assessed through a concrete definition of what is meant in this context by "political." This analysis constructed the parameters of "political" as actions concerned with political consolidation. In other words, "political" here means the attempt to maintain and strengthen the newly acquired or successfully defended control of the governmental institutions at stake. The changes in political power that occur before the creation and management of human rights trials vary in the degree that societal change preceded the point in time where trials became possible. The degree to which the winner in any given conflict has the capacity to exert political power and control also varies. In other words, once the conflict has ended or abated, the winning side, those political factions then in control, has the ability to manipulate the institutions and mechanisms of the government to varying degrees.

Sometimes the shift in power is so thoroughly complete that the victorious have little or no concern about how they treat the vanquished. The winners are not overly concerned with how they treat those on the losing side who have been accused of war crimes since those individuals no longer have any real political, military, or economic power. The victors can treat the vanquished in any fashion without much regard for justice after a total victory that leaves the vanquished virtually powerless. In this situation, the defeated simply have no recourse even if their treatment by the victorious is nothing more than summary justice as with Charles I, or even a complete absence of any justice, like the situation the Uighers are in. Other shifts in power are complete but somewhat unstable regarding the control over some aspect of some of the institutions of government. The maintenance of power by the ruling coalition depends, at least to some degree, on a continuation of the suppression of the defeated elites, but the ruling coalition is cognizant that unfair or improper treatment of the former leaders might pose a risk to the continuation of control. This situation occurs, like in Argentina, where the former elite group maintains an ability to mobilize or resurrect a political base and possibly challenge the newly installed regime. Other power shifts, like in South Africa, are incomplete and those with new power are dependent on the former elites for some critical aspect of maintenance of the system and control of the government. These two situations occur when those who are no longer in power nonetheless maintain or are able to exert some control over a critical aspect of governance like a substantial stake in the financial infrastructure or some significant elements of the military. Other power shifts end in an indeterminate resolution. For those instances, like Rwanda and in the former Yugoslav states, there is often no clear winner at the end of the conflict. The uneasy balance of, or even contestation over, power among the various competing factions continues beyond the cessation of the violent dimension of the conflict. Here, the end of the conflict is the result of a brokered agreement rather than a complete military or political victory by one of the coalitions in the conflict. In light of the variations in power distribution and political consolidation that occur when conflicts end and in light of the variations in the manner in which power can be maintained after conflict, it follows that the degree of justice achieved in human rights trials is likely a function of the political expediency and the needs of those factions that come to power after conflict rather than a function of some universal understanding of an abstract notion of justice.

Because conflict has occurred in both transnational or international and domestic venues, it is no surprise that the jurisprudence of war crimes trials has evolved and developed in both domestic legal environments and in the transnational or international legal environment. War crimes tribunals have been established in the context of both a search for transnational justice as well as a search for domestic justice. Each variation of war crimes trial or series of prosecutions about war crimes has had an impact and effect on those trials that followed. Each subsequent series of efforts to hold war criminals accountable, whether transnational or domestic, was shaped by the trials that came before. Perhaps each specific example of war crimes prosecutions could be thought of as so unique and so closely aligned with the specific facts of that conflict that each should be thought of as a singular event with no generalizable aspect. However, the historical path of development of these postconflict tribunals reveals that the jurisprudence of war crimes is not the result of some random walk through history, but rather these cases share a common function and political logic and each has shaped the development of those trials that followed. The international prosecutions, especially the Nuremberg Trials, have so shaped and informed the development of the more recent municipal or domestic trials that to consider each type in a vacuum without consideration of the other would omit an integral aspect of the evolution and pedigree of the domestic tribunals. Moreover, because many of the trials that have occurred in a transnational forum, whether the ICTY, the ICTR or the ICC, only involve municipal crimes, there is no reason to separately analyze the two types of trials as there is simply no reason to believe that the international community views the two types of trials as different in some meaningful way. There also is no reason that such a distinction would provide additional leverage to a systematic analysis of war crimes tribunals.

For the cases examined here, the political context of the cessation of violence or oppression set the foundation upon which the issues of justice were resolved or addressed. The variations among the trials that indicated the magnitude of the concern about justice for both the accused and the victim class included the level to which each trial provided for substantive due process and procedural due process. The extent to which the goals of the justice process, retribution and deterrence, were given attention also provided insight into the intent and purpose of the proceedings. In the final analysis, a comparison of the ability of the victors to consolidate political power and the magnitude of justice achieved at the trials illuminated the function of the trials as driven by political needs. This comparison established that the scope of justice delivered by war crimes trials is a product of the need for political consolidation given the capacity of the victors. The analysis also demonstrated that human rights tribunals can serve a legitimate political purpose beyond the confines of justice. Specifically, these trials have assisted in delivering peace and in the transition away from conflict.

While the analysis has demonstrated the political logic that shapes the pursuit of transitional justice, obviously not all situations in which war crimes tribunals might be established have been considered. Some conflicts, like those in Northern Ireland or between Israel and the Palestinian Liberation Organization (PLO), have been riddled with the sort of actions that give rise to war crimes prosecutions but still, none have been held. Other conflicts, like those in Chile and Cambodia, have only provided for war crimes trials after the wrongdoers have reached an advanced age and lost virtually all political power. The conflicts in Northern Ireland and between Israel and the PLO are what could be termed intractable. That is, the analysis here demonstrates that in the absence of clear political winners or losers, war crimes prosecutions are simply not feasible. Without a clear political or military victory, any prosecution of those perceived to be war heroes rather than war criminals from each side of the unresolved conflict would only increase the political justifications for the conflict and may exacerbate the violence. That is, in the absence of a clear political loser, prosecutions for war crimes are simply not feasible. The intractable conflicts around the world, where war crimes trials might be appropriate but have not happened, usually have been essentially spatially constrained. These types of conflicts center on issues about self-determination, perhaps sovereignty, and specific geographic claims, and often a conflation of all three of these issues.

The parties to the Northern Ireland conflict, a conflict driven by issues about self-determination, sovereignty, and specific geographic claims, reached a peace accord in April of 1998. The agreement, called the Belfast Agreement or the Good Friday Agreement, was reached after two years of negotiations and more than thirty years of active conflict (British Broadcasting Corporation 1998). The agreement among Great Britain, Ireland, and Northern Ireland was a significant step toward the cessation of violence arising from the hostilities that existed in the region for many generations. No side of the conflict was likely to accomplish a sustainable military or political victory. The accord established the foundation for the creation of three separate but related bodies of government (United Kingdom 1998). The Northern Ireland Assembly shares formal power between Protestants and Catholics and took over a host of powers and obligations formerly under the authority of Britain's Northern Ireland Office. The North-South Council is a forum for ministers from the Irish Republic to promote nationwide, or "all-Ireland," policies subject to approval by both the Northern Ireland Assembly and the Irish Parliament in Dublin. The East-West Council is a consortium of representatives of British, Irish, Welsh, and Northern Irish citizens who address issues of concern to all of the parties (Morgan 2000, Accord 3–17).

One of the more notable aspects of the case of Northern Ireland is the complete omission of any provision for war crimes trials or tribunals of any sort. The long and violent history of the conflict in Northern Ireland includes multiple tragedies including the killing of noncombatants, indiscriminate bombings in civilian areas, the unlawful imprisonment of opponents, and a variety of other actions that, in other contexts, have led to prosecutions for gross violations of human rights. Despite multiple examples of acts of violence that have been prosecuted after the end of other conflicts, no tribunals are established, contemplated, or considered in the Peace Accord. The language of the agreement unambiguously demonstrates that the parties did not simply omit or neglect to consider the possibility of war crimes trials. Instead, concerns for transitional justice were limited to a "fresh start" with a goal of reconciliation:

> The tragedies of the past have left a deep and profoundly regrettable legacy of suffering. We must never forget those who have died or been injured, and their families. But we can best honor them through a fresh start, in which we firmly dedicate ourselves to the achievement of reconciliation, tolerance, and mutual trust and to the protection and vindication of the human rights of all (Ibid., Accord 3).

Rather than provide for a series of prosecutions where all sides to the conflict see their heroes tried for war crimes, the agreement establishes the foundation for a reparations fund for any victim of political violence arising out of the conflict. The agreement also set out a direct and multifaceted commitment to "the protection of the fundamental rights of everyone living in the island of Ireland" (Ibid., Accord 19–20). The agreement also established A Northern Ireland Human Rights Commission with a mandate that its membership reflected "the community balance" (Ibid., Accord 19). The broad task to which the Human Rights Commission aspires is "to include keeping under review the adequacy and effectiveness of laws and practices, making recommendations to Government as necessary; providing information and promoting awareness of human rights; considering draft legislation ... and, in appropriate cases, bringing court proceedings" (Ibid.).

It is difficult to imagine a scenario in which a commission comprised of members that reflects the balance of power within the community would seek or obtain the prosecution of anyone, as every faction in the community might be liable for prosecution for pre-accord activity. In short, every faction within the community maintains a veto over the initiation of a prosecutorial action against one of their own. Moreover, because no act has been defined as a crime by the agreement and because the agreement left the definition of a court case ill-defined and vague with no specific identification of a basis for a cause of action, any prosecutor interested in bringing such an action would need to find some statute or common law basis for the charge. Obviously, there would be prohibitions on many of the more clear acts of violence, but not all violations of human rights would inherently be covered by routine criminal law. At least in the case of Northern Ireland, an institutionalized power sharing arrangement led to a de facto prohibition on any prosecution of pre-accord human rights violations. Justice is not the point of the agreement, peace is.

Oliver Cromwell claimed he was only seeking justice for the victims of the civil war through the trial and execution of Charles I. More plausibly, Cromwell realized he could only overcome the symbolic power of royalty and the crown by beheading the monarch. Cromwell's claim that even the king was not above the rule of law was a calculated effort to seize power rather than an attempt to ensure those who created the law were also bound to it. The coalition brought to power by Cromwell was soon replaced by the resurrected monarchy and the deceased Cromwell was exhumed and symbolically beheaded to underscore the revival of royal rule. Cromwell's claims of a determination to serve justice were unsupportable in the face of his clear efforts to consolidate his own power and rule England. Ultimately his efforts at consolidation of power failed because he failed to persuade the population they were better off without a monarch than with one. Of course, if Charles I had defeated Cromwell, Cromwell's head would have fallen first. The winner of the conflict, Cromwell, defined justice for his own political purposes.

Captain Henry Wirz was tried and executed because some in the United States government were not satisfied with merely the collapse of the Confederacy and the end of the Civil War. Instead, Wirz was killed as a necessary step toward the trial of Jefferson Davis because some wanted vengeance for the assassination of Abraham Lincoln. The tenuous connection between Wirz and Davis provided the justification for prosecution because others in the government were simply unhappy with allowing the Confederate rebels to reintegrate into the fabric of the nation. Whatever the motivations for the Wirz trial may have been, there is no question that he was not given a fair trial and he was convicted and hung for crimes he did not commit. The lasting legacy for Wirz is not, however, his status as a symbol of the abuses of a war department that was not very good at accommodating peace. Rather, the legacy of the trial of Henry

Wirz is that the government of the United States reacted to the public revulsion of the show trial. The hanging of Wirz was in some senses the final episode of the Civil War. The legacy of the Wirz trial dictated that, at least until the War on Terror began, the government of the United States would not deprive its enemies of at least the minimum safeguards required to conduct a fair trial.

With both the Nuremberg Trials and the Tokyo trials, because the Allies had been victorious in every conceivable dimension, they were able to impose their will on defeated countries and those soldiers who fought for the losing side. The differences in the postwar issues of concern for the United States and its allies about Germany and Japan led to the dramatically different outcomes in the two sets of trials. A serious concern about economic and social stability for the countries in postwar Europe, including Germany, led to a triumph of fundamental justice and the rule of law for the war crimes trials in Germany. The procedural due process was fairly developed and concerns about substantive due process meant that the subject matter of the prosecutions was legitimate. In Japan, however, the Allies were primarily concerned about protecting the emperor from being implicated so that the occupation of Japan would not be challenged by a popular uprising of royal loyalists. Shielding the emperor from culpability meant that any concern about notions of justice came as an afterthought if at all. For both Germany and Japan, the absolute military victory by the Allies meant that the parameters of the trials would be determined by the victorious countries only, with no concern about the interests of the vanquished. Even the victims of the German and Japanese war efforts were not fundamentally of concern to those who constructed the Nuremberg Trials or the Tokyo trials. Justice was a dimension of the prosecutions only to the extent serving justice also promoted a consolidation of power and furthered the goals of the victorious Allies.

The Dirty War trials in Argentina and the construction of the Truth and Reconciliation Commission in South Africa are examples of the administration of transitional justice constrained by clear political considerations. In Argentina, President Alfonsin had a precarious hold on his political coalition and any action that would alienate either the military that had been responsible for the gross violations of human rights or the population that had been victimized by the military might very well have spurred a reignition of the violence or even a full-blown civil war. In South Africa, President Mandela had a firm political coalition but a tenuous ability to maintain economic stability because of the breadth of ownership of assets within the coalition of South Africans that supported the previous regime. Mandela was cognizant that only an inclusive government and future, and reconciliation among the factions, could avoid more violence and conflict as well as provide for economic development.

Alfonsin and Mandela provided for only as much justice as they perceived their political coalitions and systems could withstand. While the structure of the trials in Argentina were very closely modeled on the Nuremberg experience, South Africa made dramatic modifications to the fundamental design and formally embraced reconciliation and future peace as the primary purpose of the proceedings. The former Soviet states also adopted a model based on future peace and reconciliation. Lustration, shedding light on the events that could have led to prosecution, was the most feasible path that would allow the suddenly independent states to consolidate the fledgling democracies while maintaining state administrative capacity to operate.

The international criminal tribunals for both Rwanda and the former Yugoslav states represent another variation on the development of the jurisprudence of war crimes trials. For both cases, the tribunals were vehicles for the imposition of justice created by strangers to the conflicts. The architects of the tribunals were neither victors nor victims of the conflicts. Neither Rwanda nor the former Yugoslav states were close to a cessation of the violence prior to the involvement of the international community and both regions were at a significant amount of risk that the political conflicts would again become violent once the international community pulled out. The ICTY eventually made real progress in prosecuting many of those accused of the most serious violations of human rights. At a minimum, even if the ICTY could be criticized for inefficiency or for the failure to complete the prosecution of Milosevic, it served to remove Milosevic and his aggressive hyper-nationalism from the political arena. This alone helped bring some level of political normalcy and a reduction of violence to the region. The inefficiencies of the international tribunal had a more profound impact on the dispensation of justice for the crimes committed in Rwanda because the volume of suspects magnified the problems that arose from the inefficiencies. Even if those who constructed the ICTR had been fully aware at the time of the magnitude of civilian participation in the genocidal effort, it is difficult to imagine how the system could have been structured to accommodate so many defendants. With South Africa as an example, Rwanda moved toward reconciliation over punitive justice through the *gacaca* process and resolved a tremendous volume of the claims of atrocities without the assistance of the international community. Still, it is not at all clear that the *gacaca* process would have been possible without the creation of the ICTR, which started the effort at holding those who committed the murders accountable.

Both the ICTY and the ICTR set the stage for the creation of the International Criminal Court, a permanent and independent court for the international adjudication of war crimes, crimes against humanity, and other gross violations of human rights. Both the tribunals for the former Yugoslav states and for Rwanda adopted a broad and comprehensive codification for the prosecution of the crimes, the overall administration of the trials, comprehensive provisions for a full and fair defense, and all of the formal expectations that could be desired of both procedural due process and substantive due process. Although the ICTY and the ICTR were in essence dress rehearsals for the ICC, the problems those two tribunals would face in administering justice were not yet known to the members of the international community when it moved forward with the creation of the details of the Rome Statute that created the ICC. By the time the ICC was created, the evolution and development of the jurisprudence of war crimes trials had undoubtedly arrived at a point where procedural due process and substantive due process were expected dimensions of any proper dispensation of justice. Still, while an appropriate formal structure that ensures a fair process is a necessary condition for justice to be the product of the tribunals, proper process alone is insufficient to ensure a just outcome.

The International Criminal Court institutionalized the globalization of the judicial mechanisms necessary to properly address war crimes through a tribunal. While the formal structure of the ICC from the perspective of anyone who stands before it as a defendant is essentially above reproach, the substantial jurisdictional limitations structured by the nations that created it, in particular the restriction of complementarity, means that in the end the ICC is simply a criminal court for the weakest states, administered by the most powerful ones.

In a period of belligerence around the globe, the ICC has been absorbed with pursuing suspects only from sub-Saharan Africa while completely avoiding any engagement about the behavior of the Western states during the conflicts affiliated with the so-called War on Terror. Complementarity has performed exactly as it was designed. This restriction on the jurisdiction of the court has been an absolute barrier to the initiation of any investigations by the office of the prosecutor of any acts attributable to the states that developed the court. Regardless of the intent behind the institutionalization of the court as secondary in nature, this stricture means the court is in the final analysis a permanent theater for the international criminal prosecutions of state agents from weak states. While it may be true that the jurisprudence of international war crimes trials, especially regarding substantive due process and procedural due process, matured, even if narrowly constructed, with the creation of the ICC, the most powerful nations in the world have exempted themselves from accountability before the very tribunal they created. The powerful nations that created and institutionalized the modern conception of a war crimes tribunal also rigged the institutional design to ensure they would be beyond its reach.

The United States and its allies responded to the terrorist attack of September 11, 2001 by initiating two wars, in Afghanistan and Iraq, and by detaining individuals from various countries from all over the world who often had no connection whatsoever to terrorism or either war. The Bush administration signaled its intent to prosecute those deemed terrorists as war criminals from the outset of the conflicts. The administration of President George W. Bush co-opted the concept and jurisprudence of war crimes tribunals in response to acts of terrorism in order to promote its policies and the multifaceted war effort. The War on Terror brought about a total de-evolution of the jurisprudence of war crimes trials from a mechanism for the administration of justice to a return to these trials as mere political prosecutions.

The long history of war crimes trials has been shaped by the interaction between the search for justice and the effort to consolidate political power. The criminal prosecutions that followed the conflicts in Argentina and Germany provided examples of the compelling use of criminal law processes as legitimate political tools. That is, the trials were politically, legally, and morally defensible. They also served to consolidate peace as well as power. The trials of Charles I, Captain Henry Wirz, and the defendants in Japan are examples of the exercise of power rather than the administration of justice. These trials were little more than executions staged within an artificial claim of just process. For these cases, neither the methods of prosecution nor the purposes that underpinned the political manipulation of a system of justice are defensible in any dimension. These cases led to nothing more than the executions of defeated enemies of the victors.

The efforts of the international community to solidify the norm that states and actors are to be held accountable for behavior during conflict were institutionalized through the criminal tribunals for Rwanda, Bosnia, and ultimately the International Criminal Court. However, this collective effort has been substantially undermined by the collective attempt to ensure the powerful states can never be brought before the court. The development of a nonpunitive dimension to the resolution of claims of atrocities has been positive as exemplified by the reconciliation efforts in South Africa, the former Soviet states, and Rwanda. In each of these cases, reconciliation was seemingly the only politically viable option. Likewise, in countries where there is no clear winner in a conflict, and perhaps even more important, there is no clear loser, war crimes prosecutions are not feasible and are simply out of the question. In Northern Ireland the conflict was resolved by the creation of a political power sharing arrangement that included a broad commitment by all involved parties to end human rights violations. The lesson from these cases is that, to whatever extent justice demands prosecution for gross violations of human rights, some party must be able to consolidate political power before meaningful prosecutions can be held. In short, retribution and deterrence seem to be luxuries for those who prevail in battle.

Although from the perspective of victims, justice for war crimes is a scarce commodity, procedural due process and substantive due process have become dimensions of the institutionalized prosecution that are expected by the international community. In the final analysis, politics prevails in even the best of circumstances and justice is relegated to the status of a symbolic excuse for prosecution. Finally, with the advent of the Bush administration's new worldview – entailing an American right to intervene at will regardless of international sentiment – the future of war crimes prosecutions is at a precarious stage. Should war crimes prosecution become simply another tool of imposing the will of the dominant hegemonic power on weaker states, the administration of justice in response to the most atrocious crimes against humanity will give way to ongoing political manipulation of justice for the consolidation and exercise of power.

References

Ailslieger, K. 1999. "Why the United States Should be Wary of the International Criminal Court: Concerns over Sovereignty and Constitutional Guarantees." *Washburn Law Journal* 39: 80–105.

Aghion, A. (director). 2002. *Gacaca: Living Together Again in Rwanda?* Icarus Films.

Akande, D. 2004. "International Law Immunities and the International Criminal Court." *The American Journal of International Law* 98(3): 407–33.

Allen, S. G. 2002. Letter to Constituents. Virginia. 22 July.

Almack, E. 1901. *Eikon Basilike or the King's Book*. London: Chattle and Windus, Boston: John W. Luce.

Amnesty International. 2002. *Gacaca: A Question of Justice*. London: Amnesty International.

2005. *Iraq Special Tribunal-Fair Trials Not Guaranteed*. London: Amnesty International.

Andersen, M. E. 1993. *Dossier Secreto, Argentina's Desaparecidos and the Myth of the "Dirty War."* Boulder: Westview Press.

References

Ansolabehere, S. and J. M. Snyder. 2002. "The Incumbency Advantage in U.S. Elections: An Analysis of State and Federal Offices, 1942–2000." *Election Law Journal: Rules, Politics and Policy* 1(3): 315–38.

Aquinas, St. T. 1913–25. *Summa Theologica*. Trans. Fathers of the English Dominica Province pt. II, 2nd. Pt., qu. 58, art I., London: FEDP.

Aristotle. 1994. *The Politics*. Trans. by Carnes Lord. Chicago: University of Chicago Press.

Arnold, A. 2003. "Trial by Fire: the International Criminal Court pushes ahead." *Harvard International Review* 24(4): 11–12.

Arnold, D. R. 1979. *Congress and the Bureaucracy: A Theory of Influence*. New Haven: Yale University Press.

Asmal, K., L. Asmal, and R. S. Roberts. 1997. *Reconciliation Through Truth: A Reckoning of Apartheid's Criminal Governance* 2nd ed. New York: St. Martin's Press.

Associated Press. 2006. "Sentenced to Die: Iraqi Court Rules That Saddam Hussein, 2 Co-Defendants Will Hang For Dujail Killings." *Chicago Tribune* Nov. 6, 2006, p. 6.

  2009. *A look at statistics on Guantanamo detainees past and present*. 13 November 2009. http://news.gaeatimes.com/a-look-at-statistics-on-guantanamo-detainees-past-and-present-228903/.

Aukerman, M. J. 2002. "Extraordinary Evil, Ordinary Crime: A Framework for Understanding Transitional Justice." *Harvard Human Rights Journal* 15 : 39–97.

Background Information on the I. C. C. 1998. United Nations: www.un.org/icc/justice(trigger)(crimes).

Bachrach, P. and M. S. Baratz. 1962. "Two Faces of Power." *The American Political Science Review* 56(4): 947–52.

Baird, J. W. 1982. *From Nuremberg to Mai Lai*. Cambridge, MA: D.C. Heath & Co.

Baldwin, R. E. and C. S. McGee. 1998. *Is Trade Policy for Sale?: Congressional Voting on Recent Trade Bills*. Cambridge, MA: National Bureau of Economic Research.

Barnes, J. E. 2007. "America's own unlawful conmbatants?" *Los Angeles Times* 15 October 2007, p. A1.

Barnett, M. and R. Duvall. 2005. "Power in International Politics." *International Organization* 59(1): 39–75.

Barria, L. A. and S. D. Roper. 2005. "How Effective are International Criminal Tribunals? An Analysis of the ICTY and the ICTR." *The International Journal of Human Rights* 9(3): 349–68.

Bass, G. J. 2000. *Stay The Hand Of Vengeance: The Politics of War Crimes Tribunals*. Princeton: Princeton University Press.

2003. "Milosevic in the Hague." *Foreign Affairs* 82(3): 83–96.

Baxter, R. R. 1958. "Criminal Jurisdiction in the NATO Status of Forces Agreement." *The International and Comparative Law Quarterly* 7(1): 72–81.

Becker, E. 2002. "On World Court, U.S. Focus Shifts to Shielding Officials." *New York Times* 27 September: A1+.

Belknap, M. R. 2002. "A Putrid Pedigree: The Bush Administration's Military Tribunals in Historical Perspective." *California Western Law Review* 38: 433–80.

Benton, W. E. 1955. *Nuremberg: German Views of the War Trials*. Dallas: SMU Press.

Blais, A. 1974. "Power and Causality." *Quality and Quantity* 8: 45–64.

Bland, M. A. 1995. "An Analysis of the United Nations International Tribunal to Adjudicate War Crimes Committed in the Former Yugoslavia: Parallels, Problems, Prospects." *Global Legal Studies Journal* II: 1–35.

Bodenheimer, F. M. 1962. *Jurisprudence, the Philosophy and Method of Law*. Boston: Harvard University Press.

Bolton, J. R. 2001. "The United States and the International Criminal Court: The Risks and Weaknesses of the International Criminal Court from America's Perspective." *Law and Contemporary Problems* 64:167–81.

Boyle, F. A. 1996. *Negating Human Rights in Peace Negotiations*. Helsinki: Domovina Net.

Brackman, A. C. 1987. *The Other Nuremberg: The Untold Story of the Tokyo War Crimes Trials*. New York: Quill, William, Morrow.

Brannigan, A. and N. A. Jones. 2009. "Genocide and the Legal Process in Rwanda: From Genocide Amnesty to the New Rule of Law." *International Criminal Justice Review* 19(2): 192–207.

References

British Broadcasting Corporation. 1998: "Northern Ireland peace deal reached." news.bbc.co.uk/onthisday/hi/dates/stories/april/10/newsid_2450000/2450823.stm.

Bueno de Mesquita, B., J. D. Morrow, R. M. Siverson, and A. Smith. 1999. "An Institutional Explanation of the Democratic Peace." *American Political Science Review* 93(4): 791–807.

Bugajski, J. 1996. "Balkan Myths and Bosnian Massacres." in *The South Slav Conflict*, eds. R. G. C. Thomas and H. R. Friman. New York: Garland Publishing.

Burns, J. F. and K. Semple. 2006. "Hussein is Sentenced to Death by Hanging." *New York Times* Nov. 6, 2006, p. A4.

Buscher, F. M. 1989. *The U.S. War Crime Trials Program in Germany, 1946–1955*. Westport, Conn: Greenwood Press.

Bush, G. W. 2001a. *text:Bush Announces Start of War on Terror.* September 20, 2001. (distr. by Office of International Information Programs, U.S. Dept. of State: usinfo.state.gov).

2001b. *text:President Bush Announces Military Strike in Afghanistan.* October 7, 2001. (distr. by Office of International Information Programs, U.S. Dept. of State: usinfo.state.gov).

2001c. *President Issues Military Order, Detention, Treatment, and Trial of Certain Non-Citizens in War Against Terrorism.* Whitehouse.gov/2011/11/print/2011113–27.

2003. *President Discusses Beginning of Operation Iraqi Freedom.* 22 March 2003. (whitehouse.gov/newsreleases/2003/03/20030322).

Byron, C. M. D. 2010. Report of the International Criminal Tribunal for Rwanda (15th annual report) United Nations (A/65/188-S/2010/408).

Catton, B. 1959. "Prison Camps of the Civil War." *American Heritage Magazine* 10(5): 4–13, 96–7.

Clegg, S. 1979. *The Theory of Power and Organization*. London: Routledge & Kegan Paul.

Clotfelter, J. 1970. "Senate Voting and Constituency Stake in Defense Spending." *The Journal of Politics* 32(4): 979–83.

Collier, K. and M. Munger. 1994. "A Comparison of Incumbent Security in the House and Senate." *Public Choice* 78(2):145–54.

Constitution of the Federation of Bosnia and Herzegovinia. www. soros.org.ba/project_bosnia/fed.

Corradi, J. E. 1985. *The Fitful Republic, Economy, Society and Politics in Argentina.* Boulder: Westview Press.

Crnobrnja, M. 1996. *The Yugoslav Drama* 2nd ed. Cambridge: McGill-Queens University Press.

Crocker, D. A. 1999. "Reckoning with Past Wrongs: A Normative Framework." *Ethics & International Affairs* 13(1): 43–64.

Dahl, F. "Serbia Making Steady Recovery From Assassination." *Washington Post* 8 May 2003. Available Online: http://www.washingtonpost.com/wp-dyn/articles/A28934–2003May8.html.

Dahl, R. 1956. *A Preface to Democratic Theory.* Chicago: The University of Chicago Press.

___. 1963. *Modern Political Analysis.* Chicago: The University of Chicago Press.

Daly, E. 2002. "Between Punitive and Reconstructive Justice: The Gacaca Courts in Rwanda." *International Law and Politics* 34: 355–96.

Danner, A. M. 2003. "Enhancing the Legitimacy and Accountability of Prosecutorial Discretion at the International Criminal Court." *The American Journal of International Law* 97(3): 510–52.

Doctors Without Borders. 1995. *Deadlock in the Rwanda Refugee Crisis: Virtual Standstill on Repatriation.* www.dwb.org/deadlock.

Derouen, Jr., K. and U. Heo. 2000. "Defense Contracting and Domestic Politics." *Political Research Quarterly* 53(4): 753–69.

Des Forges, A. 1999. *Leave None to Tell the Story: Genocide in Rwanda.* NY: Human Rights Watch.

Digeser, P. 1992. "The Fourth Face of Power." *The Journal of Politics* 54(4): 977–1007.

Dimitrijevic, N. 2006. "Justice Beyond Blame." *Journal of Conflict Resolution* 50(3): 368–82.

Dishneau, D. 2007. "Split Verdict for Officer at Abu Ghraib," Washingtonpost.com 28 August, 2007. Associated Press. Washingtonpost.com/wp-dyn/content/article/2007/08/28/AR2007082800359.

References

Donnelly, J. 1986. "International Human Rights: A Regime Analysis." *International Organization* 40(3): 599–642.

Draper, G. I. A. D. 1951. "The Exercise of Criminal Jurisdiction under the NATO Status of Forces Agreement, 1951." *Transactions of the Grotius Society* 44: 9–28.

Dwyer, S. 1999. "Reconciliation for Realists," in *Ethics & International Affairs* 13(1): 81–98.

El Zeidy, M. 2002. "The United States Dropped the Bomb of Article 16 of the ICC Statute: Security Council Power of Deferrals and Resolution 1422." *Vanderbilt Journal of Transnational Law* 35: 1503–44.

Ellis, M. S. 1997. "Purging the Past: The Current State of Lustration Laws in the Former Communist Bloc." *Law and Contemporary Problems* 59(4): 181–96.

England, J. F. 2001. "The Response of the United States to the International Criminal Court: Rejection, Ratification or Something Else?" *Arizona Journal of International and Comparative Law* 18: 941–78.

Engle, K. 2005. "Feminism and Its (Dis)contents: Criminalizing Wartime Rape in Bosnia and Herzegovina." *The American Journal of International Law* 99(4): 778–816.

Epstein, E. C. 1992. *The New Argentine Democracy, the Search for a Successful Formula*. Westport, Conn: Praeger.

Erro, D. G. 1993. *Resolving the Argentine Paradox, Politics, and Development, 1966–1992*. Boulder: Lynne Rienner Publishers.

Fearon, J. 1994. "Domestic Political Audiences and the Escalation of International Disputes." *The American Political Science Review* 88(3): 577–92.

Fein, E. 2005. "Transitional Justice and Democratization in Eastern Europe" in *(Un)Civil Societies: Human rights and democratic transitions in Eastern Europe and Latin America*, eds. Rachel A. May and Andrew K. Milton. Lanham, MD: Lexington Books 197–217.

Foucault, M. 1980. "The Confessions of the Flesh" and "Two Lectures" in *Power/ Knowledge: Selected Interviews and Other Writings 1972–1977*, ed. Colin Gordon, trans. Leo Marshall, John Merphaum, and Kate Soper. New York: Pantheon.

Futch, O. L. 1968. *History of Andersonville Prison*. Gainesville: University of Florida Press.

Gallarotti, G. and A. Preis. 1999. "Politics, International Justice and The United States: Toward a Permanent International Criminal Court." *UCLA Journal of International Law and Foreign Affairs* 4: 1–54.

Gastrow, P. 1995. *Bargaining for Peace, South Africa, and the National Peace Accord*. Washington, DC: United States Institute of Peace Press.

Gelman, A. and G. King. 1990. "Estimating Incumbency Advantage without Bias." *American Journal of Political Science* 34(4): 1142–64.

Ginsburgs, G. and V. N. Kudraivtsev. 1990. *The Nuremberg Trial and International Law*. The Netherlands: Martinus Nijhoff Publishers.

Global News Wire. 2002. "Britain Welcomes Ratification of ICC Statute." *Global NewsWire: Asian Africa Intelligence Wire* 11 April.

Grossman, G. M. and E. Helpman. 1994. "Protection for Sale." *American Economic Review* 84(4): 833–50.

Gurule, J. 2001. "United States Opposition to the 1998 Rome Statute Establishing an International Criminal Court: Is the Court's Jurisdiction Truly Complementary to National Criminal Jurisdictions." *Cornell International Law Journal* 35. 1–40.

Haddad, H. N. 2010. "Mobilizing the Will to Prosecute: Crimes of Rape and the Yugoslav and Rwandan Tribunals." *Human Rights Review online first* 10.1007/s12142–010–0163-x.

Hall, J. 1973. *Foundations of Jurisprudence*. Indianapolis: The Bobbs-Merrill Co., Inc.

Hart, H. L. A. 1961. *The Concept of Law*. Oxford: Clarendon Press.

Haynor, P. 2001. *Unspeakable Truths: Confronting State Terror and Atrocity*. New York: Routledge.

Highton, B. 2000. "Senate Elections in the United States, 1920–94." *British Journal of Political Science* 30(3): 483–506.

Hodges, D. C. 1976, 1988. *Argentina 1943–1987*. Albuquerque: University of New Mexico Press.

References

1991. *Argentina's "Dirty War."* Austin: University of Texas Press.

Hoge, W. 2005. "U.S. lobbies UN on Darfur and International Court." *The New York Times* 29 January. Section A5+.

Hooker, M. A. and M. M. Knetter. 1997. "The Effects of Military Spending on Economic Activity: Evidence from State Procurement Spending." *Journal of Money, Credit, and Banking* 29(3): 400–21.

Horowitz, S. 1950. "The Tokyo Trial." *International Conciliation* 45(Nov): 473–584.

Hosoya, C. et al. 1986. *The Tokyo War Crimes Trial: An International Symposium.* Tokyo: Kodansha, Ltd.

House of Representatives. 1864. Report No. 67, 38th Congress, 1st Session.

Howarth, D. R. and A. J. Norval. 1998. *South Africa in Transition: New Theoretical Perspectives.* New York: St. Martin's Press.

International Criminal Court. 2006. *Report on the activities of the International Criminal Court.* 17 October 2006.UN Doc. ICC-ASP/5/15.

2010. *Report of the International Criminal Court.* 19 August 2010. UN Doc. A/65/313.

2010. *Registry of Facts and Figures.* 3 November 2010. icty.org/sections/TheCases/KeyFigures June 30, 2010 icty.org/sections/LegalLibrary/Defence 2010.

International Tribunal for Rwanda: *A Western Show Trial.* 1996. Africa 2000: www.africa2000.com/INDX/rwanda2b.

International Tribunal for Rwanda, Rules of Procedure and Evidence, U.N. Doc ITR/Rev. 1. 1995. United Nations: www.umn.edu/humanrts/africa/RWANDA1.

James, B. J. 1964. "The Issue of Power." *Public Administration Review* 24(1): 47–51.

Jorgenson, N. H. B. 2004. "The Right of the Accused to Self-Representation Before International Criminal Tribunals." *American Journal of International Law* 98(4): 711–26.

Johnston, D. 2009. "Uighers leave Guantanamo for Palau." *New York Times* November 1, 2009. topics.nytimes.com/top/reference/

timestopics/subjects/u/uighurs_chinese_ethnic_group/index.
html?inline=nyt-classifier.

Juckes, T. J. 1995. *Opposition in South Africa: The Leadership of Z.K. Matthews, Nelson Mandela, and Stephen Biko*. Westport, CT: Praeger Publishers.

Justice for All: An Analysis of the Human Rights Provisions of the 1998 Northern Ireland Peace Agreement. 1998. Human Rights Watch. www.hrw.org/reports_98/nireland.

Kaufman, H. and V. Jones. 1953. *Community Power Structure: A Study of Decision Makers*. Chapel Hill: University of North Carolina Press.

Kami, A. 2006. *Saddam Judge Stands By Resignation: Court Spokesperson*. Reuters Jan 16, 2006.

Kaminski, M. M. and M. Napela. 2006. "Judging Transitional Justice: A New Criterion For Evaluating Truth Revelation Procedures." *Journal of Conflict Resolution*. 50(3): 383–408.

Kennedy, D. 1864. "David Kennedy Diary 1864 Jan –Sept." St. Paul, MN: Minnesota Historical Society.

Khiddu-Makubuya, E. 1994. "Voluntary Repatriation by Force: The Case of Rwandan Refugees in Uganda." in *African Refugees, Development & Repatriation*, eds. Adelman and Sorensen. Boulder: Westview Press.

Kirsch, P. and J. Holmes. 1999. "Developments in International Criminal Law: The Rome Conference on an International Criminal Court: The Negotiating Process." *American Journal of International Law* 93(2): 332–8.

Kritz, N. J. 1996. "Coming to Terms with Atrocities: A Review of Accountability Mechanisms for Mass Violations of Human Rights." *Law & Contemporary Problems* 59: 127–33.

Kyl, S. J. 2004. Interview. *Human Events*. 10 Dec.

Lagomarsino, D. and C. T. Wood, eds. 1989. *The Trial of Charles I*. Hanover, NH: University Press of New England.

Laska, L. L. and J. M. Smith. 1975. "Hell and the Devil: Andersonville and The Trial of Captain Henry Wirz, C.S.A. 1865." *Military Law Review* 68: 77–132.

References

Laswell. H. D. and A. Kaplan. 1950. *Power and Society*. New Haven Conn.: Yale University Press.

Latore, R. 2002. "Escape Out the Back Door or Charge in the Front Door: U.S. Reactions to the International Criminal Court." *Boston College International and Comparative Law Review* 25: 159–76.

Lauria, J. 2004. "Kerry Opposes Role in Tribunal: U.S. Concerns Not Yet Met He Says." *The Boston Globe* 5 October, A10.

Lesson of Slobodan Milosevic's Trial and Tribunal. "The UN's war-crimes tribunal." *The Economist*. 13 Feb. 2003. Available Online: http://www.economist.com/world/europe/displayStory. cfm?story_id=1576821.

Linzer, D. 2010. "White House Drafts Executive Order for Indefinite Detention." *Washington Post* and *Propublica* Dec. 21, 2010. www. Propublica.org/article/white-house-drafts-executive-order-for-indefinite-detention.

Lippman, T. 1997. "Ambassador to the Darkest Areas of Human Conflict." *The Washington Post* 17 November, A16.

Leigh, M. 2001. "Editorial Comments: The United States and The Rome Statute." *American Journal of International Law* 95(1): 124–31.

Locke, J. 1993. *Political Writings of John Locke*. ed. David Wootton. New York, NY: Mentor, Penguin Group.

Lukes, S. 1974. *Power: A Radical View*. London: Britich Sociological Association.

Malamud-Goti, J. E. 1996. *Game Without End: State Terror and the Politics of Justice*. Norman: University of Oklahoma Press.

Mandela, N. 1994. *Nelson Mandela Speaks*. New York: Mayibuye Books.

Maoz, Z. and B. Russett. 1993. "Normative and Structural Causes of Democratic Peace: 1946–1986." *American Political Science Review* 87(3): 624–38.

March, J. G. 1955. "An Introduction to the Theory of Measurement of Influence." *American Political Science Review* 49: 431–51.

Martin, L. 2000. *Legislatures and International Cooperation*. Princeton, NJ: Princeton University Press.

May, R. A. and A. K. Milton, eds. 2005. *(Un)Civil Societies, Human Rights and Democratic Transitions in Eastern Europe and Latin America.* Lanham: Lexington Books.

Mayer, K. R. 1991. *The Political Economy of Defense Contracting.* New Haven: Yale University Press.

Mayfield, N. H. 1988. *Puritans and Regicide.* Charlottesville: University Press of America.

McAdams, A. J., ed. 1997. *Transitional Justice and the Rule of Law in New Democracies.* Notre Dame: University of Notre Dame Press.

McCormick, T. L. H. 1997. "From Sun Tzu to the Sixth Committee: The Evolution of an International Criminal Law Regime," in *The Law of War Crimes: National and International Approaches,* eds. T. L. H. MCormick and G. J. Simpson. The Hague and London: Kluwer Law International, 31–43.

McFarland, A. S. 1969. *Power and Leadership in Pluralistic Societies.* Stanford: University of Stanford Press.

McElroy, J. 1879. *Andersonville, A Story of Rebel Military Prisons.* Toledo: D. R. Locke 1999 digital reproduction by Digital Scanning, Inc.

Mearsheimer, J. 1994. "The False Promise of International Institutions." *International Security* 19(3): 5–49.

Mencken, F. C. 2004. "Federal Defense Spending and Metropolitan and Nonmetropolitan Disparities in Economic Growth in the Southeast." *Social Science Quarterly* 85(2): 324–39.

Mignone, E. F., C. L. Estlund, and S. Issacharoff. 1984. "Dictatorship on Trial: Prosecution of Human Rights Violations in Argentina." *Yale Journal of International Law* 10: 118–50.

Milner, H. 1997. *Interests, Institutions, and Information: Domestic Politics and International Relations.* Princeton, NJ: Princeton University Press.

Minear, R. H. 1971. *Victor's Justice: The Tokyo War Crimes Trial.* Princeton, NJ: Princeton University Press.

Minow, M. 1999. *Between Vengeance and Forgiveness: Facing History after Genocide and Mass Violence.* Boston: Beacon Press.

Montgomery, D. 2005. "Death Row inmate's appeal hinges on global treaty issue." *The Miami Herald* 3/29 p 5A.

References

Moravcsik, A. 2000. "The Origins of Human Rights Regimes: Democratic Delegation in Postwar Europe." *International Organization* 54 (2): 217–52.

Morgan, A. 2000. *The Belfast Agreement a practical legal analysis.* London: The Belfast Press. http://www.cain.ulst.ac.uk/events/peace/morgan/morgan00.jpg.

Morris, M. 2001. "The United States and the International Criminal Court: High Crimes and Misconceptions: The ICC and Non-Party States." *Law and Contemporary Problems* 64(1): 13–66.

MSNBC. 2010. "Supreme Court dismisses Uighers' Appeal." 1 March. http://www.msnbc.msn.com/id/35643544/ns/us_news-security/.

National Commission on the Disappearance of Persons.1984. *Nunca Mas.*

Neier, A. 1998. *War Crimes, Brutality, Genocide, Terror, and the Struggle for Justice.* NY: Times Books/Random House.

Newbury, C. 1988. *The Cohesion of Oppression.* Columbia: Columbia University Press.

Nincic, M. and T. R. Cusack. 1979. "The Political Economy of US Military Spending." *Journal of Peace Research* 16(2): 101–15.

Nino, C. S. 1991. "The Duty to Punish Past Abuses of Human Rights Put into Context: The Case of Argentina." *Yale Law Journal* 100: 2619–40.

Obama, B. 2011. Executive Order on Periodic Review. www.whitehouse.gov/sites/default/files/Executive_Order_On_Periodic_Review.pdf.

Oppel, R. 2006. "After Remark, Judge in Hussein Trial Loses His Post." *New York Times* Sept. 20, 2006, A10.

Orentlicher, D. F. 1991. "Settling Accounts: The Duty to Prosecute Human Rights Violations of a Prior Regime." *Yale Law Journal* 100(8): 2537–615.

Osiel, M. 1997. *Mass Atrocity, Collective Memory, and the Law.* New Brunswick, NJ: Transaction Publishers.

Packer, G. 2006. "Saddam on Trial." *New Yorker* Oct. 31, 2005.

Page, J. M. and M. J. Haley. 1908. *The True Story of Andersonville Prison: A Defense of Major Henry Wirz.* NY: The Neale Publishing Company, 1999 digital reproduction by Digital Scanning, Inc.

Parenti, M. 1978. *Power and the Powerless*. New York: St Martins Press.

Partridge, P. H. 1962. "Some Notes on the Concept of Power." *Political Studies* 11(3): 107–25.

Penrose, M. M. 1999. "Lest We Fail: The Importance of Enforcement in International Criminal Law." *American University International Law Review* 15: 321–94.

Peralta-Ramos, M. and C. H. Waisman. 1987. *From Military Rule to Liberal Democracy in Argentina*. Boulder: Westview Press.

Perry, T. 2007a. "Defining the time to kill." *Los Angeles Times* 31 July, A1.

2007b. "Marine sentenced to 15 years in Iraq killing." *Los Angeles Times* 4 August, A8.

Persico, J. E. 1994. *Nuremberg, Infamy on Trial*. New York: Viking Penguin.

Petrovcic, B. 1995. *Peace in Our Times: Details of the Dayton Peace Accord*. Helsinki: Domovina Net.

Peterson, J. 2007. "Unpacking Show Trials: Situating the Trial of Saddam Hussein." *Harvard International Law Journal* 48(1): 257–92.

Popkin, S. L. 1991. *The Reasoning Voter*. Chicago: The University of Chicago Press.

Posner, E. A. and A. Vermeule. 2004. "Transitional Justice as Ordinary Justice." *Harvard Law Review* 117(3). 701–825.

Postema, G. J. 1977. "The Principle of Utility and the Law of Procedure: Bentham's Theory of Adjudication." *Georgia Law Review* 11: 1393–424.

Prunier, G. 1995. *The Rwanda Crisis: History of a Genocide*. Columbia: Columbia University Press.

Ralph, J. 2005. "International Society, the International Criminal Court and American Foreign Policy." *Review of International Studies* 31(1): 27–44.

Ransom, J. L. 1881. *Andersonville Diary: Escape and List of the Dead with Name, Company, Regiment, Date of Death and Number of Grave in Cemetary*. Philadelphia: Douglass Bros.; reprint 1974, NY: Haskell House Publishers Ltd.

References

Ratner, S. R. and J. S. Abrams. 2001. *Accountability For Human Rights Atrocities in International Law: Beyond The Nuremberg Legacy.* 2nd ed. Oxford: Oxford University Press.

Ratner, M. and E. Ray. 2004. *Guantanamo: What the World Should Know.* Gloucester: Arris Books.

Raustiala, K. 1997. "Domestic Institutions and International Regulatory Cooperation: Comparative Responses to the Convention on Biological Diversity." *World Politics* (49)4: 482–509.

Ray, B. A. 1981. "Defense Department Spending and 'Hawkish' Voting in the House of Representatives." *The Western Political Quarterly* 34(3): 438–46.

Rettig, M. 2008. "Gacaca: Truth, Justice, and Reconciliation in Postconflict Rwanda?" *African Studies Review* 51(3): 25–50.

Reuters. 2002. U.S. says detainees not protected by Geneva Conventions. January 12, 2002.

Reyntjens, F. 1990. "Le gacaca ou la justice du grazon au Rwanda." *Politique Africaine* 40: 31–4.

Riker, W. H. 1964. "Some Ambiguities in the Notion of Power." *American Political Science Review* 58(2): 341–9.

Roling, B. V. A. 1993. *The Tokyo Trial and Beyond: Reflections of a Peacemonger.* Cambridge: Polity Press.

Rosembaum, A. S. 1993. *Prosecuting Nazi War Criminals.* Boulder: Westview Press.

Roach, S. C. ed. 2009. *The Global Politics of the International Criminal Court: Global Governance in Context.* Oxford: Oxford University Press.

Rotberg, R. and D. Thompson, eds. 2002. *Truth v. Justice: The Morality of Truth Commissions.* Princeton, NJ: Princeton University Press.

Rubin, B. R. 1996. *Toward Comprehensive Peace in Southeast Europe: Conflict Prevention in the South Balkans.* New York: The 20th Century Fund Press.

Rudolph, C. 2001. "Constructing an Atrocities Regime: The Politics of War Crimes Tribunals." *International Organization* 55(3): 655–91.

Ruhlman, R. F. 2006. *Captain Henry Wirz and Andersonville Prison: A Reappraisal.* Knoxville: University of Tennessee Press.

Russett, B. 1996. "The Fact of Democratic Peace," in *Debating the Democratic Peace*, ed. M. Brown. Boston: MIT Press.

Rutherford, M. L. 1921. *Facts and Figures vs. Myths and Misrepresentation: Henry Wirz and Andersonville Prison*. Athens, GA: United Daughters of the Confederacy; undated reprint by the Alexander H. Stephens Camp 78 of the Sons of Confederate Veterans, Americus, GA.

Sadat-Wexler, L. 1999. "Association of American Law Schools Panel on the International Criminal Court." *American Criminal Law Review* 36: 223–64.

Sarkin, J. 2001. "The Tension between Justice and Reconciliation in Rwanda: Politics, Human Rights, Due Process, and the Role of the Gacaca Courts in Dealing with the Genocide." *Journal of African Law* 45: 143.

Sasaki, K. 1963. "Military Expenditures and the Employment Multiplier in Hawaii." *The Review of Economics and Statistics* 45(3): 298–304.

Schabas, W. 2004. "United States Hostility to the International Criminal Court: It's All About the Security Council." *European Journal of International Law* 15(4): 701–20.

Scharf, M. 2001. "The ICC's Jurisdiction Over the Nationals of Non-Party States: A Critique of the U.S. Position." *Law and Contemporary Problems* 64: 67–118.

2004. "Is it International Enough? A Critique of the Iraqi Special Tribunal in Light of the Goals of International Justice." *Journal of International Criminal Justice* 2: 330–7.

Scheffer, D. 1999a. "The United States and the International Criminal Court." *American Journal of International Law* 93: 12–22.

1999b. Speech to the American Society of International Law: *International Criminal: The Challenge of Jurisdiction* (March 26).

2001. "Staying the Course with the International Criminal Court." *Cornell International Law Journal* 35: 47–100.

Schultz, K. 1999. "Do Democratic Institutions Constrain or Inform: Contrasting Two Institutional Perspectives on Democracy and War." *International Organization* 53: 233–66.

References

Serrano, R. A. 2007. "Officer is acquitted of abuse at Abu Graib." *Los Angeles Times*. 29 August, A7.

Shortell, C. and C. A. Smith. 2005. "The Institutional Stability of the Judiciary in the Aftermath of Terrorism." *Judicature* 88 (4): 173–7.

Siklova, J. 1996. "Lustration or the Czech Way of Screening." *E. European Constitutional Review* 5: 5762.

Simon, H. A. 1957. *Models of Man*. New York: Wiley Publishers.

Skaar, E., S. Gloppen, and A. Suhrke, eds. 2005. *Roads to Reconciliation*. Oxford UK: Lexington Books.

Smith, B. F. 1981. *The Road to Nuremberg*. New York: Basic Books, Inc.

1982. *The Road to Nuremberg: The Documentary Record 1944–1945*. Stanford, CA: Hoover Institute Press.

Smith, C. A. and H. Smith. 2006. "The Electoral Dis-Connection: Institutional Barriers to U.S. Support for the ICC." *Eyes on the ICC* 3(I): 1–31.

Smith, C. A. 2007. "Judicialization: The Key to European Unification and Expansion," in *The State of the European Union*, ed. Y. Stivachtis, Burlington, VT: Ashgate Publishers. pp. 127–39.

2008. "Credible Commitments and the Early American Supreme Court." *Law & Society Review* 42(1): 75–110.

Smith, C. A. and H. Smith. 2009. "Embedded *Realpolitick*: Re-evaluating the U.S. Opposition to the ICC," in *The Global Politics of the International Criminal Court: Global Governance in Context*, ed. S. C. Roach Oxford: Oxford University Press, 27–53.

Smyser, W. R. 1999. *From Yalta To Berlin:The Cold War Struggle Over Germany*. New York: St. Martin's Press.

Solis, G. 2007. "Is military justice just?" *Los Angeles Times* 10 September, A17.

Sowell, T. 1994. *Race and Culture: A World View*. New York: Basic Books, Inc.

Stotzky, I. P. 1993. *Transition to Democracy in Latin America: The Role of the Judiciary*. Boulder: Westview Press.

Taylor, T. 1992. *The Anatomy of the Nuremberg Trials: A Personal Memoir*. New York: Alfred A. Knopf.

Thompson, L. 1995. *A History of South Africa*, revised edition. New Haven: Yale University Press.

Tindemans, L. 1996. *Unfinished Peace: Report of the International Commission on the Balakans*. Aspen: Aspen Institute.

Tan, C. J. 2004. "The Proliferation of Bilateral Non-Surrender Agreements among Non-Ratifiers of the Rome Statute of the International Criminal Court." *American University International Law Review* 19: 1115–80.

Tverdova, Y. V. 2011. "Human Trafficking in Russia and Other Post-Soviet States," *Human Rights Review* 12(3): 329–44.

United Kingdom. 1998. Agreement Reached in the Multiparty Negotiations: Northern Ireland. United Kingdom: www.n10.gov.UK/agreement.

United Nations. 1994. Report of the International Law Commission on the Work of its Forty-Sixth Session. 2 May 22 July 1994. UN Doc A/49/10.

Van de Kieft, C. M. 2002. "Uncertain Risk: The United States and the International Criminal Court." *Cardozo Law Review* 23: 2325–68.

Van der Vyver, J. D. 2001. "International Human Rights: American Execeptionalism: Human Rights, International Criminal Justice, and National Self-Righteousness." *Emory Law Journal* 50: 775–832.

Varadarajan, L. 1998. "From Tokyo to the Hague: A Re-assessment of Radhabinod Pal's Dissenting Opinion at the Tokyo Trials on its Golden Jubilee." *Indian Journal of International Law* 38 (2): 233–47.

Waldmeir, P. 1997. *Anatomy of a Miracle: The End of Apartheid and the Birth of the New South Africa*. New York: W.W. Norton & Co.

Waldorf, L. 2006. "Mass Justice for Mass Atrocity; Rethinking Local Justice as Transitional Justice." *Temple Law Review* 79 (1): 1–87.

Watson, C. 1991. *Exile from Rwanda: Background to an Invasion*. Washington, DC: Am. Council for Nationalities Service.

Weber, M. 1946. *Max Weber, Essays in Sociology*. Trans. and ed. by H. H. Gerth and C. Wright Mills. Fairlawn, NJ: Oxford University Press.

References

Wedgewood, C. V. 1964. *A Coffin for King Charles: the Trial and Execution of Charles I.* New York: The Macmillian Co.

Whitcomb, D. 2008. "Haditha charges dropped against top Marine officer" Reuters http://web.archive.org/web/20080624222747/news.yahoo.com/s/nm/20080617/us_nm/usa_iraq_haditha_dc.

White House Press Release. 2003. "Statements of Support from Coalition Members." 26 March 2003. http://www.whitehouse.gov/infocus/iraq/news/20030326–7.html.

Wieseltier, L. 1996. "Afterword," in *The Black Book of Bosnia: the Consequences of Appeasement,* ed. N. Mousavizadeh. New York: A New Republic Book, Basicbooks.

Williams, C. J. 2007. "Guatanamo defense lawyers see stacked deck." *Los Angeles Times* 13 November 2007. www.latimes.com/mnationworld /nation/la-na-gitmo13nov13,1,6779375.

Williamson, H. R. 1957. *The Day They Killed the King.* London: The MacMillian Co.

Wingfield-Stratford, D. S. 1950 and 1975. *King Charles the Martyr, 1643–1649.* Westport, CT: Greenwood Press.

Wirz Trial. 1880–1901. U.S. War Dept., War of Rebellion Official Records.

Wolfowitz, P. 2004. Memorandum: Order Establishing Combatant Status Review Tribunal 7 July. Department of Defense.

Worthington, A. 2007. *The Guantanamo Files: The Stories of the 774 Detainees in America's Illegal Prison.* London: Pluto Press.

Wynia, G. W. 1992. *Argentina, Illusions, and Reality.* 2nd ed. Vancouver: Holme and Meier.

Yacoubian, G. S., Jr. 1998. "Sanctioning alternatives in international criminal law: recommendations for the International Criminal Tribunals for Rwanda and the former Yugoslavia." *World Affairs* 161: 48–55.

Yacoubian, G. S., Jr. 2003. "Evaluating the efficacy of the international criminal tribunals for Rwanda and the former Yugoslavia: implications for criminology and international criminal law." *World Affairs* 165: 133–42.

Zacher, M. and R. A. Matthews. 1995. "Liberal International Theory: Common Threads, Divergent Strands," in *Controversies in*

International Relations Theory: Realism and Neoliberal Challenge, ed. C. W. Kegley Jr. New York: St. Martin's Press.

Zagaris, B. 2005. "US Tries to Stop International Criminal Court Investigation." *International Enforcement Law Reporter* 21(2):67.

Websites

Rome Statute at www.un.org/law/icc/.

The Statute of the Iraqi Special Tribunal. Coalitional Provisional Authority. 2003. (Baghdad:iraqispecialtribunal.org).

www.amicc.org/usinfo/administration_policy_BIAs.html.

www.amicc.org/docs/CGStableofBIAsbyICCstatus%2010–04.pdf.

www.amicc.org/usinfo/administration_policy_pkeeping.html.

www.amicc.org/usinfo/administration_policy_pkeeping.html# USstatements.

www.globalpolicy.org/intljustice/icc/crisis/0703annan.htm.

www.icc-cpi.int/cases.html.

www.nsgtmo.navy.mil.

www.people-press.org/reports/index.php?TopicID=6. "President's Remarks at an Ask the President Event in Clive, Iowa," 7 Flags Event Center, Iowa. 4 Oct. 2004.

Pew Research Center Surveys: 1) "A Year after Iraq War: Mistrust of America in Europe Even Higher, Muslim Anger Persists," 16 Mar.2004; 2) "Views of a Changing World 2003: War with Iraq Further Divides Global Publics," 3 June 2003; 3) "America's Image Further Erodes, Europeans Want Weaker Ties," 18 Mar. 2003.

web1.whs.osd.mil/mmid/MMIDHOME.

www.whitehouse.gov/infocus/iraq/news/20030326–7.html. White House Press Release. "Statements of Support from Coalition Members." 26 March 2003.

www.whitehouse.gov/news/releases/2004/10/20041004–12.html George Bush. Speech.

Index

Index

Index

Index

CPSIA information can be obtained at www.ICGtesting.com
Printed in the USA
LVOW12s0813190614

390748LV00005B/28/P